Ronald C. Howard - 1989

W9-BDE-707

Computers and Education

Ronald C. Howard (signature)

CHARLES S. WHITE
GEORGE MASON UNIVERSITY
GUY HUBBARD
INDIANA UNIVERSITY

Computers and Education

MACMILLAN PUBLISHING COMPANY
NEW YORK

Copyright © 1988, Macmillan Publishing Company,
a division of Macmillan, Inc.

PRINTED IN THE UNITED STATES OF AMERICA

All rights reserved. No part of this book may be reproduced or
transmitted in any form or by any means, electronic or mechanical,
including photocopying, recording, or any information storage and
retrieval system, without permission in writing from the Publisher.

Macmillan Publishing Company
866 Third Avenue, New York, New York 10022

Collier Macmillan Canada, Inc.

LIBRARY OF CONGRESS CATALOGING-IN-PUBLICATION DATA

White, Charles Stitham, 1952–
  Computers and education / Charles S. White, Guy Hubbard.
    p.   cm.
  Bibliography: p.
  Includes index.
  ISBN 0-02-427090-3
  1. Education—United States—Data processing.   2. Computer-
assisted instruction—United States.   I. Hubbard. Guy.   II. Title.
LB1028.43.W44   1988
371.3′9445—dc19   87–16831
                                                                    CIP

Printing: 1 2 3 4 5 6 7   Year: 8 9 0 1 2 3 4

ISBN   0-02-427090-3

To Douglas Edward Salomon,
  a dedicated teacher and friend [CSW],
and to Jennifer [GH]

Preface

Over the past 40 years, computers have had a steadily growing impact on our lives. The invention of miniaturized circuitry and remarkable advances in chip technology have had a dramatic effect on business, industry, and government, not to mention our daily lives. The effects of computing in our schools have followed the model set by society at large, though at a slower pace. The creation of the microcomputer in the early 1970s and the mass production of inexpensive machines beginning in 1977 provided the impetus for the more recent growth of computer use in schools. But having computer equipment available in a school is no guarantee that it will be understood well enough to be used satisfactorily. The products of past educational fads languish in school storerooms across the nation, and teachers are understandably wary of allowing their time to be consumed by projects that eventually are likely to be discarded.

The premise underlying this book, however, is that computers are here to stay, and computer-based technology is taking its place in the array of instructional media in schools. For these reasons, every educator needs to know what computers can do and what they cannot do. College students who plan to enter teaching need to be prepared in this way before they graduate, and practicing teachers need the same information even though they may be well established in their careers. Few, if any, of these people are likely to become computer specialists; yet, if they hope to remain current in their teaching, they need a general level of understanding about computer technology as it applies to their professional roles.

The debates about whether teachers—and their students—should learn to write computer programs will undoubtedly rage on. And advocates for using one language rather than another will continue to air their opinions. Similarly, champions of particular software choices—be they of word processors, filing systems, or instructional software—will also be heard. Although such discussion and debate mark the dynamism of the field, they can be very confusing to beginners. For this reason, we confine ourselves to the general foundations of educational computing rather than addressing the specifics of particular programs or special points of view. In this way you, the reader, are spared both excessive technical detail as well as the passions of advocacy. Instead, you are treated to a series of discussions about computers in general and educational computing in particular. Our goal is to steer you toward the goal of being able to think through your own rationale for using computers in your professional careers.

As a consequence, we make no attempt to provide information about how to program in a particular high-level language such as BASIC, Logo, or Pascal. Likewise, we do not attempt to provide instruction to make you proficient with a particular word processing program or to run a particular package of instructional courseware. The list of possibilities, in any event, is almost endless and is constantly changing, so any such effort has limited value. Moreover, we believe that the inclusion of practical manuals in a book of this kind would detract from the fundamental information that all teachers need to know about computing. In our opinion, instruction on practice should be handled by special publications or kits that focus exclusively on a given program or language.

In order to achieve our goal of informing educators, we have held the text to a modest length so that it can be used as a primary text for a short course that provides an overview of educational computing. Alternatively, it may be used in conjunction with one or more practice manuals in a comprehensive course that includes work with computers. Each chapter presents an important dimension of educational computing. Chapter 1, for example, consists of an introduction to the history of computing, with particular emphasis on developments during the last half century. Chapter 2 completes the historical overview by reviewing the state of the ongoing electronic revolution. Topics include computing in the workplace, government, and the home, as well as legal and ethical issues. Chapter 3 attempts to clarify the inner workings of computers for people who have had little or no instruction in electronics. The purpose of this chapter is to help readers understand the kind of activity that goes on inside computers. It is all too easy to close one's mind to the fact that a great deal of orderly activity is occurring inside the tiny, enigmatic black computer chips. Moreover, there is considerable temptation to attach mystical—and even threatening—powers to computers, just because they are typically silent and nothing visibly moves.

The counterpart to the actual computer hardware is discussed in Chapter 4 in the examination of the software programs that have been written to drive the hardware. The discussion extends to operating systems, binary code, and computer languages. In addition, the chapter introduces readers to the types of storage that hold large amounts of information. Although Chapter 5 addresses educational computing specifically for the first time, much of what appears in the preceding chapters is written from the viewpoint of teachers rather than members of the general public. This chapter outlines what has occurred in educational computing since its beginning. It describes what the pioneers in educational computing tried to do, as well as outlining common applications of computers in schools today.

Chapter 6 addresses the familiar subject matter areas of the school curriculum. Instead of writing a book that refers to educational computing only in general terms, we decided that a better service to readers would be to outline how computers may be used in numbers of subject fields. After all, even in elementary schools where teachers are expected to cover almost all curricular areas, they typically divide the school day into time periods for the various subjects. And in secondary schools, teachers typically specialize in one or at the most two areas. Individuals will understandably focus attention on the areas they are to teach. Hopefully, however, they will also read some of the other sections, and in so doing extend their understanding of the contribution that computers can make to the total school curriculum. This chapter also includes a discussion of the computer as the focus of curriculum in the subjects of computer literacy and computer science. The merits of the computer languages that are best suited to educational application are weighed. The chapter concludes with a review of two computer literacy curricula.

Chapter 7 guides readers in the vitally important task of evaluating educational software. In general, teachers will use computing equipment mostly to support the teaching of the subject matter where they feel most competent. And very few are likely ever to write their own programs for general classroom use. Consequently, you need to know how best to become a good critic of published programs. In one sense, the task is not unlike evaluating a book or a film, but the character of computer programs is such that special techniques are needed in order to make effective evaluations and thus avoid spending money wastefully on materials that are either poorly written or inappropriate for a given task.

Finally, Chapter 8 discusses the future of educational computing. No one, of course, knows what the future holds in store, but judging from school trends, not to mention what is known about pending technological advances, there are many possibilities. The purpose of the chapter is to help you anticipate where computing in education is most likely to be moving in the foreseeable future. We will accomplish our goal if, after reading the chapter, you begin to fashion your own ideas about what may happen. This has particular relevance if you decide to become more deeply involved in some aspect of educational computing. But even if expertise in computing is not your goal, you will be preparing yourself to take an active role in the profession rather than passively accepting whatever occurs. This final chapter, in effect, continues the sentiments expressed at the opening of this Preface: that computing is here to stay and that educators need to keep informed about how to exploit this technology to its fullest in the best interests of student learning.

Acknowledgments

In 1982 the School of Education at Indiana University embarked on the development of an undergraduate teacher endorsement sequence in instructional computing. The idea for this book grew from our search for an appropriate text for the initial course in the sequence—a survey of educational computing—which we co-designed and co-taught. It is thus appropriate that we credit the role played by those early development efforts in shaping our views about educational computing generally and in challenging us to reflect on what knowledge of the field is of most importance to teachers.

Naturally, our students, both preservice and inservice teachers, have also influenced our thinking over the past several years. We owe them a debt of gratitude for helping us to clarify our thinking. We hope we have conveyed some of their wisdom in what appears between the covers of this book.

C.S.W.
G.H.

Contents

CHAPTER 6
Practical Applications of Computers in Education   *122*

CHAPTER 1

The Electronic Revolution

Introduction

Not long ago, one of the authors had the occasion to visit one of those super grocery stores in upstate New York that sells almost anything one might want, except perhaps furs and houses. Patrons of the store have three options for finding what they're looking for: (1) ask someone who works there, (2) walk the width of the store looking at the signs above each of the score of aisles, or (3) go to the nearest computer terminal.

It was really rather easy to use. Let's say you're looking for onions (and you have a cold, so your sense of smell won't help). On the computer screen you see the letters of the alphabet, with the instruction to touch the letter that corresponds to the first letter of what you're seeking. You touch the "O," the screen clears, and you see the beginning of a list of all the store items beginning with the letter "O." Touching another area of the screen makes the list continue, until you see "onions." When you touch the word, the screen clears again and displays a map of the store. The orange box marks where you are; the blue box marks where the onions are. You hear a voice from the computer say, "The onions are in aisle 17B." You're off and running. Meanwhile, you notice the patrons who walk past the terminal rather quickly, intently reading each of the signs above each of the aisles. The past and the future are colliding.

A local library is in the midst of changing its card catalog. Patrons now have two choices for finding the books they want: (1) look through the traditional and familiar card catalog, or (2) go to the nearest computer terminal. Either option provides the information they're accustomed to seeing, but the person who chooses the computer terminal gets more information. While the card catalog patron begins a futile search through the shelves for the three books she wants, the computer terminal patron is told that one book is checked out and won't be back until Friday. The second book is at the bindery and will be back next week. The third book should be in its place on the shelves. The past and the future collide; the future gains the advantage.

These two very real situations reflect a period of transition in history, where we recognize that we have one foot in the past and the other in the future. As the people who avoided the computer option in these examples show, transitions can produce anxiety accented by frustration. On the other hand, as the computer users learned, transitions are a time of tremendous opportunity, not just as an observer and participant but as an active agent of change. Times of transition carry in them the opportunity for people to help shape the contours of the future, to alter the current trajectories of change to the best of human aims.

To do this requires not only a vision of the future and alertness to the present but an understanding of the contextually rich past. Knowledge of the forces that have driven technology to its current state inform efforts to mold the future. In this chapter, we focus considerable attention on the past as a means to reflect on the significance of computer technology in our lives. In Chapter 2, we extend the discussion to how we have made computers a part of our lives and where we might take them in the future.

Origins of the Modern Computer

From Abacus to Mark I

If you have ever observed a child struggling to use his or her fingers for counting, you may recall a time when keeping track of quantities was for you no small task. For small quantities there was little trouble, but as amounts increased and (even worse) kept changing, fingers came in handy as devices to help you keep track and to calculate. What the child does is not unlike what early humans did when faced with the same challenge: They used their "digits," five on each hand, to help count and calculate.

Not without resources, though, humans began to employ devices other than anatomical: knots in a robe, pebbles on the ground, marks in the sand. Perhaps five thousand years ago, these devices evolved into the abacus. The word *abacus* has an interesting entymological root. "Abacus" comes from the Phoenician "abak," which referred to a stone spread with sand in which one might make marks. A slab of stone was called an "abax" by the Greeks, with reference to the sand apparently assumed. The Romans married the idea of the stone slab and pebbles. The device they used was called variously as "abaculi" (slab and pebbles) or "calculi" (pebbles). One can identify "abacus" in the first Latin term but not the

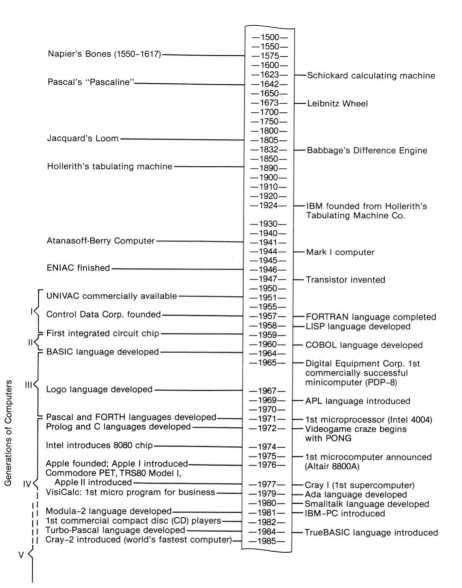

Napier's Bones (1550–1617) ———————— —1500—
—1550—
—1575—
—1600—
Pascal's "Pascaline" ———————— —1623— — Schickard calculating machine
—1642—
—1650—
—1673— — Leibnitz Wheel
—1700—
—1750—
—1800—
Jacquard's Loom ———————— —1805—
—1832— — Babbage's Difference Engine
—1850—
Hollerith's tabulating machine ———————— —1890—
—1900—
—1910—
—1920—
—1924— — IBM founded from Hollerith's Tabulating Machine Co.
—1930—
—1940—
Atanasoff-Berry Computer ———————— —1941—
—1944— — Mark I computer
—1945—
ENIAC finished ———————— —1946—
—1947— — Transistor invented
—1950—
UNIVAC commercially available ———————— —1951—
—1955—
Control Data Corp. founded ———————— —1957— — FORTRAN language completed
—1958— — LISP language developed
First integrated circuit chip ———————— —1959—
—1960— — COBOL language developed
BASIC language developed ———————— —1964—
—1965— — Digital Equipment Corp. 1st commercially successful minicomputer (PDP-8)
Logo language developed ———————— —1967—
—1969— — APL language introduced
—1970—
Pascal and FORTH languages developed ———————— —1971— — 1st microprocessor (Intel 4004)
Prolog and C languages developed ———————— —1972— — Videogame craze begins with PONG
Intel introduces 8080 chip ———————— —1974—
—1975— — 1st microcomputer announced (Altair 8800A)
Apple founded; Apple I introduced ———————— —1976—
Commodore PET, TRS80 Model I,
Apple II introduced ———————— —1977— — Cray I (1st supercomputer)
VisiCalc: 1st micro program for business ———————— —1979— — Ada language developed
—1980— — Smalltalk language developed
Modula-2 language developed ———————— —1981— — IBM-PC introduced
1st commercial compact disc (CD) players ———————— —1982—
Turbo-Pascal language developed ———————— —1984— — TrueBASIC language introduced
Cray-2 introduced (world's fastest computer) ———————— —1985—

Generations of Computers: I, II, III, IV, V

Timeline

second. From "calculi" we can derive "calculate," which was precisely what one did with an abacus. In a sense, the abacus was the Roman's calculator.

The pursuit of calculating devices continued to occupy individuals and nations as the field of mathematics evolved and matured. John Napier

(1550–1617) of Scotland labored on a device others dubbed "Napier's Bones," rods that were used in conjunction with one another to perform mathematical operations. Napier's rods were not unlike what we know today as a slide rule, another calculating device that has more recently been superceded by the march of progress. A German contemporary of Napier's, Wilhelm Schickard (1592–1635), designed a machine that would automatically add and subtract and perform multiplication and division in a semiautomatic manner. The machine had gears to accumulate numbers and a place set aside where unconnected gears could be used to enter numbers manually.

Apparently aware of Schickard's work, Blaise Pascal (1623–1662) produced his own machine, the Pascaline, to assist his father who was an import-export tariff collector in France. It also had gears and worked like a modern car odometer. Improving on both Schickard's and Pascal's machines, Gottfried Wilhelm von Leibnitz (1646–1716) developed the "Leibnitz wheel," capable of fully automatic multiplication and division.

Leibnitz's motivation for designing his machine derived less from economic or bureaucratic necessity than from the needs of science. Mathematics and astronomy by the 17th century were requiring more complex calculations than most individuals could perform efficiently. The figures appearing in astronomical tables required an enormous investment in time to calculate; at one time, a number of European governments employed commissions whose sole daily task was to calculate. One entry in one table might take the commission weeks or months to attain. Leibnitz struck at the heart of the machine's importance in observing:

> The astronomers surely will not have to continue to exercise the patience which is required for computation. It is this that deters them . . . from working on hypotheses, and from discussions of observations with each other. For it is unworthy of excellent men to lose hours like slaves in the labor of calculation which could safely be relegated to anyone else if machines were used. (quoted in Goldstine, 1972, p. 8)

Not all contributions to the development of calculating machines, and ultimately to computers, were related to calculations; sometimes contributions came from quite unexpected sources. The work of Joseph Marie Jacquard (1752–1834) is a good example. In the early 19th century, Jacquard devised a way to automate weaving machines. To weave a complex pattern on a loom, many different combinations of threads must be lifted or lowered with each pass of the shuttle. This required the weaver to be highly skilled and literate (to write down and read the pattern); it also required an assistant. Jacquard developed a system of cards in which holes were punched. In the process of operation, hooks would descend to pick up and lift particular threads, but only those hooks for which a hole was provided on the punched card would lift a thread. With a pass of the shuttle, the next card would pass into the machine; its pattern of holes denoted which threads were to be lifted in the next cycle. It is this system of punched cards that comes into play later in the same century.

The Jacquard loom was enormously successful, reducing the number of operators to one per machine and creating considerable joblessness among skilled weavers. Within 10 years, 11,000 Jacquard looms were in use in France, turning their inventor into a villain of automation. Introduction of the loom into England precipitated the Luddite protests, wherein displaced workers destroyed these automated looms and other labor-saving machines.

Following the more direct route of Pascal and Leibnitz, Charles Babbage (1791–1871) took mechanical calculating machines to new heights with his "Difference Engine." Indeed, Babbage is sometimes referred to as the father of the modern computer. Completed in 1832, the machine Babbage created could generate logarithmic and astronomical tables. The device used a set of linked adding machines to compute successive differences, hence the name Difference Engine. Based on this machine, Babbage received the first gold medal ever awarded by the British Royal Astronomical Society. His success brought him the financial backing he needed to work on a second machine, an "Analytical Engine," which was to use punched metal cards like the Jacquard loom and was to be powered by a steam engine. Unfortunately, machine tooling was insufficiently advanced in Babbage's time to produce the finely tooled gears he required, and the Analytical Engine project was never completed. Nonetheless, Babbage made a lasting contribution to the development of computers by identifying in his machines five fundamental parts of modern computers: a means to enter information (input), a means for doing the calculations (arithmetic unit), a mechanism for controlling the sequence of machine operations (control unit), a place to store information temporarily during the process (memory), and a means to see the results of the process (output).

Babbage's key comrade in his work was Lady Ada Lovelace, the daughter of Lord Byron. She provided both the encouragement and the financial backing needed to build the machines. More important for us, she wrote several of the operating instructions for the machines, something at which Babbage was rather inept. Ada Lovelace has rightly been referred to as the first programmer, and she is remembered today in a computer language used by the government and military called Ada.

Babbage undoubtedly depended considerably on the work of his younger contemporary, George Boole (1815–1864), who pioneered the distillation of logic into algebraic terms. Boolean algebra is based on a binary system, where 1 represents all the members of a particular set and 0 represents the empty set. There are two operations in this system: AND and OR; a third operation, NOT, can be added, but the system works with only the first two. From this system, one can construct a series of statements that represent a complex web of logical conditions and relationships. Boole's system lent itself well to the kinds of computing machines developed a century later.

Following the adage that "necessity is the mother of invention," more than one advance in computing technology has sprung from an urgent need. Indeed, a major step in the development of computers was in answer to a need of the United States government in the late 19th century. The 1880 census took more than seven years to tabulate, and rapid population increases threatened to lengthen this process to a full decade and beyond. Fearing that it would fall hopelessly behind as the years passed, the U.S. Census Bureau staged a contest to see if anyone could produce a machine that would speed up the tabulating process for the 1890 census. The winner was Herman Hollerith, whose tabulating machine used punched cards, the holes corresponding to census information to be gathered. The machine that read the cards had a series of counters representing all the categories of information. A counter would advance when it received an electrical impulse generated when a hole on the card corresponded to that counter and an electrical circuit was completed. Then the next card would be read, and so on.

Hollerith's machine was twice as fast as its nearest competitor and had the additional feature of allowing the collection of cards to be sorted in a variety of ways to get different arrangements of information. The U.S. Treasury provided all cards needed (all dollar-sized, of course), and the 1890 census proceeded. Within a month of the arrival in Washington of the last returns, the Census Bureau could announce the total population: 62,947,714. All the major reports of the 1890 census were completed within two and a half years, having collected categories of information not formerly possible. By 1911, the Hollerith Tabulating Machine Company had made its founder a millionaire and had merged with several other companies. In 1924, just five years before Hollerith's death, the company changed its name to the International Business Machine Corporation, or IBM.

With the entrance of the 20th century, development of calculating and computing machines took quantum leaps. As World War II loomed, Howard Aiken of Harvard University designed an automatic calculating machine that IBM agreed to build. Completed in 1944, the Mark I was hailed as Charles Babbage's dream come true. Rather than using gears, though, the Mark I used electromagnetic relays that would click open and closed. The sound it made was reminiscent of a room full of people knitting. The Mark I was over 50 feet long and 8 feet tall; it had 1 million parts and 500 miles of wire. A multiplication problem could be solved in a mere 6 seconds and division in 12 seconds. (There is a story associated with the Mark II, Mark I's sister machine, that during one of its occasional malfunctions, technicians discovered a moth mortally caught in one of the relays. The hapless insect was removed but remains infamous as the first computer "bug.")

Mark II log entry noting removal of the first computer "bug." *(U.S. Navy photo, courtesy of the Naval Surface Weapon Center, Dahlgren, Virginia.)*

With the introduction of electromagnetic relays came another significant development. The older mechanical devices had gears that were turned to represent different numbers. The form of operating instructions that Lady Lovelace had developed for Babbage was based on this use of gears. This had to be changed, though, to accommodate a system based on these two states: open and closed, on or off. Developers of the Mark I and its descendants used the binary number system to represent these two states: 0 represented off, 1 represented on. (We'll come back to this idea again.) From this point forward, computers would use this kind of machine language to carry out the instructions intended by the operators.

War-Time Developments: 1937–1946

World War II produced a strong demand for large-scale computers to handle the calculations involved in establishing trajectories for continually developing military ordnance. Not surprisingly, then, efforts to design increasingly powerful computing devices were going on simultaneously across the country. The electromagnetic avenue proved to be a dead end with the almost concurrent advance of electronics. John Vincent Atanasoff and Clifford Berry appear to be the first to abandon relays, creating a special-purpose machine called ABC (Atanasoff-Berry Computer) to solve linear equations. Its application of electronics via vacuum tubes influenced the development of the first general-purpose, electronic digital computer, the ENIAC.

Although intended to assist the war effort, ENIAC (Electronic Nu-

ENIAC with its co-inventor Eckert.   *(Courtesy of Unisys Corporation.)*

merical Integrator And Computer) was not completed until late 1945, born of a collaboration between John W. Mauchly and John Presper Eckert, Jr. It had no mechanical parts, no counters, and no wheels. It used on-off electric circuits in the form of vacuum tubes. Its 18,000 tubes required 130,000 watts of power. It was said that the lights in Philadelphia dimmed whenever ENIAC was turned on (Hooper and Mandell, 1984). The computer required two floors of air conditioned rooms because of the heat generated by the tubes. Even so, ENIAC could only be run for an hour or so before a tube was lost. Nonetheless, what Mark I could do in a week, ENIAC could do in 1 hour; the latter was about 1,000 times faster that the former. To change a program, however, the machine had to be rewired by manually setting internal switches.

Improvements on the basic electronic computer followed quickly. ED-SAC (Electronic Delay Storage Automatic Computer) incorporated John von Neumann's idea of storing the sequence of operating instructions (the program) within the computer itself, each instruction executed one at a time. This avoided the problem with ENIAC of resetting switches. The same strategy was followed in the development of EDVAC, completed in 1949 (Goldstine, 1972). By 1951 the first commercially avail-

UNIVAC was the first computer to predict a presidential election (1952). The historic event was covered by CBS correspondent Walter Cronkite. *(Courtesy of Unisys Corporation.)*

able computer had been completed: UNIVAC (Universal Automatic Computer).

The Four Generations of Computers

The advent of the vacuum tube as the basis of the electronic digital computer marks the beginning of four generations of true general-purpose electronic digital computers (see also Hopper and Mandell, 1984).

THE FIRST GENERATION (1951–1959) While vacuum-tube-based computers had been in use for five years, 1951 was the year UNIVAC I arrived on the scene. It is significant in that it was the first such device to leave the confines of the government, the military, or the scientific laboratory and to impress its impact on society more generally. From this small beginning in the *business* marketplace, the computer has reached the *mass* marketplace in the form of the microcomputer.

Computers of the first generation continued to fill entire rooms, although their size did tend to shrink as vacuum-tube technology advanced. Instructions were read into the computer by way of punched cards and were stored in the computer's memory. As an aid to programmers, symbolic languages were developed that were easier to use than the machine's language of zeros and ones. These languages would then be translated into machine language and executed.

THE SECOND GENERATION (1959–1964)   In 1947 John Bardeen, Walter Brattain, and William Shockley at Bell Labs invented the transistor, a kind of circuit that performed the same function as the vacuum tube but was smaller, faster, and more reliable. (The transistor's inventors were awarded the Nobel Prize in physics in 1956.) While the Japanese seized on the transistor for use in radios in the 1950s, it would be 1959 before transistors replaced vacuum tubes as the basis of electronic circuitry in computers. IBM, by this time the premier computer company in the nation, marketed a number of computers for business orientations during this time.

THE THIRD GENERATION (1964–1971)   Transistors had helped improve the reliability of computers, had reduced their size, and had increased their speed. To a certain extent, the invention of the transistor had also reduced production costs, in that transistors required less manual assembly than the vacuum tube. However, the individual transistors still had to be attached to a plastic board and soldered, and even in an automated process, the number of parts limited the speed of production and kept the price of computers relatively high. Although heat was less of a problem, transistors did stop functioning when they became as hot as a cup of coffee. For the military, whose new rocket-based weapons required resistance to high temperatures, transistors simply would not do. Consequently, considerable military funding went into the development of better circuitry.

By the early 1960s such a circuit had been developed, based on the inventive designs of Jack Kilby of Texas Instruments. This "integrated" circuit lies flat on a chip made of silicon, a semiconductor material. Integrated circuits held a lot of advantages over previous designs. First, more circuits could be packed into the same physical space, making computer components smaller. Indeed, hundreds of components could be placed on a single chip less than one eighth of an inch square. Second, the distance between circuits could be reduced, resulting in faster computers. Third, integrated circuits used less power and produced less heat.

This era also saw a number of other developments. Programming languages became more widely used, and new languages were developed. One was BASIC, developed by John Kemeny at Dartmouth University in 1964. The purpose of BASIC (Beginners All-purpose Symbolic Instruction Code) was to serve as a language students could learn easily.

Four generations of computers, represented (from back to front) by vacuum tubes, transistors, integrated circuits, and microprocessors. *(Courtesy of I.B.M. Archives.)*

More will be said about BASIC and other languages in Chapters 3 and 4.

The third generation of computers also saw the introduction of mini-computers, that is, computers possessing similar capabilities to larger machines but with smaller internal memory and taking up less physical space.

Finally, time sharing became a standard for interacting with the computer. Large computers could accommodate multiple users at what seemed to be the same time. Actually, users would share computer time, but the computer was so fast that the individual user would be unaware of delays caused by numbers of other people using the computer at what appeared to be the same time. The user could be in the room next to the computer or could be some distance away and communicating with the computer by telephone.

THE FOURTH GENERATION (1971–1980+)   Once the integrated circuit became a reality, the story of further developments centered around how many circuits could be packed on a single silicon chip. Large-scale integration (LSI), for example, made possible the pocket calculator and the digital watch.

By 1971 developers at Texas Instruments had developed a single-chip microcomputer, also called a microprocessor. This was an integrated circuit that incorporated all the basic elements of a computer: the arithmetic and logic component, the control unit, memory, and input/output circuitry (these parts and their function are explained in detail in Chapter 3). Intel Corporation also introduced a microprocessor in 1971, and by late 1974 produced the 8080 chip used along with additional memory chips in the Altair microcomputer kit marketed in 1975. The Altair was the first commercially available microcomputer. Other microcomputers soon appeared in the marketplace.

Advances in microprocessor technology were paralleled by the development of memory chips, that is, chips designed to hold all the zeros and ones needed to express commands in programs. The microprocessor would direct information to be stored in these chips, to be drawn from the chips in the course of executing programs. Intel produced the first practical, low-cost memory (RAM) chip by 1970. Three years later, a single chip could store over 1,000 pieces of information. By 1977 this

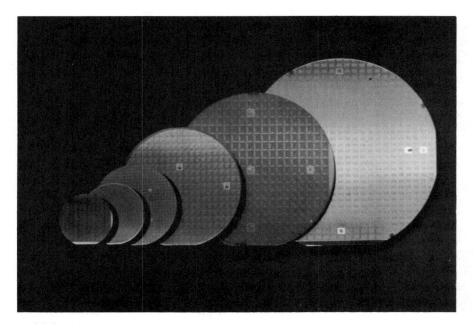

Multiple chips (the tiny squares) are photographically etched onto silicon wafers. Over the years, wafers have grown from 1 inch to 6 inches in diameter. *(Courtesy of National Semiconductor Corporation.)*

After testing, chips are separated from each other and each good chip (like the one on the fingertip) will be placed in a plastic holder. *(Courtesy of General Motors Corporation.)*

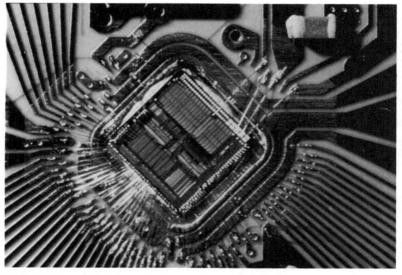

This 32-bit CPU chip, with wires radiating in all directions, can now reach out to other parts of the computer system. *(Photo courtesy of Hewlett-Packard Company.)*

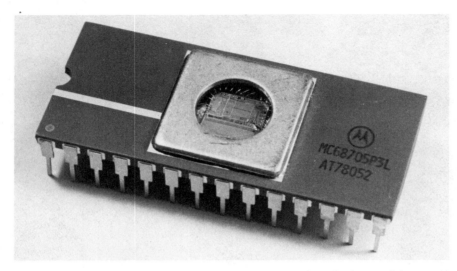

The chip, visible through the top of its holder, is ready to be inserted into a circuit board. *(Courtesy of Motorola, Inc.)*

figure had quadrupled, and it had increased sixteen times by 1980. A year later, over 64,000 pieces of information could be stored on a single chip, and by 1984 commercially available memory chips could store more than 256,000 pieces of information.

As a consequence of these advances, computers during the fourth generation continued to shink in size while growing in computing power. Moreover, the cost of computers fell during this period to the point where the computing power of ENIAC became affordable to a mass marketplace.

Summary: Trends in Computer Technology

It is said that humanity's scientific knowledge from the dawn of time to fifty years ago has been outstripped by the growth of science over the last half century. Computer technology, as machines that extend humankind's intellectual powers, has enjoyed an analagous growth spurt. In the last quarter century, silicon-chip technology advanced from a point where a chip held only a single transistor circuit to the point where a chip can hold half a million transistors today.

Even more graphically, consider a given computer task that in 1965 took a computer 29 seconds to process at a cost of 47 cents. Ten years later, the same task took 4 seconds and cost 20 cents. By 1985 that task was accomplished in barely four tenths (0.4) of a second and cost a mere 4 cents ("Computers' Next Frontiers").

There is little doubt that the trends we've noted over the last fifty years will continue. This new machine, the digital computer, has produced, and will continue to produce, profound social, psychological, economic, political, and educational changes. The trajectories of many such changes have already been set by the course of past events we have described. Let's see if we can catch a glimpse of what those changes are.

Impact and Significance: Digital Computers as Information Technology

Digital and Analog

We have already used the term "digital" in referring to four generations of electronic computers, and we have made reference to the use of zeros and ones as the fundamental language used by computers. Let's put those pieces of information together to explain more fully the significance of computer technology across many kinds of communication.

Humans used to count by using their "digits" or fingers. (Children today still do.) Because we have ten fingers, a system of counting based on ten became a standard, each finger representing a single digit. As a consequence of representing this system with arabic numerals, we are accustomed to seeing 1, 2, 3, 4, 5, 6, 7, 8, 9. Of course, the Arabs added the idea of 0, which is very handy when you have nothing of something. Note that when you get past 9, the next number is represented by two digits: 10. Now having a numbering system based on ten is fine for humans, but it is not as suitable for computers with switches that have only two conditions: on or off. For computers, a system based on two digits makes more sense, thus the use of 0 and 1 as the only digits employed. Extending this a bit further, a digital representation of any piece of information uses only numbers, and, in the case of computers, only the two digits at their disposal (0 and 1). And this is precisely what modern computers do; they convert all information into combinations of zeros and ones based on an organized code.

The usefulness of digital representations extends beyond just the convenience of computers, and this can be seen most clearly when considering how people communicate. When speaking to a friend, you are really sending out sound waves that vary in frequency (how close together the wave crests are) and in amplitude (how tall and deep the crests and troughs are). As you can see, both frequency and amplitude change constantly as you move along the waves. When you speak to your friend through a telephone, the microphone converts these sound waves into an exact electrical replica referred to as an *analog signal* (analog as in "analogy," a replica). That signal is carried through the telephone

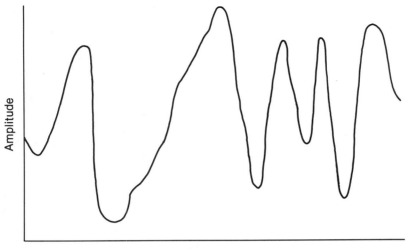

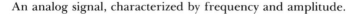

An analog signal, characterized by frequency and amplitude.

lines to the speaker of your friend's phone and converted back into sound waves. Analog signals are at work not only in telephones, but in most of today's music recordings ("analog recordings") and in radio and television transmissions.

There is a fundamental disadvantage with analog signals, however. As they are transmitted over wires (whether by telephone or in recordings) or through the air (as in radio and television), electrical interference (from cars, planes, and other machinery) gets mixed in with the communication signal. Moreover, because all signals weaken over distances, they have to be amplified at the receiving end. Unfortunately, the interference gets amplified right along with the real signal that was originally sent. This "noise" can mean you often can't hear what your friend is yelling at you over the phone, or your TV picture is fuzzy, or the music you're listening to isn't as clear as it was when it played by the musicians. Some of this noise can be filtered out, but it's hard to decide in an analog signal what is noise and what is really part of the original signal.

Here is where one benefit of digital technology comes in. It is possible to "digitize" analog signals, that is, to break the waves into regions and to give each region a digital code. So converted, what gets transmitted are series of ones and zeros, or, more accurately, series of pulses and non-pulses. At the receiving end of a digital transmission, the same interference noise has invaded the signal as before, but it's much easier to remove it. If the signal is below a certain strength, it must be a non-pulse or a 0, regardless of what variations in noise have been received. If the signal is above an expected level, it must be a true pulse or a 1.

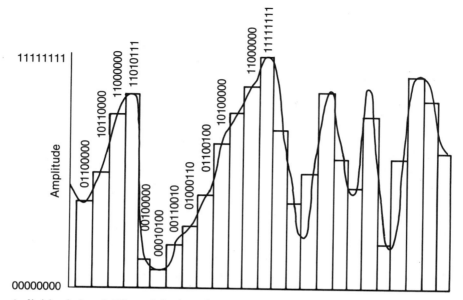

A digitized signal. The original analog signal is periodically "sampled" (vertical bars), and these sampled levels are assigned a digital value. The digital values are then transmitted. This process is reversed at the receiving end.

This filtering results in a stream of zeros and ones as pure as the stream originally sent. In this way, when the digital code is reconverted into an analog form (that is, sound waves), the clarity of the original is preserved. Thus, if your conversation with your Parisian friend is digitized, it will sound as if he or she is speaking from next door.

Unification of Diverse Technologies

Of course, the implications of digital technology go far beyond clearer telephone conversations. If voice communication can be digitized and transmitted, other forms of communication can be digitized as well. If I wanted to use a computer in Michigan, and I had my own microcomputer at home in Virginia, my computer could communicate with that distant computer over telephone lines, just as easily as your long-distance telephone conversation. The zeros and ones of my communication are changed into tones sent over the wires, and changed back into zeros and ones when they arrive at the Michigan computer in exactly the same way. Airline companies can use computer-based communications to transmit and record booking information rapidly, and I can use the same system to find out an airline's flight schedule and to make a reservation.

Or maybe I'll just tele-order some live lobsters to be delivered to my door. . . .

Many other communications media can also be digitized. The music that used to be recorded on an album and required a needle dragged through grooves may also be recorded on disks read with lasers. Motion pictures can also be stored on disks and reproduced on the screen in a similar fashion. The written material that could only be stored on sheets of paper may now be stored on disks and tapes and transmitted at lightning speed over telephone lines or beamed worldwide through satellite transmission. And formerly unused sectors of television signals can now carry digital communications.

At the heart of this discussion is the idea that forms of communication that used to be produced, recorded, transmitted, and reproduced in different ways can now be reduced to a single, digital system based on computer technology. The computer, in essence, has embraced the diverse forms of human communications and has united them in all sorts of interesting and valuable ways. Think of how many ways forms of communication can be mixed together: telephones that carry sound and pictures; entertainment centers that carry music recordings with video; televisions that send pictures, sound, and text.

The Information Age

Leibnitz's observation regarding the usefulness of machines has been borne out. Problems that formerly took teams of human calculators months to solve can now be arrived at painlessly in fractions of a second. Beyond relieving some elements of drudgery, the advance of information technology has also precipitated an accelerating volume of information. Not only is the amount of information that is generated daily increasing, but the capacity of electronic technology to store, retrieve, and manipulate information is also increasing.

The technology that handles all this information has its own handlers, of course—the people whose occupation involves working with the technology to shuttle information from place to place. Rather than wrestling with a jackhammer, these men and women wrestle with a keyboard ultimately connected at some point to a computer. Instead of building edifices of concrete and steel, they build data bases of facts and figures. These are the information workers, the workforce of the Information Age.

John Naisbitt (1982) dates the Information Age as beginning around 1956 and 1957, when, respectively (1) white-collar workers outnumbered blue-collar workers for the first time, and (2) *Sputnik* became the catalyst for rapid technological change. And while it would be misleading to suggest that the Information Age has reached maturity, it is reasonable to believe that it is approaching its tempestuous adolescence. A brief inspection of three manifestations of the Information Age may convey a sense of the ungainly development of this era as it moves beyond childhood.

The first of these exemplars of the Information Age is on-line data retrieval. In brief, a large computer and its equally large memory capacity stores, updates, and manages a large amount of information—conventionally referred to as *data*. This collection of data is called a *data base*. If you subscribe to a commercial service that owns a large computer in which are stored one or more data bases, you can connect to their computer (get "on line") by way of a telephone and retrieve the data of your choice. If the computer stores a variety of data bases on different topics, you may have to subscribe to each one separately. The data you have retrieved appears immediately on your computer monitor screen. You may then have it printed out on paper if you have a printer attached to your computer, or you may "download" the information from the large computer onto a memory storage medium attached to your own computer (see Chapter 4 for a discussion of storage media).

The number of on-line data bases has mushroomed, growing at more than 35 percent annually, according to one estimate ("Total Databases Top 2000"). As of April 1984, more than 2 thousand data bases were available for business and individuals. The topics, of course, are wide ranging. For example, for those of us who have difficulty keeping up with all the articles written about computers in the plethora of computer magazines, there are data bases that provide abstracts of all these articles. You can of course search for computer topics you're particularly interested in without looking at all the abstracts. These include a directory of the latest computer dating services or what high school physics software has been reviewed recently. If you need information about U.S. legal cases and legislation, or about British and European law, then you might subscribe to Westlaw (the U.S. data base) or Eurolex (the European version) and access information from either side of the Atlantic.

While some of these data bases seem rather obscure, several large data base services have become quite popular among individual computer enthusiasts, such as The Source and Compuserve. Many manage collections of data bases and, because communication between computers can be two-way, some provide on-line "browsing" through catalogs of consumer goods and, of course, on-line ordering (like the lobsters we were telling you about).

Taking the idea of two-way communication a bit further brings you to the second manifestation of the Information Age, computer conferencing. Here's how it works. My computer can tie into my telephone using a modem, a device that translates my computer's zeros and ones into those tones that can be transmitted over the phone. My fellow conference participants and I "converse" by sending messages by telephone to a central computer to which we are all connected. Each person dials the

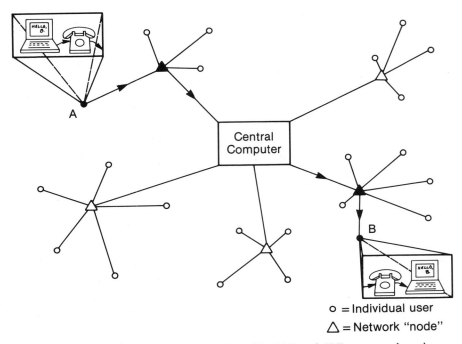

o = Individual user

△ = Network "node"

A computer conferencing network. Users (like "A" and "B") connect by telephone to a network node, which in turn connects to the central computer. Real-time conversations can occur or messages can be left for later retrieval.

computer's telephone number, the central computer answers, and it stores each message for other participants to read and make a response. One of the beauties of computer conferencing is that participants don't all have to be connected to the central computer at the same time. The central computer holds all messages and delivers them to the participants of my choosing whenever they connect. Recipients then read their messages, mull them over, and respond at their convenience. Their replies are waiting for me the next time I tie in. There are no busy signals, no being put on hold, and no waiting until Joe or Mary gets back to the office or back home.

The University of Michigan sponsors one such computer conferencing system called CONFER, designed especially for those interested in computers and computing. You can join one or more ongoing conferences concerning computers in general, computers in education, and other more specialized topics. Within each conference, an agenda is maintained that lists the specific topics participants have discussed, so that you can read what has been entered and reply if you like. Public items can be displayed for all participants, or you can send private messages to one or more individuals in the conference. Surprisingly lively debate can ensue, and the quality of discussion can generate very useful ideas.

Computer conferences can also be sources of information or assistance. Those who wish to tap participants' knowledge in a certain area can "post" a message requesting help. Looking for a computer program for a high school American government class? Ask if anyone has seen or used any. Several dozen, or several hundred, people will see your message. Compare this to other alternatives for seeking the same information, ways that may be time-consuming and painfully slow.

On-line data base retrieval and computer conferencing are unique features of the Information Age that relate to obtaining already-produced information and to communicating information. A third manifestation of the Information Age focuses on the production of information at its earlier stages: when it gets thought of and written down. Examples of this dimension of computer technology include word processors and outline processors.

Word processors are programs that allow a person to sit at a computer keyboard and use it like a typewriter, except that what gets written appears on a monitor screen and is simultaneously stored in the computer's memory. In itself, this capability doesn't sound very impressive until you consider editing what you've written. We all remember how we felt at school the first time a teacher critiqued our first draft, when we had really hoped it was the final draft. Rewriting was a drudgery to be avoided, mainly because it really meant writing the whole thing over again, the good parts and the bad. We may also remember typing a ten-page paper flawlessly (with liberal applications of "white-out") and discovering to our horror that we'd left out maybe the most important paragraph—on page 2? Herein lies the beauty of word processors. They allow you to edit, correct, rearrange, add, and subtract text before it ever appears on paper. Thus, ideas remain central to the writing process, where they belong, and mechanical tasks assume a subordinate status, as they should.

Word processors also take care of those messy little details like renumbering pages if necessary and maintaining the consistency of margins. And if you have difficulty with spelling, grammar, even writing style, a computer program can help. It will warn you if your sentences are too ponderous, if you use passive voice too frequently, if your punctuation is off, and if you've slipped into sexist language. If you persist in believing that your style (or someone else's) is preferable to the computer's standards, you can reprogram the software to adopt new standards ("Poetry Writ by the Numbers" p. 79).

What does all this mean for the production and use of information? First, considerable time can be saved. Improvements are simple to make, and small variations needed across several documents no longer require starting from scratch. And, of course, the words that can be stored in a computer's memory can as easily be transmitted digitally to whatever destination is appropriate. With the more sophisticated adjuncts to the simple word processor, the way people learn to write may be significantly altered.

Unlike word processors, outline processors aid in the writing task before the actual writing takes place, that is, at the idea stage. While outline processors are a bit difficult to describe succinctly, a quote from one who did is appropriate:

> Basically, [outline processors] allow users to create an outline very much like the one most students learn in grade school. The difference is that, because of the computer's power to manipulate information quickly, the outline information can be entered randomly—in fact, it can be entered long before the author has any idea of what the outline will include. As the information begins to pile up, it can be labeled, reorganized, and structured like an outline. . . . Because users can start the process by typing in virtually any idea and organizing it later, some call [these programs] "brainstorm" processors. ("Outline Processors Catch On," p. 30)

What we have, then is another computer-based tool serving the needs of people who invest increasing amounts of their time as producers and manipulaters (in the best sense of the word) of information. For school children learning how best to express their ideas and to use information effectively in support of their ideas, both word processors and outline processors are especially appropriate.

Summary

In this chapter, we have traced the development of computing technology from abacus to microcomputer. In so doing, we have described two of the most significant results of advances in computer technology: the digitization of information and the subsumption of historically discrete media under a single, unifying digital technology. Propelled by these advances, our society entered what has been dubbed the Information Age, three manifestations of which we briefly surveyed.

In the next chapter, we will examine in more detail current applications of computer technology and will speculate a bit about the shape of things to come in the Information Age. Both carry implications for how the technology may be used in the schools.

References

"Computers' Next Frontiers," *U.S. News & World Report*, August 26, 1985, pp. 38–41.

GOLDSTINE, HERMAN H. *The Computer from Pascal to von Neuman*. Princeton, NJ: Princeton University Press, 1972.

HOPPER, GRACE MURRAY, & MANDELL, STEVEN L. *Understanding Computers.* New York: West Publishing Company, 1984.
NAISBITT, JOHN. *Megatrends.* New York: Warner Books, 1982.
"Outline Processors Catch on." *Infoworld,* July 2, 1984, pp. 30–31.
"Poetry Writ by the Numbers," *Newsweek,* September 2, 1985, p. 79.
"Total Databases Top 2000." *Information Today,* no. 4 (April 1984), pp. 1, 3.

CHAPTER 2

The Present and Future of Electronic Technology

Introduction

In the preceding chapter, we saw the evolution of electronic technology and recognized how evolution turned to revolution in the period after World War II. Our purpose was to underscore the significance of this revolution by looking back to where we've been. In this chapter, we propose to examine the range of current applications of electronic technology and to consider where we might take this technology in the future.

Notice that we said "where we might take this technology" rather than "where it might take us." A key assumption in this book is that the future is not preordained and is as yet unformed with respect to technology. This assumption applies as well to our view of education—that its future is similarly malleable. How we might shape education in the future depends on whether we maintain a clear view of general purposes of education—the "big picture," if you will. We ought to ground the educational use of technology not on the technology, but on those general purposes. Some preliminary thoughts about what those general purposes might be and how they might be interpreted in light of the new technologies conclude the chapter and set the stage for closer scrutiny in later chapters.

The Scope of Current Computer Applications

In the Arts and Sciences

In the arts, we have already mentioned the digital recording of music. The compact disk (CD) is gaining in popularity, valued for its high fi-

This CD ROM half-height drive accommodates 5.25 inch compact disks and is designed for integration into a microcomputer. External CD ROM drives are also available. *(Courtesy of Laser Magnetic Storage International, a joint venture between Philips and Control Data.)*

delity to the original performance. Beyond this, however, CDs are likely to last almost indefinitely because of their construction and the method used to play them. The digital information is stored in spiral tracks and is read optically with a laser beam. No piece of equipment is in actual contact with the disk, unlike the needle of a standard record, so that there is virtually no wear. The disk itself is covered with a substance that protects the information from the environment but allows the laser beam to pass through and access the information. The disk is thus not susceptible to decay from the environment.

Optical disk technology is applied to a wide range of uses in the arts. Disks that store video digital information (videodiscs) are also widely available and equally indestructable. The zeros and ones in the grooves express every detail of every frame of every scene you see on the screen.

Disks that store data in the same manner are also appearing in the marketplace. A 5¼-inch disk, capable of storing the equivalent of 1 million typewritten pages, is now available for microcomputers. Such disks and the equipment to read them are prohibitively expensive for the individual user now, but prices can be expected to decline as the equipment becomes more plentiful.

For large-scale users, applications of optical data disks have been impressive. The print-based card catalog of the Library of Congress, for example, would extend the length of a football field. Now, all that information is on thirty 14-inch optical disks, each holding 200,000 library cards. On a smaller scale, schools with the right equipment can use the complete *Grolier Encyclopedia* on optical disk.

Beyond optical disks that store large amounts of information, the computer itself has come in very handy in the arts. Several Broadway theaters have used computers to control stage lighting. Musicians have used computers in the form of music synthesizers, capable of reproducing nearly every musical "voice" in a full orchestra. Needless to say, musicians' unions are wary of this particular innovation. On the other hand, musicians themselves have found computers useful for producing complete orchestrations. An individual can sit at a piano, play a tune, and watch what is being played appear in the form of written sheet music, complete with the lines of the staff, sharps and flats, time signatures . . . the works.

The visual arts are also exploiting computer technology. Computer graphics is a new art form, a new artistic medium, producing works of art and design heretofore unimagined, or at least unrealized. Computer graphics are creating what look like photographs and motion pictures of objects and phenomena only possible in one's own mind. Industry and business, advertising design, television graphics, and motion picture imagery have become heavily dependent on a multitude of forms of computer-generated graphics.

Medicine is an arena where such formerly unimaginable forms are appearing. A thoroughly detailed human skeleton can be electronically produced and then may be viewed from any direction, close up or at a distance, stationary or in motion. The CAT (Computerized Axial Tomography) scanner is capable of producing images of microscopic slices of the brain or other organ, without scalpels and anesthesia, to aid in medical diagnosis. Medical research has been significantly assisted by the ability to display molecular structures in three dimensions.

In astronomy, the dramatic photographs of the windswept surface of Mars and the looming faces of Jupiter and Saturn would have been disappointingly blurred images without computer-enhanced photographic techniques. Even the relatively close-up photographs of Uranus and its moons taken by *Voyager 2* required some means to compensate for the space probe's incredible velocity (9 miles per second). Sophisticated use of the probe's on-board computer made such image motion compensation (IMC) possible, yielding dramatic results (Beatty, 1986). The discovery of distant galaxies as old as the universe itself would similarly remain beyond our grasp without computers.

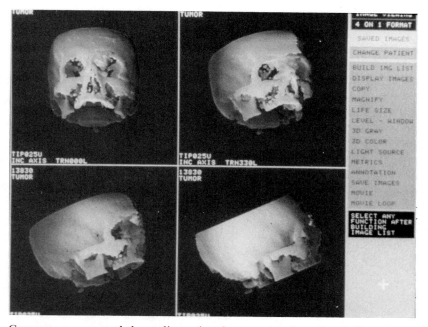

Computer-generated three-dimensional reconstruction of a skull, revealing the location of a facial tumor. *(Courtesy of CEMAX, Inc., Santa Clara, California.)*

In the Economy and the Workplace

The computer has also affected how business does business and how employees do their work. For manufacturing enterprises, CAD/CAM will continue to have a significant impact. The first part of the acronym, CAD, stands for *computer-aided design*. Rather than sketching out a new car design on paper, the designer uses the computer to help put the car design together, complete with a visual model that can be viewed from a variety of angles. Such imaginary, computer models can then be "tested" for wind resistance and any number of other factors important to the efficiency and sales appeal of cars—all before a physical model has been produced. Everything from cars to computers can be designed through CAD.

CAM stands for *computer-aided manufacture*. Consider a petrochemical factory where refining and production require a complex set of conditions to be maintained at multiple stages in the process. The temperatures have to be just right, and for the precise amount of time required. Fitting all the pieces of the process together and keeping them together is difficult for humans but easy for a computer. Well-designed computer-aided manufacture can result in production lines that run faster, more

An automobile engineer uses a CAD system to create new car models. *(Courtesy of Chrysler Corporation.)*

smoothly, and more efficiently than other production lines, with a minimum amount of disruption when problems appear in the process. Add a few robots to the picture, and businesses find that they can increase the overall productivity of the factory.

The petrochemical factory may be only one of dozens owned and operated by a large, multinational corporation, requiring a high degree of coordination in their daily operations. The decision makers in this far-flung enterprise need to conduct business across many miles without going bankrupt with airfares. The solution is teleconferencing. Executive offices in every factory in the corporation can be tied together with sound, picture, and data transmission, giving the distinct impression that everyone is in the same room. The cost savings, communication speed, and efficiency of decision making are considerable.

A related computer application may affect both employers and employees. If a person's job involves primarily information tasks, why must this necessarily be done in the office? Why not stay home and be a "tele-commuter"? Why not "ride to work" over the telephone lines rather than being stalled in traffic lines? As "tele-commuting" has entered the busi-

Another impact of technology on the auto industry: on-board navigation systems. *(Courtesy of Chrysler Corporation.)*

ness lexicon, so has "flexiplaces," connoting flexibility in the sites where one earns a living.

Other computer applications are allowing businesses to reach out to consumers, expedite communication, and centralize billing. Here are some recent examples:

Videotex: in Oklahoma and around the world. A system of two-way information transmission, computer-based and displayed on a monitor. In Oklahoma City, public access terminals have been placed in forty locations, including the city's airport and major hotels, catering especially to consumers, tourists, and shoppers.

In Europe, where communications systems traditionally have been more unreliable and sparsely distributed compared to the U.S. telephone system, more advanced applications of videotex are emerging (need as mother of invention). In France, videotex services provide electronic phone directories, financial services, classified ads, farm crop and equipment information, consumer rights data, timetables, restaurant guides, disease diagnosis, and the like.

Britain's Prestel system of information services and electronic mail was started by the British post office. Electronic mail is somewhat of a misnomer in this instance, since Prestel, and many systems like it, are really computer-based message systems. Most messages don't take the place of letters, but they do replace short telephone calls. Electronic mail has proven to be relatively inexpensive and efficient, not unlike the benefits described in connection with computer conferencing. It is interesting to note that the U.S. Postal Service attempted an electronic mail service called E-COM, but it eventually failed. A needed price hike would have placed it out of the market. Moreover, the Postal Service was limited in its charter, according to which it could provide only paper-based mail service; the computer-to-computer transmission typical of most electronic mail services was out of the question.

A French company, Intelmatique, is currently issuing Multi-Service Smart Cards, plastic cards shaped like credit cards, but with one or more microchips embedded in the surface. The chips are programmable and have memory storage capacities. Capable of containing a hefty amount of information about its bearer, a Smart Card can provide higher security in transactions. The card is used for public pay telephones, for videotex service payment, for decoders to use France's fourth television channel (pay TV), and for payment mechanisms for delegates attending conferences and special events at permanent exhibition/convention sites. Similar cards have begun to appear in the United States as well.

Undercutting the costs of telephone transmission of information, electronic publishing by satellite is a teletext system in which information is transmitted to a central location, digitized, and beamed by satellite to a receiving station. (Though similar to videotex, teletext differs from videotex in the manner of its transmission and its capabilities for two-way communication.) In the case of financial or news services, subscribers retrieve what they want from the data base that is transmitted. Such systems are now being used by such businesses as Reuters Limited,

UPI, Associated Press, and Dow Jones. The Associated Press purchased its 10,000th earth station in 1984. Using the same system, other companies can construct and control their own private data communications networks.

Looking for a job? Put your resume in the Career System computer, a California-based job search/recruiting service. Major companies like American Express, W. R. Grace, Prudential, Marriott, Tandem, and Data General subscribe to the system in searching for a match between job criteria and the resumes stored in the data base. Individuals can add their resumes to the system for free, since it is the employer who pays the subscription fee.

Are you a farmer looking for the high tech solution? Join the Eastern Computing Farmers Association. Members get free agricultural computing consultation by phone, access to an agricultural software library, conferences and seminars, and group discounts on computer supplies.

The role of computers in the economic life of nations is growing rapidly, with the number and variety of applications only hinted at by the brief list of examples we have provided here.

In Politics and Government

In the 1984 presidential election, the use of computers figured prominently, specifically at the Democratic National Convention in San Francisco. According to one of the deputy convention managers, "In 1980 the only use we had for computers was basically our housing system. . . . It's nothing like it is now, with computers as our eyes and ears" ("Democrats Computerize Politics," p. 23). Delegates were able to vote electronically and have their votes tabulated instantly. According to a computer consultant for the convention, though, "They'll still do the roll call for the benefit of the TV and the folks back home" (Ibid). Videotex monitors replaced bulletin boards; conference attendees could watch to see if they had messages and then retrieve them from one of the terminals in the convention hall or in several hotels.

The convention chose as its presidential candidate Walter Mondale, whose own computer resources were considerable. His headquarters kept track of the 3,000 delegates, 1,300 alternates, and 2,000 volunteers almost 24 hours a day. Detailed records were kept on each delegate and alternate, 45 variables in all, including name, address, issues preferences, and spouses. A Mondale computer aide described how the system worked: "Let's say a floor fight breaks out and we need to find a group concerned with the [nuclear] freeze. We could identify them in seconds on the tracking system and go talk to them directly" ("Mondale's Electronic Running Mates," p. 25). As an article on Mondale's electronic campaign noted, "this potential allows a group as diverse as, say, all 'pro-freeze feminists from the Sunbelt under 35' to be isolated and reckoned with even before they have a chance to raise a picket sign" (ibid).

Placing this computerized politics in perspective, however, it is important to note that Walter Mondale lost the presidential election to Ronald Reagan.

In the Military

Not long ago, a movie called *War Games* depicted the frightening possibilities of tampering with a computerized war simulation game used for military training and strategic planning. Although one may justifiably take issue with some of the technical aspects of war games as depicted in the movie, the use of computer-based simulated wars by the military is no secret. Indeed, they have become quite sophisticated.

A vivid example is one that is used for officer training. Placed in command of units engaged in battle, the officers must make strategic decisions, including whether to call for nuclear weapons. Some officers, in desperate situations, take the nuclear option. The officer's initial elation at stopping the enemy is tempered rather quickly by the realization that his own forces have been decimated along with those of the enemy. The simulation displays the effects of the nuclear action, including its effects downrange from the blasts based on wind speed, humidity, and other atmospheric conditions.

In a less foreboding arena, the military has also made extensive use of interactive video, the electronic coupling of a computer and a videodisc. A number of highly motivating simulation games provide training, for example, to tank repair personnel, allowing the trainee to take actions via the computer and view the results on the video screen.

Computers are also very good at keeping track of and controlling a large number of individual devices, and herein lies the computer's big advantage over humans. "The fuel-control system alone in a modern fighter jet has more than 5,000 parts" ("Military in a Fix," p. A16). The navy's Aegis radar has 6 million parts. When the interplay of all those parts must be flawless, only a computer can monitor such a complex system.

One outcome of military use of computer technology has been the development of "smart" weapons, weapons whose operation can be altered and adjusted even after they have left the launch site. A hand-held missile launcher developed for the army can continue to direct its missile directly to the target with the aid of a laser beam. The Cruise missile is even more sophisticated in this regard. After launch, the Cruise flies near to the ground and scans the lay of the land. It then searches its computer memory to match the terrain it "sees" to terrain it "knows." When it makes a match, the Cruise can then navigate itself around or over hills and other obstructions.

One particularly smart weapon is available beyond just the military. The **PROWLER** (Programmable Robot Observer With Logical Enemy Response) is equipped with sensing devices attached to a microcomputer running artificial intelligence software (described later), and can be used to guard military bases, prisons, or perhaps even a department store parking lot. The advantages are numerous; it doesn't get bored or fall asleep, it doesn't have to be paid, and it does what it is told. According to an article in *Newsweek*, "purchasers will specify the sensors and weaponry they desire—and also whether or not the robot will need human permission (from a remote monitoring station) before it opens fire" ("Birth of the Killer Robots," p. 51).

Clearly, the military has displayed considerable initiative in exploiting the computer's potential, not only for weapons production but also for training. The investment in computer-based training and development by the military may well have implications for computer-based education in the schools.

In the Home

The home, of course, enjoys some of the benefits of the applications we have already described. Compact discs and videodiscs are prime examples.

Computers allow you to reach out from your home, not just for work but for everyday chores and interesting diversions. If you can tele-commute, you can tele-shop. A computer store in Nevada runs an electronic bulletin board offering tips on computer operation, product information, and even community bulletins. You can preview computer programs for 15 minutes, and, while you cannot copy then, you can place an order by computer. On the other hand, a Torrance, California, software distributor will actually send the program to your computer and store it permanently on a blank storage disk (after you've charged it on your credit card, of course).

Have you just gotten a computer and need some guidance with a program or two? There is a 24-hour cable news network devoted entirely to news of the computer industry that now combines television transmission and computer-to-computer communication. While you receive a picture on your television, you can be receiving computer software through a separate cable channel. While watching a televised demonstration of a computer program, you can practice the program at your home computer ("Computer News Shows Planned," p. 13).

Need a greater sense of security in your home? Register your belongings with Secure 24, a 24-hour emergency identification, security, and information retrieval service. You can store medical information, insurance data, and even descriptions of your children should they become lost.

In these areas of our lives and others, the computer is becoming a

force of change, offering opportunities and presenting challenges, be-
stowing benefits and exacting costs. We consider next what some of those
costs might be.

The Price of Technological Progress

> Isaac Asimov once wrote that the important thing to predict is not the
> automobile, but the parking problem; not the radio, but soap operas; not
> the income tax, but expense accounts; not the Bomb, but the arms race.
> Similarly, the important thing to forecast is not that schools and universi-
> ties, homes and industries will add videodisks, microcomputers, satellite
> telecommunications, and interactive "artificial intelligence" simulations to
> the repertoire of instructional techniques. Rather, the crucial question be-
> comes, "What new 'social inventions' will spring from these devices to en-
> hance learning?" (Dede, Bowman, and Kierstead, 1982, p. 174)

Asimov's "social inventions" may be viewed as desirable or undesirable,
depending on one's point of view. Having described some of the more
obvious, and glowing, outcomes of technological change, we need to explore some social inventions that are less obvious and less positive.

Computer Crime

When new technologies emerge, questions about the legality of various
uses are frequently difficult to answer. Our legal system is faced with
trying to catch up, applying traditional concepts to new contexts. Sometimes, a computer use is questionable, maybe illegal, but falls into a gray
area; sometimes those who exploit computers in questionable activities
find themselves exploited by the computer. Other computer uses are less
ambiguous. One observer of the rising wave of computer-related crime
attempted a classification system to describe the wide-ranging manifestations of this fast growing "social invention." The types of crime
BloomBecker (1981) described were based on what he saw as emerging
from varying perceptions of computer systems on the part of the per-
petrators of these crimes.

One type of crime grows from a view of a computer system as "the
land of opportunity." Frequently, this involves an employee who stum-
bles upon (and exploits) a vulnerability in the system with which he or
she is working, discovered perhaps in the course of learning the job.
Imagine the operator of a check-printing device who presses the RE-
PEAT button when her check is being produced. Not unrelated to this
accidental discoverer is the person who is simply unaware of the power
he or she is wielding in operating the computer as part of the job. For
them, the computer is "fairyland," divorced from reality. Consider the

Computer Takes Its Revenge for Wick's Misuse

WILLIAM SAFIRE

Never abuse a computer; it has a way of getting even.

USIA Director Charles Wick has been taking advantage of the government computer in his office for years.

He puts all kinds of stuff in: household files, personal tax information, Christmas card lists, personal diary notes that could be useful in a memoir, files marked "fantasy," "the sayings of Walter Annenberg," and instructions to government secretaries to keep his smile bright ("Mary—remind me to buy some toothbrushes today") and to find his favorite stories ("Peggy—in my jokes, give me one 'Shoes ready Tuesday.' ")

Peggy Gugino Pape, described as a "transcriptionist," dutifully listens to all the tape-recorded notes from her boss and types them into a word processor. These have included portions of telephone conversations secretly taped by Wick.

Robert Earle, the foreign service officer who is Wick's chief assistant, has been looking over these notes as they come out of the printer, and has "routinely discarded—burned or shredded—some of them.

After Wick was forced to admit his secret taping, which violated federal regulations, the Senate and House demanded to see all the tapes or transcripts on hand. He sent over a bunch; among those taped without their knowledge were columnist John Loften, new-right publisher Richard Viguerie, and comedian Bob Hope.

Wick's associates showed no great worry about this limited submission of transcripts to Congress: after all, the other, perhaps more embarrassing stuff had been thrown away and the computer purged. And the Congress had not even asked for the "CZW Daily Notes" in which the secret transcripts were embedded.

But Senate investigators found one item that completely escaped the bumbling House Foreign Affairs Committee Staff: one call was apparently taped by Wick in California, where state law forbids secret taping in many circumstances. Los Angeles District Attorney Robert Philibosian was informed.

Then the abused USIA computer, fed up with 7,000 ill-phrased documents that it had been forced to engorge, and indignant at having to run off 160 "personal" apologies from Wick to his victims, struck back. Someone tipped off Senate investigators that a copy of the complete Wick file—unpurged—was on "backup" magnetic tapes in a USIA vault.

"I do not now know how the magnetic backup tapes came to be

prepared," swears Earle in a Freedom of Information affadavit. ". . . I do not recall being informed that a copy of Office files was routinely retained by the Computer Center on electronic media."

Thus, while the aide was shredding his hard copies and the typist was purging the processor at her desk, a master computer was just as busily remembering everything. It is supposed to forget within 48 hours, but in this case—perhaps with the nudge of a technician who did not like what Rep. Dan Mica Thursday called Wick's "climate of fear"—the computer made a copy, perhaps unknown to Wick aides.

As a result, another installment of transcripts was sent to the Congress by a USIA that had previously assured us that all preserved conversations had been submitted. And lo—in this batch of 47 taped or eavesdropped-on calls is one in July 1983, from Senate Foreign Relations Chairman Charles Percy. The conversation with Sen. Percy in Washington, seems to have been secretly recorded by Wick at a telephone in California, where we all now know such taping may be illegal if the statute covers interstate calls. (If this were a news story, I suppose that would be the lead.)

The Senate staff knew of this evidence of a second California call for three weeks without informing the Los Angeles DA; Philibosian's staff had been promptly notified by Wick's counsel, but did not get in touch with the Senate for the transcript until asked about it Wednesday. In this investigation, only the computer is showing any fervor.

Moreover, thanks to The Computer That Refused to Forget, a complete set of Wick's "DRS"—his Direct Record System, which Earle calls "the Director's public affairs contact system"—is preserved intact. The USIA shrugs this off as no more than a list of names and addresses, but has been resisting a Freedom of Information request for four months.

Moral: Those who secretly use technology to record may be confounded by machines that secretly refuse to forget.

SOURCE. Copyright © 1984 by The New York Times Company. Reprinted by permission.

employee who daily and routinely transfers millions of dollars from one account to another; there is an unreality here that can lead that employee to being either unwittingly used by others or insufficiently observant in detecting potential crimes in progress.

Quite a different kind of computer criminal views the computer as a "war zone," using it to retaliate against employers. BloomBecker recounts the story of a disgruntled programmer who arranged to have the computer erase all the company's records automatically two years after he left the company. And those of us who have ever harbored a desire to bend, fold, spindle, or mutilate a computer card received in the mail can understand the "soapbox" perspective, where aggression is directed at the computer itself.

The final category of computer crime that has received much press of late derives from a view of computer systems as "playpens." Some individuals, sometimes derisively referred to as "hackers," delight in seeing if they can compromise computer security, get into a computer system (the same way a legitimate user of a computer's service gets on line), and play around with the data stored therein. Criminals of this type are motivated by the challenge of getting past whatever security (often little) stands in the way of unauthorized users. While such activity constitutes trespassing and is an invasion of privacy when the computer stores personal data about people, many commentators on this type of crime applaud the ingenuity of the hacker, without regard to the real and potential harm that can be done.

Examples are legion of individuals acquiring computer time without paying for it and sometimes altering data stored in the computer. Someone sitting at a home computer dialed up the Sloan-Kettering Cancer Center computer and played around with passwords until the right one was found, erased part of the memory concerning accounts, and allowed access to other "invaders." Fortunately, none of the data relating to patient treatments had been disturbed. When the culprit anonymously called the center, he said he was just playing. This "playing" was not halted until the FBI intervened and identified the alleged perpetrator. Similar intrusions have been made into computers at the Los Alamos Nuclear Testing Ground, Brown University, and TRW's credit reporting agency.

So serious has unauthorized entry into computers become that the U.S. Congress has considered legislation to make such activity a felony. In the meantime, a growing sector of the computer industry is devoted to the development of computer security systems, including "encryption" devices that code computer information so that even if accessed by a hacker (or business competitor), the information is uninterpretable without the encryption key. A particularly sobering fact for educators is that many of the computer hackers caught by the authorities are junior and senior high school students.

Copyright Law

A large area of concern related to computer crime centers on copyright law. While this applies occasionally to copyright on parts of the computer itself (hardware), as in the recent law that gives copyright protection to chip designs for the first time, it most typically involves computer programs (software). When people copy a computer program without

New Wave Computer Crime

WILLIAM D. MARBACH WITH JENNET CONANT IN NEW YORK
AND MICHAEL ROGERS IN SAN FRANCISCO

When he walked into his office in a computer center at New York's Memorial Sloan-Kettering Cancer Center on the morning of June 3, Chen Chui knew right away that something was wrong. A message on the main console indicated that the computer had crashed—broken down—briefly during the night. Chui, a systems manager, immediately started investigating. Sloan-Kettering's VAX 11/780 computer monitors the cancer center's five radiation-treatment machines, keeps patients' records and is also used by about 80 hospitals around the country that consult it to calculate how much radiation to use for patients. Chui quickly discovered that someone had erased part of the computer's memory containing accounting information, and then he found that the computer had been authorized to allow access from half a dozen new users' accounts. None of the names was familiar. Someone had broken in. "It was very unnerving," said Radhe Mohan, director of the facility. "If the files are altered, then a patient could get the wrong treatment."

Alarmed, the Sloan-Kettering officials erased the phony accounts and changed the passwords of the privileged users. They could find no evidence that the intruder had damaged any of the therapy records stored in the computer for 6,000 current and former Sloan-Kettering patients. But the following Monday morning the computer again indicated that it had failed briefly during the night. More new accounts had been created. The intruder had struck again. This time a spy program had been planted in the computer, a program that trapped legitimate users into unknowingly revealing their secret passwords. Officials disabled the program, notified the police and the FBI, began monitoring the system and left messages telling the intruder that he had entered a hospital computer and pleading with him to stop. "He called, but did not want to identify himself," says Mohan. "He said he was just playing."

BAFFLING

Hospital officials gave the intruder a limited "demo" account in the computer, and the New York City Police began tapping the incoming calls. Over the next two months, there were 20 to 30 separate uses of the demo account—and more than 20 unsuccessful attempts to break into privileged and other accounts. It was baffling.

Last week the mystery was apparently solved. An FBI affidavit filed in Milwaukee claimed that Gerald R. Wondra, 21, of West Allis, Wis., had tampered with Sloan-Kettering's computer system in New York. Wondra was allegedly one of the loose-knit group of Milwaukee-area computer enthusiasts—or hackers—who called themselves the 414s. That group has been linked to break-ins at Los Alamos National Laboratory, Security Pacific Bank (NEWSWEEK, Aug. 22), a Dallas consulting firm and a Canadian cement company. According to the FBI document, Wondra used his Apple II personal computer, gaining access to the system over Telenet, a nationwide computer data-link network and then cracking Sloan-Kettering's password security system.

The hospital was only the latest victim of the darker side of the computer revolution. Experts warn of a growing computer crime wave accompanying the explosion in personal computers and computer literacy. "There's an epidemic of malicious system hacking going on across the country," says consultant Donn B. Parker of SRI International in Menlo Park, Calif. "Every high school and university that teaches computer technology has this problem—either as a victim or as the source of students who do it." The movie "WarGames" popularized the underground culture that considers breaking into a computer system an indoor sport. Yet many potential victims are largely unaware of the threats they face. "We thought we had a very secure system," says Sloan-Kettering's Mohan.

Incidents like the Sloan-Kettering break-in are spurring efforts to improve computer security. "Regrettably most on-line systems are vulnerable to this kind of attack," says Stephen W. Liebholz, president of Analytics, a Pennsylvania computer-security firm. "Most people tend to choose passwords that are easy to remember—like 'Joshua' in 'WarGames'." More stringent systems rely on other ways to enforce security. Several companies are now marketing dial-back systems to verify entry; the user signs in with a name and password and the computer immediately disconnects the call, searches its memory for the legitimate user and, if the call is verified, dials the user back at a preprogrammed number.

SCRAMBLED

High-security military computer systems use sophisticated encryption and elaborate physical security precautions, but most commercial computer data traffic is not encrypted. Each day more than $400 billion is transferred—mostly unencoded—over the nation's financial networks. "In the next three to four years we'll see much more encryption as other aspects of the system become more protected," says Parker. Analytics, for instance, is selling an encryption security system—dubbed Sherlock—to the government, banks and other corporations. Sherlock, which is based on the Data Encryption Standard (DES) issued by the National Bureau of Standards, uses scramblers and special keys containing built-in microchips that can be programmed with secret codes. Other systems store data in the computer in scrambled form so that if an unauthorized user gains access the data appears only as gibberish.

Still, because high-security systems are not yet widely used, incidents like the Sloan-Kettering break-in—or worse—may be all too common. It is only a question of time, warns Adam Osborne, chairman of Osborne Computer Corp., before the financial community faces a catastrophic computer crime—a Three Mile Island-like financial disaster. "If this is what kids can do on a lark," says Osborne, "can you imagine what people are doing who are serious about this?"

SOURCE. *Newsweek*, August 29, 1983, p. 45. Copyright 1983, by Newsweek, Inc. All rights reserved. Reprinted by permission.

the permission of its producer, they are engaging in *software piracy*. This is analogous to photocopying an entire textbook rather than having to buy it. Commercial producers of software claim that they are losing money because of this piracy, citing ten pirated copies of programs for every one program legitimately purchased. Pirates claim that software is overpriced and that there are too few consumer protections against inferior products. In return, producers argue that lost sales must be made up by higher prices, and that anti-piracy techniques that must be included in the software also add to the cost.

Because computer software is a relative newcomer to the legal arena, the application of copyright law to software still generates heated debates as contending factions—producers and consumers—attempt to protect what they view as their rights. For educators, with limited budgets for everything, the temptation is great to pirate copyrighted educational software, or to participate in software swapping of illegally copied programs, "for the benefit of the kids." The International Council for Computer Education (ICCE) has formulated guidelines for the copying of software directed both at the potential educator-pirate and at commercial software producers (1987). In recent months, representatives of this group have displayed greater willingness to permit site licenses (allowing multiple copying rights on site) and to market "lab packs" (multiple copies at a reduced price). Whatever course you as a teacher decide to take in this regard, you should weigh carefully the consequences of breaking software copyright, not only in view of your own legal status but in the message you may convey to your students about the legitimate rights of others.

1987 Statement on Software Copyright
An ICCE Policy Statement

Background

During 1982-83, educators, software developers, and hardware and software vendors cooperated to develop the **ICCE Policy Statement on Network and Multiple Machine Software.** This Policy Statement was adopted by the Board of Directors of the International Council for Computers in Education (ICCE) in 1983, and was published and distributed. It has received support from hardware and software vendors, industry associations and other education associations. One component of the Policy Statement, the "Model District Policy on Software Copyright," has been adopted by school districts throughout the world.

Now, three years later, as the educational computer market has changed and the software market has matured, ICCE has responded to suggestions that the policy statement be reviewed by a new committee and revisions be made to reflect the changes that have taken place both in the marketplace and in the schools.

The 1986-87 ICCE Software Copyright Committee is composed of educators, industry associations, hardware vendors, software developers and vendors, and lawyers. All the participants of this new Committee agree that the educational market should be served by developers and preserved by educators. To do so requires that the ICCE Policy Statement be revisited every few years while the industry and the use of computers in education are still developing.

Responsibilities

In the previous Policy Statement, lists of responsibilities were assigned to appropriate groups: educators; hardware vendors; and software developers and vendors. The suggestion that school boards show their responsibility by approving a district copyright policy was met with enthusiasm, and many districts approved a policy based on the ICCE Model Policy. The suggestion that software vendors adopt multiple-copy discounts and offer lab packs to schools was likewise well received; many educational software publishers now offer such pricing. It is therefore the opinion of this committee that, for the most part, the 1983 list of recommendations has become a *fait accompli* within the industry, and to repeat it here would be an unnecessary redundancy.

Nevertheless, the Committee does suggest that all parties involved in the educational computing market be aware of what the other parties are doing to preserve this market, and that the following three recommendations be considered for adoption by the appropriate agencies.

School District Copyright Policy

The Committee recommends that school districts approve a District Copyright Policy that includes both computer software and other media. A Model District Policy on Software Copyright is enclosed.

Particular attention should be directed to item five, recommending that *only one* person in the district be given the authority to sign software licensing agreements. This implies that such a person should become familiar with licensing and purchasing rights of all copyrighted materials.

Suggested Software Use Guidelines

In the absence of clear legislation, legal opinion or case law, it is suggested that school districts adopt the enclosed Suggested Software Use Guidelines as guidelines for software use within the district. The recommendation of Guidelines is similar to the situation currently used by many education agencies for off-air video recording. While these Guidelines do not carry the force of law, they do represent the collected opinion on fair software use for nonprofit education agencies from a variety of experts in the software copyright field.

Copyright Page Recommendations

The Committee recommends that educators look to the copyright page of software documentation to find their rights, obligations and license restrictions regarding an individual piece of software.

The Committee also suggests that software publishers use the documentation copyright page to *clearly* delineate the users' (owners' or licensees') rights in at least these five areas:

1. How is a back-up copy made or obtained, how many are allowed, and how are the back-ups to be used (e.g., *not* to be used on a second machine at the same time)?

2. Is it permissible to load the disk(s) into multiple computers for use at the same time?

3. Is it permissible to use the software on a local area network, and will the company support such use? Or is a network version available from the publisher?

4. Are lab packs or quantity discounts available from the publisher?

5. Is it permissible for the owner or licensee to make copies of the printed documentation? Or are additional copies available, and how?

ICCE—Suggested Software Use Guidelines

The 1976 U.S. Copyright Act and its 1980 Amendments remain vague in some areas of software use and its application to education. Where the law itself is vague, software licenses tend to be much more specific. It is therefore imperative that educators read the software's copyright page and understand the licensing restrictions printed there. If these uses are not addressed, the following Guidelines are recommended.

These Guidelines do not have the force of law, but they do represent the collected opinion on fair software use by nonprofit educational agencies from a variety of experts in the software copyright field.

Back-up Copy: The Copyright Act is clear in permitting the owner of software a back-up copy of the software to be held for use as an archival copy in the event the original disk fails to function. Such back-up copies are not to be used on a second computer at the same time the original is in use.

Multiple-loading: The Copyright Act is most unclear as it applies to loading the contents of one disk into multiple computers for use at the same time. In the absence of a license expressly permitting the user to load the contents of one disk into many computers for use at the same time, it is suggested that you *not* allow this activity to take place. The fact that you physically can do so is irrelevant. In an effort to make it easier for schools to buy software for each computer station, many software publishers offer lab packs and other quantity buying incentives. Contact individual publishers for details.

Local Area Network Software Use: It is suggested that before placing a software program on a local area network or disk-sharing system for use by multiple users at the same time, you obtain a written license agreement from the copyright holder giving you permission to do so. The fact that you are able to physically load the program on the network is, again, irrelevant. You should obtain a license permitting you to do so before you act.

Model District Policy on Software Copyright

It is the intent of [district] to adhere to the provisions of copyright laws in the area of microcomputer software. It is also the intent of the district to comply with the license agreements and/or policy statements contained in the software packages used in the district. In circumstances where the interpretation of the copyright law is ambiguous, the district shall look to the applicable license agreement to determine appropriate use of the software [or the district will abide by the approved Software Use Guidelines].

We recognize that computer software piracy is a major problem for the industry and that violations of copyright laws contribute to higher costs and greater efforts to prevent copying and/or lessen incentives for the development of effective educational uses of microcomputers. Therefore, in an effort to discourage violation of copyright laws and to prevent such illegal activities:

1. The ethical and practical implications of software piracy will be taught to educators and school children in all schools in the district (e.g., covered in fifth grade social studies classes).

2. District employees will be informed that they are expected to adhere to section 117 of the 1976 Copyright Act as amended in 1980, governing the use of software (e.g., each building principal will devote one faculty meeting to the subject each year).

3. When permission is obtained from the copyright holder to use software on a disk-sharing system, efforts will be made to secure this software from copying.

4. Under no circumstances shall illegal copies of copyrighted software be made or used on school equipment.

5. [Name or job title] of this school district is designated as the only individual who may sign license agreements for software for schools in the district. Each school using licensed software should have a signed copy of the software agreement.

6. The principal at each school site is responsible for establishing practices which will enforce this district copyright policy at the school level.

The Board of Directors of the International Council for Computers in Education approved this policy statement January, 1987. The members of the 1986 ICCE Software Copyright Committee are:

Sueann Ambron, American Association of Publishers
Gary Becker, Seminole Co. Public Schools, Florida
Daniel T. Brooks, Cadwalader, Wickersham & Taft
LeRoy Finkel, International Council for Computers in Education
Virginia Helm, Western Illinois University
Kent Kehrberg, Minnesota Educational Computing Corporation
Dan Kunz, Commodore Business Machines
Bodie Marx, Mindscape, Inc.
Kenton Pattie, International Communications Industries Association
Carol Risher, American Association of Publishers
Linda Roberts, US Congress—OTA
Donald A. Ross, Microcomputer Workshops Courseware
Lary Smith, Wayne County Int. Schl. Dist., Michigan
Ken Wasch, Software Publishers Association

For more information write to the ICCE Software Copyright Committee, ICCE, University of Oregon, 1787 Agate St., Eugene, OR 97403.

Reprinted by permission of ICCE Software Copyright Committee.

Another branch of the copyright conundrum precipitated by the development of computer technology relates to the status of words and ideas that are transmitted electronically. Let's consider this example. You are participating in a computer conference along with 157 other individuals scattered across the country; the conference was made possible by someone who wrote the computer program that manages all the information residing in the central computer somewhere in Kansas, let's suppose. Another person is the conference organizer, who takes care of arranging the agenda for discussion and for indexing messages for easy access by you and your colleagues. In the course of the electronic discussion, the group develops some insights about teaching sign language to fourth graders; this just happens to be the topic of a paper you're working on in your education methods course. You include these ideas in your paper. Now what do you give as a citation? To give no citation would suggest that these insights are original. If you quote some of the electronic text from the computer conference, do you need to cite that specific person who entered that text, assuming it is possible to keep track of who says what in a "discussion"?

Let's make things even harder. Suppose your paper was so good that you got it published. And suppose further that several conference participants saw your article and also saw ideas that belonged (in the copyright sense) to them because they expressed those ideas in the computer conference. Could they sue you? Maybe you included someone's offhand remarks that he or she never intended to appear on the printed page. Would this get you into trouble? What if the organizer of the computer conference decided to have the contents of the conference, currently stored in the computer's memory, printed out, made into a book and sold? Would you demand to receive royalty payments for your slice of the conference's contents? Or would the profits go to the organizer, or to the owners of the computer, or to the person who wrote the software that made the conference possible? In short, who owns what in the context of a computer conference? The answer, or answers, are still elusive in this new realm of communication born of computer technology.

Robotics and Employment

We mentioned robots briefly in conjunction with computer-aided manufacture. The introduction of robots, or "steel-collar workers," surely carries some genuine benefits: They can perform work that is either hazardous or tedious for humans, they don't ask for raises or go on strike, they don't have to put their kids through college, and the list goes

A line of robots applies welds to auto bodies. *(Courtesy of General Motors Corporation.)*

on. Surely, new jobs have been and will continue to be created as a result of technology, many of which we cannot even guess at today. There is also a downside, however. Robots displace human workers today. At General Electric's revitalized locomotive plant in Erie, Pennsylvania, officials project that *"two* workers in the future will do in 16 *hours* at General Electric what *70* employees did in 16 *days* before the plant received its electronic facelift" (Shane, 1983). Some labor unions are fighting for the right to strike for "technological" reasons; some would argue that such efforts are doomed to failure.

Social Intercourse and Invisible Dialogs

With tele-commuting, tele-shopping and flexiplaces, there may come a time when there is little need to come into contact with other people in the course of a day, or a week, or a month. How will our self-image and our beliefs about people and our ability to relate intimately with others be affected by a trend toward what Toffler (1980) referred to as "the electronic cottage"? One response is suggested by Kurland (1983), commenting on the quality of personal interaction in computer conferences. Communication, he notes, seems lifeless and impersonal; you never see conferees, words may have been sent days or weeks ago, there is no body language, and voices/tones are missing. "The electronic conferencer confronts only disembodied words and knows fellow conferees sometimes only by nicknames" (Kurland, 1983, p. 125).

One manifestation of invisible dialog, offered by CompuServe, is called CB Simulator, where individuals develop relationships sight unseen. Less formal than most computer conferences, several hundred people participate for a variety of reasons. Most are looking for friendship and companionship free of the obstacles that looks, dress, voice, and other visual impressions convey. Others praise the built-in egalitarianism—CB Simulator as a great equalizer, for example—though of course participants must be sufficiently upscale to afford the computer, the subscription fee, and the on-line telephone charges. It is an outlet for the shy and introverted, and a source of stability for people whose jobs and life-style preclude stable face-to-face relationships. It is also a fantasy land, where some people take on imaginary roles.

The anonymity that the medium provides encourages participants to reveal quite a bit more than they would in relationships that develop face to face. The potential for being exploited is considerable. One participant reported baring his soul to a female participant, only to discover that he had been part of a sociological study carried out by a male researcher.

What is apparent in all this is that communication based solely on the electronic medium is stripped of the other modes of communication to which people are accustomed. The benefits that its enthusiasts cite must be tempered by the costs its participants at times experience. But perhaps our concern for the negative consequences of invisible dialogs is unnecessary. John Naisbitt believes that no matter how "high tech" life becomes, people will purposefully seek out the "high touch" that face-to-face interpersonal contact provides. People will choose to go to the office, not because they have to conduct work there, but because that's where other people are.

Infoglut [1]

The exponential growth of information technology brings with it a rapid growth in the amount of information and in its dissemination. Daniel Bell (1973) estimated that the amount of information coursing through society will double every two years. Others suggest that scientific and technical information alone will double every 12 months.

Estimates for information in business are equally astounding. According to one, there are 21 trillion pages of paper stored in offices. "Businesses churn out roughly 600 million pages of computer printouts, 235 million photocopies, and 76 million letters daily." The volume of such information is growing at a rate of 911 million pages every workday, and this might double every four years. At a cost of twenty-five cents per document per year, the computer is seen as the answer ("Paper Weight," p. 14). It is interesting to note, though, that an alternative answer seems to have been ignored: throw out the information you no longer need or that is not essential.

Being able to store information is one issue; another issue is its selection and use. Consider this. The Information Age will give us full control over the information we choose to receive, through the cable channels and satellite beams we choose, the information services we choose, and the tele-courses we choose to take. John Naisbitt speculated about this trend as well, suggesting that "in the future, editors won't tell us what to read: We will tell editors what we choose to read" (1982, p. 26). Alan Hald (1981) fears that the information technology we laud may produce a "reality gap," with each person's perception of reality the product of his or her own self-filtering of information received.

Techno-dependence

Perhaps you have heard the query "If we let kids use calculators to do their arithmetic, what's going to happen when the battery goes dead or the electricity goes out?" People are genuinely concerned that society is

---

[1] According to futurist Harold Shane (1983), the term "infoglut" is attributable to Michael Marien, editor of *Future Survey*.

becoming far too dependent on technology and that we are building a new world of high technology on a hill of sand.

Good examples, though (to be fair) not the only examples, can be drawn from the military. More and more of the U.S. military system depends on sophisticated tracking and communications satellites. The development of anti-satellite devices by an adversary is troublesome enough. Even more troublesome, though, is a curious phenomenon that would occur during a nuclear war. When a nuclear device detonates in the atmosphere, even 25 miles up, the blast produces an EMP, or Electromagnetic Pulse. The effect of EMP disrupts at least temporarily, and perhaps permanently, any devices that are electrically and electronically based. Just when the military's need for rapid communication is most crucial, all the fancy electronics will be for naught.

Techno-dependence also raises the possibility that the very machines we have created to help us will turn against us, that we will lose control of our creation. Consider a current reality: the PROWLER robot. It can as easily play security guard in a shopping mall parking lot as it can be an unmanned tank in wartime. How much autonomy dare we bestow on these robots? Should a human always be the final decision maker when life and death are at stake? Extending this even further, how intelligent dare we make robots? As one commentator stated, "While it's naive to assume that robots won't be used in warfare, it could be none too soon to insist that no robot should ever be given the ability to start its own army" ("Birth of the Killer Robots," p. 51).

While we might be able to maintain control over our machines, how tempted will we be to apply the technology rather than seek alternate solutions? The military might be very reluctant to engage in armed conflict that produced human casualties, but would they be as reluctant to do so if they could "just send in the robots"?

At the heart of this question is whether we will come to view technology as the answer to everything, trading farsighted solutions for shortsighted gains. We'll come back to this issue later.

Anticipated Developments

More Speed in a Smaller Package

The more complex the task, the more minute steps are required. The tasks current computers can accomplish are in part limited in how many steps can be handled in a reasonable amount of time. Two ways that computers can take on bigger and tougher tasks is by increasing the number of circuits working together or by increasing the speed at which each circuit operates, or a combination of the two. Future computers will have many more circuits per square inch, each of which will be able to complete one on-off cycle in increasingly less time.

Efforts at further miniaturization of circuits are ongoing and will continue. Current computer chips are produced by photographically reducing the components of one chip from a wall-size layout to a microscopic "mask" the size of one physical chip. Photographic methods also transfer this miniature pattern onto the chip. Future circuitry may be etched directly on the chip rather than transferred photographically. Researchers at the National Research and Resource Facility for Submicron Structures have used a Scanning Transmission Electron Microscope to create what are believed to be the smallest human-made structures ever produced—patterns 50,000 times smaller than the diameter of human hair. These are 200 times smaller than the patterns on the smallest chips used today. To dramatize the accomplishment, researchers there have etched on a salt crystal letters that are so small that the entire *Encyclopedia Britannica* could be written in a space smaller than a postage stamp (Friedland, 1984).

Even more minute circuitry could be attained with biochips. In this case, on and off signals would be carried by molecules, rather than the metal and silicon in today's circuits. Billions of molecules would inhabit the space now given to silicon chips. Scientists are investigating whether they can "train" bacteria, through genetic engineering, to produce the needed molecules.

Both these techniques would increase the speed of computers as well, since the distance the signals would have to travel would be significantly reduced. The world's fastest computer, the Cray 2, can perform 1.2 billion calculations per second and send internal signals so quickly that the heat produced requires placing the computer in liquid coolant. That speed, stated differently, means that one computational cycle is completed in 4.1 billionths of a second, or the time it takes light to travel 5 feet ("Computers' Next Frontiers," p. 40). Super-cool liquid helium is also used to increase speed by reducing electrical resistance to near zero, allowing electrons to flow at near the speed of light. Further development of so-called "super-conducting" materials will permit such low levels of resistance without extreme cooling. Speed is also increased by having many programming commands executed simultaneously using a collection of microprocessors, rather than one command at a time by one microprocessor. Such "parallel processing" will become increasingly typical, far outdistancing and superceding the current "serial processing" standard established by von Neumann. (In fact, these new computers are sometimes called non–von Neumann machines, or "non-vons.")

Whatever technical limits exist are still in the distance. And continuing advances in both speed and miniaturization set the stage for a wide range of anticipated, and surely many other unanticipated, developments.

Expert Systems

One emerging application of more sophisticated computer technology is the expert system, "a computer program that has built into it the knowledge and capability that will allow it to operate at the expert's level" (Feigenbaum and McCorduck, 1983, pp. 64–65). A true expert system should not only be able, for example, to arrive at a medical diagnosis, but also to explain how it arrived at it and why it rejected other alternatives. As you might guess, this is a pretty tall order, requiring reasoning ability. The program must process the data on the patient (the data base) and must reason on the basis of its knowledge of medicine (the knowledge base) using rules, laws, and those illusive things called "heuristics" or "rules of thumb" that make human reasoning so intricate. An example of a medical expert system is MYCIN, used at Stanford University in California to diagnose blood and meningitis infections and to recommend the appropriate treatment. Other expert systems exist in biology and chemistry.

Some programs are currently available that allow you to design your own knowledge-based system. Many such systems lack the ability to acquire automatically more knowledge based on experience and might thus be better referred to as "knowledge systems" to connote more modest capabilities. You write in a set of rules that will help the program arrive at the appropriate answers, expressed in everyday language, to questions posed on a particular topic. Other systems come already designed and built, and may be customized by the producer to meet the needs of particular users. The cost of these systems is, at the moment, beyond the resources of most of us, from several thousand to tens of thousands of dollars.

Current expert systems are mere children compared to the ambitions scientists have for artificial intelligence (AI) in the future. AI researchers are looking far beyond to find general laws of thought, in order to produce machines that can learn and become knowledgeable in any field.

Fifth-Generation Computers and Intelligent Machines

Artificial intelligence is the idea that human intelligence can be reproduced by a machine. The field of artificial intelligence, or AI, has catapulted new theories of human intelligence to the forefront, especially information-processing theory—the view of humans as essentially systems that process information. If this is true, why can't a computer, albeit a sophisticated computer, do the same thing. After all, computers are systems that process information, too.

Expert systems have been a small step in this direction, but the Japanese are making major commitments of money and human capital to produce the fifth generation of computers: truly intelligent machines. "Their goal," according to Edward Feigenbaum and Pamela McCorduck, "is to develop computers for the 1990s and beyond—*intelligent* computers that will be able to converse with humans in natural [conversational] language and understand speech and pictures. These will be computers that can learn, associate, make inferences, make decisions, and otherwise behave in ways we have always considered the exclusive province of human reason" (1983, p. 12). Such machines will draw upon the anticipated developments in chip technology and upon the ingenuity of program designers.

Advances of these Japanese artificially intelligent machines will require further development of chips, packing 10 million on-off circuits in the same space that a few hundred thousand occupy today. Special artificial intelligence languages have been developed, like LISP (for List Processing) and PROLOG (for Programming in Logic). The Japanese have chosen PROLOG over LISP for their ambitious undertaking, the latter having been until recently the language of choice in artificial intelligence community. Finding ways to communicate easily with users will also require refinements in "natural language," with the ability to understand continuous human speech with a vocabulary of 50,000 words and 95 percent accuracy, according to Feigenbaum and McCorduck. This is, in short, a large puzzle with many little pieces and only a vague understanding of what the final picture will look like.

Assuming the Japanese (and others) overcome the daunting obstacles in achieving fifth-generation goals, let us look forward a bit at perhaps a somewhat frivolous example of how a fifth-generation computer might be applied. Consider the following by Alan Hald:

> Imagine a house called Fred, who, while performing routine roof maintenance, discovers a leak. Fred first seeks help. Not from you, but from Slim, a ranch-style home down the block. Slim has recently undergone roof repair and can provide Fred with needed advice. Fred then calls you at the office to present his plan of action. You've learned to trust Fred's judgment, so you approve the repairs. The rest is rather straightforward. Fred calls the roofer and directs her to the leak. After it is repaired to Fred's satisfaction, funds are electronically transferred from your account to the roofer's account. Fred promises to give her a good reference and stores the entire experience in his memory banks for future use, to share with other homes and humans. (1981, p. 21)

General Electric and Mitsubishi already have bit more modest versions of Fred the House called HouseMinder and Housekeeping System, respectively. Fred's capabilities are only part of a growing assortment of abilities that will be built into intelligent machines, flowing from the work currently being conducted in computer research labs.

A Catalog of Anticipated Developments

- Machines that recognize handwriting.
- Talk-writers: machines that convert the spoken word into written text.
- Machines that recognize gestures, read lips, track eye movements.
- Car computers that will warn of drowsiness, display maps, and require a chemical sobriety test before allowing the owner to drive off.
- Memory chips that can each contain 1 billion transistors by the year 2000.

. . . AND FOR THE MILITARY

- Unmanned robot tanks that can travel 40 miles per hour on unfamiliar terrain and fire very accurate weapons.
- Computers in aircraft that automatically take evasive action against approaching missiles, following the spoken commands of the pilot.
- System that monitors pilots' biological systems and provides them with only the amount of information the computer judges they can absorb.

SOURCE. "Computers' Next Frontiers," *U.S. News & World Report,* August 26, 1985, pp. 38–41.

One wonders, though, about the perhaps underestimated impact of intelligent machines on humans' self-image. Evans (1979) suggests that Ultra-Intelligent Machines (UIMs) might produce such considerable culture shock, forcing humanity to doubt the significance of its accomplishments and its strivings, that our self-confidence in the knowledge that the intelligence gap between the machines will always be unbridgeable will diminish. "As long as the UIMs are solidly under control, we ought to be able to prevent them from flinging us into a terminal case of culture-shock. Even so, we shall have to re-appraise our role, our goals, our future and, so far as this is possible, our purpose in the universe" (Evans, 1979, p. 278).

"Megatrends" and the Role of the Computer

Evans's observations echo Asimov's view that technological advances produce a wide range of effects that may be rather far removed from the technology itself. What might the anticipated technical developments we've discussed mean for other semitechnical or nontechnical developments.

John Naisbitt took on the role of seer in his book *Megatrends* (1982), predicting a number of emerging effects of technological change. The mass production of information will continue, exacerbating the problems we identified as infoglut. Not only the volume, but the speed of information will accelerate, through the collapse of what Naisbitt called "information float," the lapse of time between the transmission and the reception of information. Because everyday people will have increasing access to information, Naisbitt's prognosticating contemporary, Christopher Evans, predicts the decline of the professions, whether medical, legal, or educational. The status of the professions has been based traditionally on exclusive repositories of specialized information, of which they were the disseminators. With high-speed, widespread access to a plethora of data bases, these keepers and distributors of information lose their significance and relevance.

The manner in which people read and write information will change as well. Books will decline in use, replaced by portable display screens. Eventually, to find a book one will have to seek out book museums (looking a lot like libraries of the "past"), collectors, and those still attached to the sensations of flipping pages.

The home will increasingly become the center of everyday life: the workplace, the entertainment center, and the information center. All the information you might need, for example, in choosing a presidential candidate could be accessed at your home information center. Moreover, the home may become your voting booth. Some cable television viewers in Columbus, Ohio, subscribe to QUBE, which allows two-way communication. Viewers can now observe debates on local issues and then enter their opinions using a small box attached to the television. It is only a small step to casting your ballot for governor or for president.

Indeed, think of the possibilities here for a renaissance of pure democracy, like ancient Greece. When the spread of technology reaches widely and becomes as commonplace as the telephone or the car, there would be no further need for representatives to vote on national legislation. Everyone could vote on legislation, everyone could participate fully in the decisions that guide the nation. Democracy in Greece flourished because towns were small, like the small towns in New England today. Electronic technology will overcome the obstacle of distance, and citizens of the nation will be joined into an electronic village. Even if this ideal is never fully reached, the diffusion of information technology will hold the potential for increasing the quantity and quality of political participation.

Given the chance to participate so completely in the political and governing process, how many of us would take advantage of the opportunity? How much time would we be willing to devote to this? Given the opportunity to vote on hundreds of issues, great and small, how many of us would take the time to research the issues rather than to cast our votes hastily and thoughtlessly? If it were easy to cast a quick ballot for president at home, rather than having to go to the polling place and fill out a ballot, would more uninformed citizens vote, just because it's so much easier now? Given a world of information at our fingertips, how much of it would we really take the time to see? These are questions technology cannot answer.

Summary: Implications for Education

In this chapter we have described how computers and their electronic brethren have become a part of many facets of our lives. We have suggested that the electronic technology of the Information Age has brought with it both blessings and curses, just as new mechanical technology brought both good news and bad news during the Industrial Age. And while we might reflect considerable optimism when peering into the future, we should not be surprised that emerging technologies will similarly produce a mixed bag of effects.

How will education change and how much in light of the current and future development of computer-based information technology? One view was provided by the U.S. government's Office of Technology Assessment:

> The so-called information revolution, driven by rapid advances in communication and computer technology, is profoundly affecting American education. It is changing the nature of what needs to be learned, who needs to learn it, who will provide it, and how it will be provided and paid for. (Office of Technology Assessment, 1982, p. 3)

Chapter 8 will discuss in some detail how we and others think education and teaching will change in the future, but let's plant a seed for that discussion by attempting a general link between technological change and education.

In Chapter 1 we noted that digital technology was rapidly uniting formerly diverse information technologies into a single entity. In an article titled "Going Digital," William H. Sanders (1982) provides some interesting insights into the significance of this technological change and its relevance to what needs to be learned.

Sanders begins with two definitions. First, information technology is anything related to the "storage, retrieval, and manipulation of information." Second, literacy is defined as the ability to "manipulate successfully the dominant information technology" of one's time. Sanders noted that for the last 500 years, print has been the dominant information technology, and thus, literacy has been viewed as the ability to read and write the printed word. Much of the development of education over the last 200 years has focused on this understanding of literacy.

With the advent of the computer and digital technology, print is losing its preeminence as the dominant information technology. By association, literacy that is conceived of narrowly as a print manipulation skill is losing its relevance. The task education must assume is a new literacy, one founded on the new dominant information technology. Failing to do so, education will court not just disaster, but, to use Sanders's word, obsolescence.

This is not to suggest that the ability to read and write are to be abandoned. On the contrary, these abilities are to be expanded from print to all the other media unified under digital technology. In concurring with Sanders, John Naisbitt observed, "In this literacy-intensive society, when we need basic reading and writing skills more than ever before, our education system is turning out an increasingly inferior product" (1982, p. 19).

Some would suggest that the "product" leaving schools at the moment has still been prepared according to specifications required for the Industrial Age and its factories, rather than for the Information Age and its computers. For some critics, the economic consequences of continuing along this course are potentially catastrophic. They cite the expected percentage growth in information occupations, from computer operators and technicians to systems analysts. They call for massive efforts, many at the national level, to move the education system into the age of high technology.

Other interested observers are more sanguine in their assessment of the schools' task. Harriet T. Bernstein of the Council for Basic Education argued that "our vision of the future must rest on something more

Copyright 1986, Jules Feiffer, reprinted with permission of Universal Press Syndicate. All Rights Reserved.

substantial than revolutionary technological advances" (1983, p. 108). She pointed out that in terms of absolute numbers, jobs in the information sector will lag behind jobs in the service sector, most of which require little technical training. Moreover, the trend in computer use is away from technical complexity toward "user-friendliness," requiring less rather than more technical knowledge—a belief confirmed by a *U.S. News & World Report* article ("Computers' Next Frontiers," pp. 38–41) reporting on the "faster, smarter and friendlier" computers under development.

More fundamentally, overemphasis on high tech education betrays an overestimation of technology's ability to solve problems, whether local, national or global. According to Bernstein:

> Our troubles are compounds of historical, economic, political, social, psychological, technical, and moral forces. They can only be addressed by Renaissance men and women, adept in all of those realms, capable of synthesizing knowledge (as distinct from information), able to inspire and motivate others, and willing to persevere. (1983, p. 109)

In this, Bernstein echoes Naisbitt, who sees the decline of the specialist (whose expertise rapidly becomes obsolete) and the rise of the generalist (who is able to adapt to change). He also underscores Bernstein's distinction between information and knowledge: "We are drowning in information but starved for knowledge" (1982, p. 24).

Bernstein concludes:

> If we are to stand any chance of solving our social and economic problems, we need to create a large pool of citizens with a basic liberal arts education, in touch with the best thinking from other places, times, and cultures. . . . [A truly visionary] system of public education will prove itself by producing citizens with a deep understanding of political democracy, a tolerance for ambiguity, an abiding curiosity, and a firm grip on the values that sustain both family and civilization. (1983, p. 109)

Running below the surface of Bernstein's argument is an opposition to what seems to be a modern trend, the reification of science at the expense of the humanities, a laudatory to intellect at the expense of character. Joseph Weizenbaum, computer scientist turned skeptic, summarized this tendency as a turn away from judgment to calculation (1976). Perhaps the description of how computers have been used in politics is indicative of the latter in particular.

The counterpoint provided by Bernstein and Weizenbaum challenges educators to not lose sight of fundamentals in pursuit of a new literacy. What use is more information if one has not learned how to make knowledge out of it and then to act on that knowledge? Keeping the "big picture" in your sights means understanding the context in which computers developed over time, how they are being used now, and how they could be used in the future. Calls for computer literacy, and what meanings are attached to this term, are discussed at greater length in Chapter 5, but the foregoing discussion invites educators to contemplate the nature of computer literacy in light of the general purposes of education in a free society. It is clear that schools can easily find themselves in the middle of a heated debate, especially when each faction advances its claims on the limited budgets available to schools. As you continue through the pages of this book, consider where you stand in this debate over the future of education.

References

BEATTY, J. KELLY. "Voyager 2's Triumph," *Sky and Telescope*, 72, (1986), pp. 336–342.

BELL, DANIEL. *The Coming of Post-Industrial Society: A Venture in Social Forecasting.* New York: Basic Books, 1973.

BERNSTEIN, HARRIET T. "The Information Society: Byting the Hand That Feeds You," *Phi Delta Kappan*, October 1983, pp. 108–109.

"Birth of the Killer Robots," *Newsweek*, June 25, 1984, p. 51.

BLOOMBECKER, JAY. "Who are the Computer Criminals?" *Recreational Computing*, September/October 1981, pp. 16–20.

"Computer News Shows Planned," *Infoworld*, August 6, 1984, p. 13.

"Computers' Next Frontiers," *U.S. News & World Report*, August 26, 1985, pp. 38–41.

DEDE, CHRISTOPHER, BOWMAN, JIM, AND KIERSTEAD, FRED. "Communications Technologies and Education: The Coming Transformation," in Howard F. Didsbury (ed.). *Communications and the Future: Prospects, Promises, and Problems.* Bethesda, MD: World Futures Society, 1982.

"Democrats Computerize Politics," *Infoworld*, July 23, 1984, p. 23.

EVANS, CHRISTOPHER. *The Micro Millenium.* New York: Washington Square Press, 1979.

FEIGENBAUM, EDWARD A., & McCORDUCK, PAMELA. *The Fifth Generation.* Reading, MA: Addison-Wesley, 1983.

FRIEDLAND, LOIS. "The Incredible Shrinking Microchip," *Sky*, April 1984, pp. 20–26.

HALD, ALAN P. "Toward the Information-Rich Society," *The Futurist*, August 1981, pp. 20–21+.

International Council for Computer Education. "1987 ICCE Statement on Software Copyright: An ICCE Policy Statement," *The Computing Teacher*, March 1987, pp. 52–53.

KURLAND, NORMAN D. "Have Computer, Will Not Travel: Meeting Electronically," *Phi Delta Kappan*, October 1983, pp. 124–126.

"Military in a Fix," *The Washington Post*, August 18, 1985, pp. A1, A16.

"Mondale's Electronic Running Mates," *Infoworld*, August 20, 1984, p. 25.

NAISBITT, JOHN. *Megatrends.* New York: Warner Books, 1982.

"New Wave Computer Crime," *Newsweek*, August 29, 1983, p. 45.

Office of Technology Assessment. "Informational Technology and Its Impact on American Education." Washington, D.C.: OTA, Autumn 1982, p. 3.

"Paper Weight," *Family Weekly,* June 24, 1984, p. 14.

SAFIRE, WILLIAM. "Computer Takes Its Revenge for Wick's Misuse," *Sunday Herald Times,* May 13, 1984, p. A13.

SANDERS, WILLIAM H. "Going Digital," *Instructional Innovator,* March 1982, pp. 14–16.

SHANE, HAROLD. "The Silicon Age II: Living and Learning in an Information Epoch," *Phi Delta Kappan,* October 1983, pp. 126–129.

TOFFLER, ALVIN. *The Third Wave.* New York: Morrow, 1980.

WEIZENBAUM, JOSEPH. *Computer Power and Human Reason: From Judgment to Calculation.* San Francisco: W. H. Freeman, 1976.

CHAPTER 3

Microcomputers: How They Work and Which to Choose

Introduction

Review

In Chapters 1 and 2 we established the groundwork for computers in education. Chapter 1 consisted of an outline of the history of computing, first as a means of reducing the drudgery of calculation and subsequently as a means of manipulating information in a broad range of areas that called for solutions to predominantly mathematical problems. Chapter 2 extended this review into the present and foreseeable future, and in it we discussed the degree to which computers have entered every corner of our lives. We also attempted to predict some of the changes that are immediately ahead of us. However, since this book is intended for teachers, we tried at every stage to maintain an educator's perspective on the material. Chapter 1 includes information that teachers need to know, but it also includes information that students in school need to know. Much of it is general knowledge for all people living today, while particular topics have special significance for certain areas in the curriculum as well as for school in general. What follows, however, addresses areas of special knowledge about computers that you as a teacher in a contemporary school need to know in order to be effective in this new age of electronic information and problem solving. We should emphasize, however, that this book is written for teachers and prospective teachers whose work will focus on the conventional teaching areas rather than for individuals who intend to specialize in computing technology, either as programmers or engineers. As a consequence, we have attempted to present the technological aspects of computing in as nontechnical a way as possible, where the goal is one of general understanding rather than technical expertise.

Why Teachers Need to Know How Computers Work

Some readers may feel that for school use only students and teachers of computer science need understand how computers work. They may think that most computer users need only learn to press the keys that will enable them to operate a particular machine or program. Yet, if you hope to able to control computers and not be controlled by them, then you need to have at least a general understanding of the parts that are common to all machines. This task involves learning what the components of a computer are and how they work together to perform the diverse tasks that have become familiar everywhere in daily life and are now becoming equally familiar in schools. You will then have a general understanding of the main characteristics and will be able to recognize them when you meet them. This may be particularly useful for troubleshooting problems you encounter when operating the equipment, saving time and frustration. If nothing else, such knowledge removes some of the aura of mystery—and threat—often associated with present-day electronic technology. And since an increasing proportion of school-age youth is growing up with computers as a part of their everyday lives, much as an earlier generation grew up with television, you need to have at least a passing knowledge, regardless of your teaching area—if only to be able to maintain conversation with students.

Computers have five distinct parts: input, a primary storage unit, a processing unit, a control unit, and output. You will recall that this five-part system had its origins with Charles Babbage (see Chapter 1). The ways in which these parts interact will be explained. A description of the three units that compose the central processing unit (CPU) comes first, because the CPU—memory, processing, and control—constitutes the "brain" of the computer. Input and output are integral parts of the overall process, but they actually involve peripheral devices. The chapter continues with a review of what "input" and "output" mean and the kinds of input and output devices commonly found in school, together with the ways in which they may be used. Although schools are equipped almost exclusively with microcomputers, part of the chapter explains the characteristics of larger computers such as those found in school administrative offices, and comparing them with microcomputers. This topic is included partly because small computers are rapidly acquiring the memory capabilities formerly found only in very large machines (much as present-day microcomputers are as powerful as the largest computers of 40 years ago). Not least, school-sized machines are being used increasingly to access information held in memories of large computer data bases located in distant places.

Computer resources for schools are no longer restricted to what can be done on small stand-alone machines. As a consequence, the information available to students and teachers is rapidly expanding. Knowing that these resources are now becoming available to schools is important. You will become acquainted with the actual techniques for operating these systems when you find yourself in a teaching position with particular resources to hand. While many variations of machines will be found, their structure and the ways in which they work remain essentially the same.

The final section of this chapter addresses the task of choosing suitable computer hardware from what is available on the market.

The Basic Parts of the Computer

The Central Processing Unit (CPU)

One of the most difficult aspects of first learning about computers is that there is nothing tangible to see. Steam and gasoline engines with distinctive moving parts can be heard and observed and are relatively easy to understand. You may not plan to become an auto mechanic, but it does not take much effort to understand what the various parts of a car engine are and what they do. Even electro-mechanical machines, such as vacuum cleaners and electric drills, have distinctive moving parts. No such condition exists in computing. The operation is silent and without apparent movement. Moreover, components are miniaturized to the point that a microscope is needed just to see the circuitry. In addition, these silicon "chips" are encased in protective shells that give no clue about what is inside other than identification numbers stamped on the outsides.

Thus, the main circuit board (or "motherboard") of a microcomputer, with its array of plug-in chips and circuitry, is not helpful to trying to understand how it works. Many people, therefore, have a tendency not to think about the inner workings of computers. Yet, to have no knowledge about the inner workings of a computer is to be put at a disadvantage.

Nonetheless, before proceeding, we need to explain how communications occur within the CPU, and then we need to mention the ways that have been devised to enable people to communicate with the electronic message systems of the CPU.

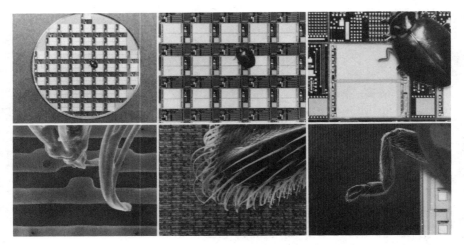

This series of photographs demonstrates the extent of miniaturization in microcomputers. Clockwise starting from the upper-left, a ladybug sitting on a silicon wafer of chips is magnified thousands of times to reveal circuitry no wider than a hair on its toe. *(Courtesy of Texas Instruments, Inc.)*

Bits, Bytes, and Wordlengths

The only system of operation inside a computer is binary. Unlike the more familiar decimal number system, binary numbering has a base of two. It is particularly well suited to computing, because computers are run by electricity. As explained in Chapter 1, the current is either on (1) or off (0), hence the name *binary digit* for the smallest unit of information that can be handled. The term binary digit is abbreviated to "bit."

In order to make binary digits (bits) useful, they are clustered together. While numbers of groupings are possible, eight is most typical in school microcomputers today. A cluster of eight bits represents a single character such as a letter or a number. In the computer memory such a cluster is called a "byte." The primary memory, or what can be stored in the CPU at any one time, can hold one or more bytes of memory at a time at any location depending on the CPU structure. Some computers are described as 8-bit machines, while others are 16-bit, 32-, or 64-bit machines, depending on whether their bytes are 8 bits, 16 bits, or 64 bits long. These variable byte sizes are called *wordlengths* and indicate the number of bits of information that can be held in primary memory and can be processed at one time. The larger the wordlength unit involved in data transfer within the computer, the faster the processing ability of the machine. As technology advances, computers continually increase their

8-Bit Byte

Sample 8-Bit Byte	0	1	0	1	0	0	1	0
(place values)	128	64	32	16	8	4	2	1

Value of Sample   0 + 64 + 0 + 16 + 0 + 0 + 2 + 0 = 82

0 = 00110000	A = 01000001
1 = 00110001	B = 01000010
2 = 00110010	C = 01000011
3 = 00110011	D = 01000100
4 = 00110100	E = 01000101
5 = 00110101	F = 01000110
6 = 00110110	$ = 00100100
7 = 00110111	* = 00101010
8 = 00111000	) = 00101001
9 = 00111001	SPACE = 00100000

Bit representations of selected ASCII (American Standard Code for Information Interchange) characters. ASCII code uses 7 of the 8 bits in each byte to represent numbers, letters, and other symbols. In ASCII, the sample byte at the top (01010010) represents the character *R*.

capacity to handle greater wordlengths and thus increase speed of operation. While most school microcomputers are 8-bit machines, newer ones frequently have 16-bit memories.

Higher-Level Language

Only a few years ago, data had to be loaded into the CPU by means of *machine language* consisting of combinations of 0s and 1s. While the internal mechanisms of computers continue to require instructions to be this *binary code,* other codes have been invented that enable people to communicate with computers more easily. One such language is assembly language. The instructions look like abbreviated English and can be used more easily by a programmer to enter instructions into the computer than working with 0s and 1s. But assembly language is much too different from everyday communication to be useful except for professionals.

More recently computer languages called *high-level languages* that are much more like English have been invented. The most familiar high-level languages have names like BASIC (Beginners All-purpose Symbolic Instruction Code), FORTRAN (FORmula TRANslation), as well as others such as Logo and Pascal. More will be said about languages in Chapter 4, where the focus is on software.

Starting in the Middle: The Arithmetic-Logic Unit (ALU)

The CPU microprocessor consists of three integrated but clearly definable components—a control unit, a primary storage unit, and an arithmetic-logic unit. As we said, it is the brain of the computer. At the core of this brain lies the arithmetic-logic unit (another name for it is processing unit). Here the actual "thought work" of the computer is performed. As the names imply, binary information is acted on in two ways: by executing arithmetic calculations, and by making logical comparisons.

The logical operations of the arithmetic-logic unit (ALU) are based on the algebra of George Boole (see Chapter 1) in which the truth and falseness of statements is determined. "Truth" in this system is denoted by the number (1) and "falseness" is denoted by zero (0)—in exactly the same way as the general communication within the CPU. In the ALU, data are also compared to determine the relationships between two similar items. Thus data entries may be equal to, less than, or greater than each other.

The Control Unit

The processing or arithmetic-logic unit performs the actual computations, but in order for that to happen the process must be controlled. The control unit regulates this process—as well as all other parts of the computer system—and in doing so it isolates and picks up (or "fetches") program instructions from the memory in the primary storage unit. It also translates program instructions into machine operations to be executed by the arithmetic-logic unit.

The control unit also maintains a record of what parts of a program have been executed and which ones are yet to be executed. And it checks them off one by one as they are completed. The control unit also transfers data between the ALU and primary storage and collects the output from the ALU. Finally it sends the data to an output device such as a printer or monitor screen. Extremely precise timing is required for all these tasks to be executed satisfactorily, especially since calculations inside a computer are measured in billionths of a second (nanoseconds) that approach the speed of light. Accurate timing is accomplished with an internal quartz crystal clock that measures time by means of extremely precise oscillations. In sum, the control unit is occupied most of the time with moving the instructions in a program around in order that the data may be executed properly.

Since computers can transmit information at very high speeds, data have to be stored temporarily during execution, so that it will not be processed out of sequence or missed entirely. These temporary storage locations are called *registers.* "Storage" in an everyday sense means keeping something for a considerable period of time. Because of the great speeds involved in computing, however, the process of storage in the CPU is virtually instantaneous in human terms. Registers serve as temporary storage only for managing the processes of the ALU and to speed transfer of data and instructions within the CPU. Moreover, registers should not be confused with primary storage, which will be discussed next.

The Primary Storage Unit

The CPU can only access data that are already present in the computer, which means that all the data and instructions for a program must be entered into primary memory storage before a computer is able to perform any task. The primary storage unit also stores all the data after it has been processed, as well as the intermediary results of any calculations. All this information is held in specific memory locations called *addresses.* These addresses are specific locations in primary memory and are identified by variable names embedded in a program. It is the task of the programmer to keep a record of the variables for a given program.

Because primary storage resides inside the computer (not in some external storage device), access time is reduced to a minimum. The speed of execution of all internal functions on the CPU is extremely rapid and is accomplished by means of wired pathways, or *buses.* Buses are de-

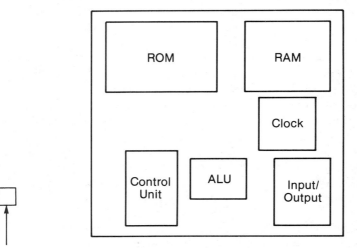

Actual size (¼″ square)

A calculator's microprocessor. In today's microcomputers all functions except those of the control unit and ALU are usually performed by other chips.

signed to carry a certain number of bits of information. A simple bus can carry information in only one direction at any one time. Microcomputer buses are normally of this kind. Buses on more complex computers are designed to carry data in two directions at once, which greatly increases the efficiency of the machine and enables it to perform numbers of computations simultaneously. By this means, the CPU "reaches out" to the information at its disposal in primary storage, including the instructions (the "program") that the CPU is to execute.

This *stored program concept* is particularly effective, because once in storage a program can be executed without human intervention over very short distances at electronic speeds. As we mentioned in Chapter 1, the concept was developed by John von Neumann over 40 years ago and permits much faster execution of instructions than was possible earlier. Before that time, a computer had to be plugged into special control panels that carried instructions before a program would operate. More recently, "non–von Neumann" computers have been designed that instead of handling one piece of data at a time work with multiple data and as a consequence are faster and have greater capacity.

When problems are encountered with present-day limitations of the primary storage unit, programmers often divide a large program into sections that the primary storage unit can handle at one time. Each section is called a *page*. Thus a page of programming is entered into primary storage and is executed while the remaining pages remain in auxiliary memory, that is, outside the computer, until the first page has been processed. By this means, programs of almost any length can be executed where primary storage is unable to handle an entire program at one time. Someone using the computer can recognize this technique by observing whether the computer occasionally activates the auxiliary memory device during the execution of a program. Today's more sophisticated educational software uses this memory allocation approach.

This primary memory that the CPU "addresses" is of two types. Both are forms of *semiconductor memory*, where hundreds of thousands of electronic circuits have been photographically etched on to minute chips of silicon. The chips are plugged into the motherboard of a computer where they are tied directly to the CPU via the bus system. The circuits operate in response to electronic *gates* that open or close in response to the presence or absence of electrical impulses. One form is called read-only memory (ROM), while the other is called random access memory (RAM). Read-only memory stores program information that the typical user will need regularly, such as routines for solving square roots. The contents of these chips cannot be altered: they remain permanently in the computer even when the external power has been turned off. This type of memory is said to be "hard wired."

While read-only memory saves user time because it contains information that is frequently needed, the major form of primary storage is

The "motherboard" for an Apple IIe microcomputer. The CPU is encased in the single, long chip holder just to the left of center on the motherboard. Three of the ROM chips are housed in the shorter holders in the row below the CPU. A row of eight RAM chips appears at the bottom of the motherboard, slightly obscured by the Apple's case. *(Courtesy of Apple Computer, Inc.)*

random access memory (RAM). Random access memory might be better named "read/write random access memory" because it is nonpermanent. When data are no longer needed, a user can write over it—much like recording a new sound track over an old one on audio tape. Since RAM is nonpermanent, when electrical power is cut off, the contents are instantly lost—something that disconcerts most inexperienced users at one time or another. However, the great value of this "volatile" semiconductor memory lies in its advantages over the forms of memory that preceded it, such as magnetic core memory. Integrated circuits (ICs) are faster, more reliable, less costly, and require less power than earlier forms of memory. And as we mentioned in Chapters 1 and 2, even greater miniaturization—large-scale integration (LSI) and very large scale integration (VLSI)—are adding dramatically to primary storage capacity. In fact, the point has been reached where increasingly complex programs can now be run on small machines that formerly were restricted to very large computers. One consequence of this change is that computers without any provision for memory expansion rapidly become obsolete as newer, more complex programs become available. Only a few years ago, school microcomputers with 16K (kilobytes) of primary storage were thought to be adequately supported. Since then, memory capacities for microcomputers have increased to 32K, 48K, 64K, and 128K as base levels of memory. Now manufacturers are regularly advertising 256K and 512K of primary storage, with expandability to over 1,000K (1 megabyte) and beyond. This trend toward larger primary storage memories is likely to continue either with the purchase of more powerful machines or by plugging in replacement chips that have much greater memory.

RAM and ROM are the most common forms of internal memory found in computers used in education. Two other forms are to be found serving specialized needs, however. One is programmable read-only memory (PROM), and the other is erasable programmable read-only memory (EPROM). Both are similar in that they are programmed rather than hard wired, but unlike random access memory, they are programmed permanently to satisfy the special needs of an individual user. A PROM chip is programmed by a manufacturer to fit a particular user's needs and is unalterable. An EPROM chip is shipped to a user where it is programmed to fit a particular need. Unlike a PROM, an EPROM may be erased when subjected to a special process using ultraviolet light. It can then be reprogrammed for some other need.

A potential successor to the predominant semiconductor memory is *bubble memory*. Instead of having circuitry etched into a silicon chip, bubble memory is composed of magnetized spots, or "bubbles," placed on semiconducter material. Bubble memory has the capability to extend storage far beyond what is possible with current semiconductor memory, and unlike semiconductor memory, bubble memory is not volatile. At present, however, it is expensive and difficult to manufacture. So while bubble memory is not likely to appear in educational hardware for some time yet, the long-term message is unmistakable: computer memories in all sizes of machines will continue to increase. When once this expansion of memory has been perfected, the use of computers in all walks of life—including education—will expand greatly.

Summary of the Machine Cycle

Each piece of information is treated in the same way within the computer. The process is called the *machine cycle*. The control unit fetches an instruction from primary storage where it is decoded so that the control unit knows what task is to be performed. This is called *instruction time*. The control unit passes the decoded instruction to the processing unit, which performs the required operations. The results of the processing are then sent back to the primary memory to complete the cycle. This latter part of the cycle is called *execution*. To give some idea of the speed of computing, machines can perform variously ranging from thousands to millions of such cycles every second.

Input and Output (I/O)

The central processing unit can perform tasks only when fed with information to compute or compare, together with instructions on what to do once the tasks have been completed. The first relates to entering information into the computer and is usually called *input*. The second relates to the presentation of results and is called *output*.

Input and output data are the most obvious of all the computer acts, and they are the steps in the computing process that affect users most obviously. Other than teachers of computer science or electronic engineering, however, educators need to have only a general understanding of what occurs. On the other hand, information of all kinds is the stock-in-trade of teachers and students regardless of subject matter specialty and levels of schooling. And where computers are concerned, this information is usually of a kind that students either need to learn or, having learned, need to be able to use. Computers can be helpful for both tasks. However, for information to be made available, it must first be entered into a computer, this is the act of input. And the only way a person can become aware of information or the consequences of various input is for it to be made known to the user. This is the output.

For convenience, and because input and output are closely linked with the discussion of software and storage media, they are developed more fully in Chapter 4.

The Main Types of Computers

While schools primarily use microcomputers, three types of computers are in general use. The largest and oldest type is the *mainframe* computer. Middle-sized machines are called *minicomputers*. The one most recently developed is the *microcomputer,* which was made possible through the technology of extreme miniaturization that occurred during the early 1970s. However, as a consequence of continual technological developments, any clear distinction that may have existed among these three types of machines has been muddied to the point where considerable overlap now exists. Nevertheless, differences do exist that warrant consideration here.

Mainframe Computers

The word *mainframe* derives from a computer where the three subunits (control, memory and ALU) of the CPU are in a single enclosure, but since computers of all sizes now possess a mainframe or its equivalent, the term is no longer very meaningful. The term has now come to apply only to very large, very fast, and correspondingly very expensive computers. Mainframe computers typically use up to 64 bits to a word, and processing speeds are commonly measured in millions of instructions per second. Another distinction is that mainframe computers have much more auxiliary memory than smaller machines because they are designed to handle very large amounts of data. Moreover, the operating systems (see Chapter 4) of mainframe computers are very complex, which again calls for more primary and auxiliary memory. The largest and fastest mainframe computers are often called *supercomputers* and are the largest and fastest computers in existence. These very large machines are used for such tasks as weather forecasting, special effects for motion pictures, and complex engineering problems. They work at such phenomenal capacities as 200 million computations a second. As a consequence of the density of the memory, supercomputers have to be surrounded with coolant. Mainframe computers tend to be used by organizations that need to process extremely large amounts of information at high speed.

Minicomputers

The word *mini* is an abbreviation for "minimal" and was used for computers built to meet the limited computing needs of factories and to serve specialized industrial purposes. Originally they were middle-sized machines with highly specific functions such as controlling manufacturing processes, temperature control, and performing accounting tasks. Minicomputers are still middle-sized machines, but they have now become general purpose computers. Unlike the very large mainframe and supercomputers, minicomputers are much less expensive, ranging from $50,000 to $500,000. They do not generate large amounts of heat and consequently do not need to be housed in expensive air-conditioned or super-cooled environments. And because they may also be plugged into normal power supplies, the cost of using them is much less than the costs of running mainframe machines. Words are normally either 16 or

32 bits in length, so that the speed of operation is less than the typical mainframe computer.

Microcomputers

When a computer is relatively portable and inexpensive, it is described as a *microcomputer*. Most microcomputers cost less than $15,000 and are normally self-contained—or "stand alone"—that is, they can be used without any additional attachments. They are further distinguished from larger computers by using 8- or 16-bit microprocessers. For this reason microcomputers are slow by computer standards. And whereas the multiple buses on more complex machines are designed to allow information to travel in both directions simultaneously, microcomputer buses typically transmit information in only one direction at a time. Microcomputers also have small primary memories and consequently depend more heavily on auxiliary storage media such as diskettes and cassette tapes than the larger machines, although additional circuit boards can be used to expand memory to some extent. For all these reasons, microcomputers process information much more slowly than larger machines.

A current microcomputer system designed for home and school use. *(Courtesy of Apple Computer, Inc.)*

Choosing Hardware for School Needs

For many years computing equipment was too costly for use in schools except for such administrative functions as inventories, accounting, and student and personnel records. Only in the late 1970s as a consequence of miniaturization were relatively inexpensive microcomputers available to the general public and to classroom teachers. At first, when a school or district would decide to purchase computing equipment, those who had to make the decision about what to buy were faced with a confusing array of new products to choose from and many plausible salespeople. While this problem persists, it has been simplified because stiff competition has caused numbers of manufacturers to withdraw from the educational market. Moreover, several brands of machines have now been in schools long enough to have acquired reputations for both their suitability to school applications and also their reliability under the punishing conditions of classroom use.

The primary question facing educators remains the same, however, and that is deciding what computers will be used for in a school. It has always been too easy to become involved with discussions about the merits of the various brands of machines rather than with the tasks for which they are to be used in the instructional program. The task has also been made more complex. At the outset, business, mathematics, and science were often believed to be the areas where computers were most suited. And even where the best thinking went into the earlier school needs assessments, the actual applications often proliferated to the extent that teachers of quite unexpected subject areas recognized the value of computers. In sum, the selection of computing equipment has now become a school-wide responsibility rather than one for teachers in a narrowly defined group of specialties. Moreover, as teachers become more at home with computers, there is a growing realization that they are as useful for art and home economics as they are for science and language arts and also that they are as useful in grade four as in grade eleven.

The Choice of Computer

Once school needs have been identified, the next task is to decide on the most suitable model of computer. A list of suitable machines for school use can easily be found by looking through some of the computing magazines published for educators or visiting schools and talking to teachers. While such issues as reputation for reliability, availability of service, and cost must be considered, one of the more important issues has to do with the size of the memory. Although most school computer needs can presently be satisfied with either 48 kilobytes (48K) or 64 kilobytes (64K) of primary memory storage (in this case, RAM memory), manufacturers are continually increasing this capacity. At the same time, software companies are publishing ever more elaborate programs for making full use of increasing primary memory.

School decision makers may decide that the speed and ease of working with integrated software programs combining several programs that formerly were separate (such as word processing with spreadsheets) is sufficiently important that they should purchase computers that have the largest memories available. For other educators, the issue of large memories is more a matter of anticipation of a time when the better software will no longer operate on 48K or 64K machines. Some computers already satisfy this desire for much larger memories but cannot be expanded. Other computers are manufactured with a conventional 48K or 64K capacity but have the capability for expansion as the need arises.

In no case, however, should the selection of any computer hardware he determined without giving both teachers and students the opportunity to try it out thoroughly first, for as long as necessary to feel comfortable with it. While information from manufacturers about their machines is useful, reviews published in computer magazines should also be studied. Once the range of possible equipment has been tried out and comparisons made, the decision should be based on local school needs, available funding, and servicing arrangements.

Until recently, keyboards and cathode ray tube (CRT) monitors were constructed within a single shell that also houses the CPU; the current trend seems to be toward detachable keyboards. Some models also have the disk drives included within the same case. The advantages to a single case are that each computing station then consists of one item of equipment only and a minimum of external wiring. However, a single unit may be heavy and clumsy to move and consequently awkward to transport from room to room in a school unless it is on a specially designed cart. Furthermore, if any one component needs repair, the entire unit has to be taken out of use. Work stations consisting of separate components, on the other hand, can easily be connected to other machines— for example, linking three disk drives to one computer to perform a particular task.

The arrangement of the keys on the keyboard as well as their action as they are depressed also deserves attention. The arrangement of the letters of the alphabet typically adheres to the QWERTY keyboard found on typewriters, including the shift key. A few rather unique keyboard arrangements have been developed, including the Dvorak keyboard, where the letters most frequently used are placed in the "home row." But the QWERTY arrangement predominates, with a few twists. Numbers may run across the top as a conventional typewriter, or they may be grouped separately to form a numeric keypad, or both arrangements may be available. Where a school program requires the constant entry of numbers, a separate pad speeds up the process considerably. Frequently used

A standard QWERTY keyboard, named for the order of keys in the uppermost letter row.

keys such as RETURN, CONTROL, and RESET (or their equivalents) and the four directional arrows may be located in various places, all with an eye to helping the user work more easily. Even the shapes and sizes of these much-used keys may be modified. Other keys will have special functions or will be individually programmable to fit the unique needs of a user. Most schools are unlikely to require these special keys, however, unless the level of work is fairly advanced, though software operation can be simplified by means of function keys.

More recently, some manufacturers have separated keyboards by means of flexible cables to permit users to sit more comfortably than in the conventional typing posture. Whether this is desirable for school use needs to considered by those about to make a purchase. For example, were several students to be working together at a machine, it might be much more convenient to pass a keyboard from one to the other than to be continually changing places. From quite another point of view, separate keyboards add to the likelihood that they will fall on the floor and be damaged.

With all the different keyboard arrangements, the task of reaching a decision on which one is best for a particular setting may be a problem. If, however, new machines are being added to some that are already in use, then confusion can be minimized if the keyboard arrangement is similar to that found on existing machines. When purchasing new equipment, the keyboard arrangement is not as likely to be a major issue, since most people soon adjust to whatever arrangement they work with. A more important consideration is that the keys be comfortable to the touch and that the action when the keys are depressed be precise without being stiff. Readers of this book may also need to address this same question at some time or another, since an increasing number of teachers are purchasing their own machines. You will naturally want to make a purchase that satisfies your own personal needs, but it is much easier to work on the same model of machine at home and at school than it is to move between different machines that have different keyboards and different command systems, and that use different software.

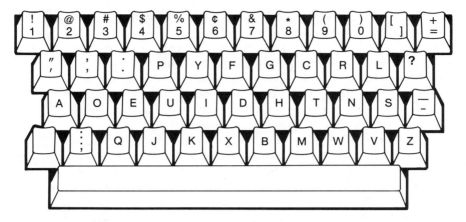

The Dvorak keyboard places the most frequently used keys in the home (middle) row of letter keys. Some 4,000 words can be typed just using the Dvorak home row keys, compared to only about 100 words from the QWERTY keyboard's home row.

Monitors

When choosing a monitor, the first task is to determine whether the need is for a monochrome display or one in full color. If both color and monochrome are needed, just what proportion of each type of monitor will satisfy the school needs? Monochrome monitors all have dark screens, but the characters may be displayed in green, amber, or white. Color monitors consist either of standard television sets or RGB (red, green, blue) monitors that are specially designed for displaying computer programs in color. Monochromatic monitors are less expensive than color models, but since much of the better educational software makes good use of color graphics, the decision may favor color monitors, although most software is adjusted for display on both color and monochromatic screens. If graphics are to play a significant part in the instructional program—as in art—then color monitors are essential. On the other hand, if most of the computer uses are to be in word processing, mathematics, or accounting, then color monitors may not be necessary.

In view of the fact that two or three monochromatic monitors may be purchased for the same cost as a good quality RGB color monitor, it is not uncommon for a school to equip a computer laboratory with monochromatic monitors for the student work stations and have one or two color monitors available for those tasks that require color displays. And since schools are likely to own color television sets already, these can be linked to computers at comparatively little cost to provide additional color displays. Television images, however, are normally not comparable with those displayed on RGB monitors.

Among monitors of all kinds, there is a range a quality—and with it corresponding cost differences. Some color monitors do not display colors well, and text can be quite difficult to read. The quality of the characters may also vary quite considerably; some will display letters and numbers where the points that compose the letters are packed together closely and make very legible shapes. Others display characters where the points are quite far apart and result in broken shapes that are difficult to read. The proportions of the characters also vary, and this can affect legibility. With constant use this illegibility contributes to student fatigue and a decline in accuracy. Moreover, when fewer than twenty-four lines of characters are visible on the screen at one time, users may have problems maintaining continuity of thought, whether with a passage of text or lines of program code. Screen size can also be a factor to consider, depending on where monitors are to be placed relative to students. A 13-inch diagonal screen may be quite satisfactory when placed immediately in front of a student on top of a keyboard and CPU housing but not if placed high up on a shelf some distance away. As with all these decisions, the only test is to work with the equipment for a while before making a purchase.

Disk Drives

Paired disk drives in a single case with a cable connection to a plug-in port at the back of the computer may be more convenient than single drives connected individually by ribbon-like connections. On the other hand initial purchases of starter equipment often include only one disk drive. And if budgets are strained by an initial outlay, single drives may be all that can be purchased at that time. Very soon, however, most users recognize the need for a second drive, especially for transferring files from disk to disk. Because one circuit board operates both drives, the second drive is less expensive.

Printers

The choice of printer is certainly next once the basic equipment has been selected. A monitor will output much important information, but "soft copy" only will not usually satisfy all needs. Printed information on paper, or "hard copy," is essential for all school computing needs. Many brands of printers are available, although typical school needs eliminate many of the more expensive and more sophisticated machines. Letter-quality daisy-wheel printers, for example, produce handsome copy, and a principal or a superintendent may need such a printer. But except for a few special tasks, classroom needs are best met with a dot matrix printer. Making a decision about which dot matrix printer to choose is no easy matter, however. Numbers of good machines are available. Obviously, a printer should be compatible with the computing equipment that is in place or about to be purchased.

The next task is to study the quality of the standard printing text. A wide variety of alphabet designs will be encountered. With some, there are no descending letter strokes. Some printers will do double striking to make boldface letters for special headings. Others can be programmed to make large, decorative letters for special effects. Not least, some printers will produce pictures when linked to a circuit board designed for the purpose. Some printers use a friction feed with rubber rollers to advance the paper, while others use a tractor feed that advances the paper by means of studded wheels that engage perforations along the edges of the paper. And some machines are designed to use both methods, so that either single sheet or fan-fold paper may be used.

All printers suitable for school use will need to take the narrow measurement of a piece of standard typing paper (8 1/2 inches by 11 inches), while some will need to take 11 inches or 14 inches (legal size) paper lengthwise. The decision about which printer should be purchased thus requires that all these considerations be weighed against what students will be doing.

Other Hardware

Other hardware that can be useful for school computing including modems, graphics pads, joy sticks, paddles, light pens, mice, and electronic music keyboards. Various brands of each of these devices are manufactured in a wide range of cost and quality, from those designed for home use to professional-level products. For example, modems that communicate with other computers slowly have a speed (baud rate) of 300 and are comparatively inexpensive, while speeds needed in business or by computer professionals (1,200 baud rate and higher) are several times more expensive. Similarly, graphics tablets range in quality and price from hand-held pads where images are created by the presence of any pointed object to pads the size of large sheets of drawing paper where images are generated with an electronic stylus. Pads of the latter quality are used in advertising agencies and by engineers and are quite costly. Musical keyboards also tend to be expensive for school unless a strong commitment has been made to composition and electronic music.

Most joy sticks and paddles, together with several models of light pen and mouse devices are manufactured for the microcomputer home and school market and fall well within an affordable price range for schools.

A problem with all these peripheral devices is that only one student can use any one of them at any given time. As a consequence, multiple purchases have to be considered if group work is contemplated, which can escalate costs even though the per item cost is moderate.

Environmental Decisions

The fundamental task of choosing hardware includes the selection of the computer (CPU) itself, keyboard, monitor, and auxiliary memory storage. While the CPU and the keyboard are almost always manufactured by the same company, monitors and memory storage units may often be purchased from other manufacturers. The first consideration is, of course, that they be compatible with the primary equipment. Together, these items constitute a single work station, although other hardware may eventually be needed. And since a school will typically purchase a number of computers at one time in order to equip a laboratory, it is desirable to think in terms of complete work stations.

A work station is more than computer hardware, however. The computing machinery needs to stand on a stable, flat surface. Space is needed around the computer, so that students have room to make notes and study manuals. Moreover, ease in working at a keyboard calls for a work surface that is at the level of a typewriting desk, which is lower than a conventional table top. Seating—as for typing—needs to be such that a student can work easily and maintain a good posture. And the CRT needs to be at such a level and at such an angle that students can read from it easily, without having to hold their heads at an uncomfortable angle, while also avoiding reflections and direct light falling on the surface of the screen.

The room also needs to have adequate electrical outlets for all the anticipated machinery without running the risk of overloading the power supply. Furthermore, the room must have adequate cooling and airflow, since computers will malfunction if overheated. Finally is the decision about how to secure the equipment against theft. One method is to attach each unit with a steel cable to its table. Another is to place each machine in a specially designed case that is permanently attached to the table. Yet another is to make the doors and windows secure. None of these choices will prevent theft and damage entirely—and they may interfere with the most flexible use of the machines—but the decisions are an integral part of the process of choosing computer hardware for school uses.

Summary

After we considered the big picture of computer technology in the first two chapters, Chapter 3 began to illuminate how computers work by focusing first on the hardware (the equipment). This look at the little picture endeavored to describe the fundamental parts of computers generally, with specific reference to microcomputers, and to explain how those parts work together to produce the results we as computer users see. Finally, we discussed some considerations to bear in mind when choosing computer hardware, whether the microcomputer itself or the various other peripheral hardware that may be part of a computing station.

In explaining how computer hardware works, we could not avoid mentioning the other side of the coin—software. The two are inextricably linked, one being worthless without the other. Chapter 4, then, completes this second half of the story by examining software and software storage devices.

CHAPTER 4

Software and Storage Media

Introduction

This chapter on the nature of software and how it is stored really extends the presentations of the first three chapters. In each of the preceding chapters, discussing the origins of modern computers and the nature of computer hardware invariably included mention of software. Software, the electronically coded commands that the computer executes, works in concert with hardware. Indeed, as we said at the end of Chapter 3, without software, hardware would be no more than odd conversation pieces requiring periodic dusting.

The rationale for teachers learning about software and storage media is also an extension of the rationale provided in Chapter 3. We wish to demystify the operation of computers, stripping away some of the technical veils to reveal the essential nature of how computers work. With demystification comes the discovery that the computer's power can be seized and harnessed for your own purposes, whether personal or professional. Beyond this, however, are practical considerations. Understanding how computers manipulate software can help you avoid making errors in software selection and to troubleshoot some of the simpler hardware or software failures that occasionally occur. Finally, this introduction to software should provide a first step to those who want to pursue more in-depth examination of software and storage media.

System Software: Operating Systems

Software is frequently divided into two categories: system software and applications software. *System software* is the collection of programs containing instructions that help the computer system operate. *Applications software* is programs that make the computer accomplish specific jobs like word processing, simulations, tutorials, and the like.

Most of you have become (or will become) acquainted with applications software; the software resides on a disk or cassette or other *storage medium* that you or your school have purchased. You place this in the proper piece of input hardware, turn on the machine, and the computer and you proceed to accomplish whatever job the software was intended to perform. Simultaneously, though, system software residing either on the storage medium or in the computer or both regulates the execution of the applications software. To the user, the workings of system software are invisible, and this is as it should be. But a closer look at some of this system software (specifically, the operating system) is necessary for a keener understanding of its importance.

Purpose

An operating system is a collection of programs that a computer uses to monitor its operation, including the sequence of commands to be executed, the orderly loading of programs and routines needed, the allocation of internal resources (memory, calculation), and the retrieval of data required while an application is running. In the early years of electronic computers, many of these set-up and management processes were handled manually by a human operator, at the expense of computer efficiency. Now they are handled by software.

Components

Operating systems contain several components that perform specialized monitoring and regulatory tasks within the computer, whether a large mainframe computer, a smaller minicomputer, or a microcomputer. The particular components of operating systems vary, however, to suit the typical user needs and particular tasks to be performed by different kinds of computers.

SUPERVISOR PROGRAMS   One set of programs within most operating systems is called the *supervisor* or *monitor*. The supervisor controls the flow of work to be performed by the computer, including the sequence of computer tasks from beginning to end. The supervisor also makes sure that the "resources" of the computer are allocated properly; these resources include the memory, input and output operations, and use of peripheral devices (those attached to the computer from outside), among others.

PROCESSING PROGRAMS   Assuming that the supervisor does its job, other programs take care of the actual processing. A very important task that this part of the operating system performs is the translation of programs you might write in BASIC, Logo, Pascal, or some other language into machine language (we'll take a closer look at this function a bit later). Other programs maintain a record of the program files on your floppy disk (a list of which you can see by requesting the CATALOG or DIRECTORY). Finally, a number of utility programs may be available to facilitate, for example, file transfers from disk to disk.

DATA MANAGEMENT PROGRAMS   Operating systems also have programs that control how data are brought into the computer, how data are organized for efficient processing, and how they are stored on your disk.

An operating system thus provides a structure or framework within which applications software accomplishes the tasks for which it was designed. In so doing, an operating system must bridge the gap between the program written in a language that the programmer understands and the instructions that the machine understands. Here is where the importance of computer languages enters the scene.

Programming Languages

Low-Level Language: Machine Language

As we have discussed in earlier chapters, the computer processes commands in its own machine language, the 0s and 1s that reflect the operation of the integrated circuits. (Another machine language called octal is also used by some computers. It is a base-8 system, with bit values ranging from 0 to 7). Machine language can be referred to as a low-level language because it is closest to what the machine understands. Indeed, machine language is as low as they go.

Programming in machine language produces some rather positive results. At the top of the list is speed of executing, because the program does not need to be translated from its language to the machine's language. On the negative side, programming in machine language is terribly laborious, resulting in hefty amounts of code to perform even simple computer tasks. To reduce the labor, other languages have been developed that are easier for programmers to use.

We said that one such language is assembly language, which uses a kind of shorthand for the zeros and ones in machine language. Easier to use while retaining some of the benefits of machine language, assembly language is widely used by experienced programmers. However, assembly language is still pretty distant from the users' language, so programming language development has pursued languages more understandable to humans than to machines, to produce higher-level languages.

```
ASSEMBLY                                    OCTAL
    LMJ   X11,NINTRS            7413  13  00  0  000000  0003
    +     0000,0                0000  00  00  0  000000

    SZ    TEST                  0500  00  00  0  000000  0000
    LA    A0,(1.000000+ 0)      1000  00  00  0  000004  0000
    SA    A0,OUTPUT             0100  00  00  0  000001  0000

IL  LA    A0,(1.000000+ 0)      1000  00  00  0  000004  0000
    FA    A0,TEST               7600  00  00  0  000000  0000

    SA    A0,TEST               0100  00  00  0  000000  0000
    FM    A0,OUTPUT             7602  00  00  0  000001  0000

    SA    A0,OUTPUT             0100  00  00  0  000001  0000
    LA    A2,TEST               1000  02  00  0  000000  0000
    FAN   A2,(1.000000+ 2)      7601  02  00  0  000005  0000
    JP    A2,$+2                7402  02  00  0  000016  0001

    JNZ   A2,1L                 7401  02  00  0  000005  0001
    LMJ   X11,NPRT$             7413  13  00  0  000000  0004
    +     0100,2F               0000  04  00  0  000002  0000
    +     0110,0                0000  04  10  0  000000
    +     0040,OUTPUT           0000  02  00  0  000001  0000
    SLJ   N102$                 7201  00  00  0  000000  0005
    LMJ   X11,NSTOP$            7413  13  00  0  000000  0006

    +     (0050505050505)       0000  00  00  0  000006  0000
```

```
FORTRAN                         BASIC
    TEST=0                      10 T=0
    OUTPUT=1                    20 K=1
1   TEST=TEST+1                 30   T=T+1
    OUTPUT=OUTPUT*TEST          40   K=K*T
    IF (TEST.LT.100)  GOTO 1    50 IF T<100 THEN 30
    PRINT 2,OUTPUT              60   PRINT K
2   FORMAT(F15.0)               70   END
    END
```

```
PASCAL
PROGRAM OUTPUT(OUTPUT);
VAR TEST, OUTPUT:REAL;
BEGIN
  OUTPUT:=1.0; Test:=0.0;
  DO TEST:=TEST+1.0; OUTPUT:=OUTPUT*TEST UNTIL TEST>=100;
  WRITELN (OUTPUT:15:0)
END.
```

Comparison of programs in different languages. These programs above were written for the UNIVAC 1110 computer. *(Classroom Activities and Reference Guide for Use with the Computer Parts Kit. Cambridge, MN: Educational Computer Shoppe, 1978. Reprinted by permission.)*

High-Level Languages

The first programming language many of us are introduced to is BA-SIC, Beginner's All-purpose Symbolic Instruction Code. The language is "built into" the permanent memories of some microcomputers and is widely available for most microcomputers. It is a high-level language because its commands are closer to human language than to the machine's language. PRINT, INPUT, FLASH, INVERSE, FOR . . . NEXT, IF . . . THEN are examples of commands that one might use in BASIC, certainly a lot easier to handle than a long list of 0s and 1s.

Of course BASIC is only one among many programming languages available for microcomputers, and still others are available on larger computer systems. Increasing numbers of high school students are learning Pascal in preparation for later work in computer science. At the other end of the spectrum, many elementary school children are exploring new "microworlds" through the language of Logo. COBOL, C, FOR-TRAN, LISP, Prolog, FORTH, Smalltalk, APL, PL/1, and RPG are other examples of high-level programming languages (see Appendix A).

At even higher levels are the authoring languages, such as PILOT (Programmed Inquiry Learning or Teaching), GENIS I, BLOCKS, and others; these are particularly well suited to the development of instructional applications programs. Moreover, word processing, spreadsheet, and instructional programs usually have their own language-like commands that must be adhered to in order for a user to be able to interact with the computer. The same is true for special programs that permit the generation of graphics images and musical composition. In general, however, the closer a computer language is to everyday language, the more memory that it consumes, with the consequent reduction of memory space to work in. On the other hand, with the continuing advances made in memory storage in recent years, this obstacle is becoming less of a problem.

Making the Translation: Interpreters and Compilers

High-level languages permit greater ease of programming because they are closer to language that the user understands. On the other hand, these languages are more distant from the machine, meaning that programs written in high-level languages must be translated into machine language before the programs can be executed. That translation is done in one of two ways: through an interpreter or a compiler. Here's how they work.

INTERPRETER   The programmer writes a program in BASIC, let's say. This is called the *source* program. When the source program is executed, it first goes to the interpreter, part of the system software whose purpose is to translate each line of the source program into machine language. The interpreter translates one line at a time into machine language, that machine language code is executed, and then the next line of the source program (the one done in BASIC, in this example) is translated and executed. If there is a problem in the source program, the computer will stop executing the program at the line where the error occurred, and the interpreter will not translate any further lines.

There are some real advantages to translating a high-level language through an interpreter. Most microcomputers have a BASIC interpreter built into them, so you don't have to acquire the interpreter software elsewhere and load it into the computer's memory before executing the program you wrote (the source program). Interpreters also do not take up much space in the computer's memory, leaving lots of room for other things. Programs translated though an interpreter tend to be easier to debug or correct if errors occur, because the program stops executing right at the point of the error.

Interpreters also have a disadvantage. They tend to execute programs slowly. Let's say that there is a command at the end of your BASIC program ordering the computer to return to the top of the program and do the same things over again. Even though the interpreter will be seeing the same program lines for a second time, it doesn't remember them, so that the lines have to be translated again into machine language.

COMPILER   A compiler works a bit differently from an interpreter in translating high-level source programs into machine form. Let's presume you've written a program in FORTRAN (the source program). Instead of translating one line of the program at a time, a compiler takes the source program and translates it all into a machine-language program (called the *object* program) before sending it along to be executed. It is this object program that gets executed, rather than line-by-line translations of your source program, as is the case with interpreters.

The big advantage of a compiled program over an interpreted program is that the former executes programs more quickly. Taking the same example as before, if the computer must return to the top of the program and repeat lines, it does not have to retranslate those lines. This is because the compiler has already translated the entire source program into the machine-language object program, and it is the object program that is really being executed.

Unfortunately, few microcomputers have compilers already installed when you buy them. Compiler software has to be purchased separately. A second disadvantage to compiled programs is the increased difficulty of debugging source programs with errors, due largely to the creation of a separate object program.

COMPILERS, INTERPRETERS, AND LANGUAGES   The use of BASIC in the interpreter examples and FORTRAN in the compiler examples was not coincidental. There is a relationship between the language in which a program is written and whether it is translated through an interpreter or a compiler. BASIC is an interpreted language, meaning that it was developed and is designed to be used in conjunction with an interpreter rather than a compiler (though compilers for some versions of BASIC are available). Other interpreted languages include Logo, LISP, and APL. Similarly, FORTRAN is a compiled language, designed to be used with a FORTRAN compiler. Other compiled languages include C, Pascal, and COBOL.

For most computer users, system software and programming language remain largely hidden in everyday interaction with the machine. Of more salience is the applications software, the programs the user employs to accomplish particular tasks.

Applications Software and Computer Compatibility

The counterpoint to system software is applications software, broadly defined as encompassing programs chosen by the user to perform certain work. In education, a distinction is often made between instructional programs (drill-and-practice programs, tutorial programs, simulations) and application programs like data-base management, word processing, and spreadsheet programs. But in a larger sense, both these categories are applications software because they are all intended to perform work and accomplish tasks for the user (or his or her students) as distinct from system software.

In choosing the applications software, educators must weigh a wide range of factors. In Chapter 7 we'll discuss evaluating software in terms of instructional design and reliability considerations. In this chapter, we will focus on more technical prerequisites for selecting applications software, flowing from our discussion of systems software and languages.

Fitting Software to Machine: Operating Systems

You may have discovered that the operating system of a computer performs some pretty crucial tasks for the system. What you may not have realized is that operating systems vary considerably, not just among computers of different sizes (microcomputers, minicomputers, mainframes) but also among microcomputers. For example, the operating system programs for the Apple microcomputer are very different from those of the IBM, Commodore, Atari, TRS-80, and the rest. Each operating system handles data differently, communicates with external devices differently, and allocates machine resources differently.

These differences in operating systems are responsible in part for the incompatibility among applications programs. A program written for use with an IBM PC, for example, will not work on an Atari 800. Even within the same machine brand, different operating systems for that machine can create compatibility problems. For example, an applications program that is designed for use with the ProDOS operating system for the Apple IIe will encounter some problems if the older DOS operating system is the only one available in the Apple IIe's memory. It's the same computer, but different operating system. When you're shopping for applications software, then, check to make sure it is compatible with your computer—that there is a match between applications software and system software requirements.

Fitting Software to Machine: Programming Language

Since application programs may be written in many different languages, you also need to be sure that the computer you're using can translate that language into machine language. That is, your computer must have the interpreter or compiler for the particular language in which your application program is written. If the application program is written in Pascal, for example, your computer needs to have a Pascal compiler program. Often, the proper interpreter or compiler is included on the same floppy disk as the application program and is automatically loaded into the computer's memory first when you start the program. It's a good idea to check, though, to see whether you need any additional system software in order for your applications software to work properly.

Fitting Software to Machine: Memory Requirements

Both system and applications software can take up widely varying amounts of computer memory. For this reason, you must be sure that the memory of the computer you are using has sufficient memory capacity, stated in terms of K or thousands of bytes (see Chapter 2). If the application program you want requires 256K of memory, but your computer's memory will only hold 128K, you're out of luck. If someone were interested in programming in FORTRAN on a microcomputer and purchased FORTRAN compiler software, the application programs she or he would write would be relatively small because the compiler itself takes up so much memory.

Having considered the issue of software-to-hardware compatibility, we turn our attention to how these two aspects of computing work together, allowing us to get information into and out of the computer. First we will consider the former—how computers receive information from the outside world.

Getting Information Into the Computer: Input Mechanisms

In Chapter 3 we briefly discussed the concept of auxiliary memory, involving storage media and devices whose purpose is to save information outside the computer itself for later use. Computers vary in the range of storage media they will accept; thus, you must make the correct match between the computer's requirements and the medium on which the application program is stored. These media and devices, plus the keyboard, form the basis for getting software into the computer for execution, that is, input.

Input

The most familiar device today for the input of information into a computer is a keyboard, and while learning the keyboard may present a considerable obstacle for some students, it is far superior to the alternatives. At one time, the commonest method of inputting information was with cards that had holes punched in them in positions that corresponded with specific information (see discussion of Hollerith in Chapter 1).

One of the weaknesses of keypunching, however, lay partly in the very considerable time taken to translate information from source documents to cards. Another disadvantage was the human error that occurred easily while punching the cards. As a consequence, all cards had to be thoroughly checked before the data could actually be entered into the computer. Punched cards were well suited to calculations and for repetitive tasks such as inventories, payroll checks, and maintaining records of people or materials in business and industry. However, they are not suited at all for the interactive task of helping students learn school content and then use it.

Two other input methods deserve mention, though, again, they have little or no application in the classroom. One is magnetic tape that is stored on reels. Information stored by this method can be accessed 25 times faster than that on punch cards and also requires less storage space. But like punch cards, it is designed for high-volume execution of computations and record keeping and not for the interactive needs that are central in teaching and learning. A third form of entering data into computers that has a place in daily life but not in school is Source-data Automation. An example is the computer at a point-of-sale terminal that reads an optical mark on an object (such as the Universal Product Code or UPC mark on items you buy at the grocery store). Another form occurs when the computer reads characters printed in magnetic ink, a method used in banks for check processing and in the post office to determine correct postage.

Input Devices for School Computing

The primary method of input for education is by way of the computer keyboard. Other methods are also used, such as joystick, mouse, and light pen, and they are described later. While voice recognition is still in its infancy, it is quite likely that verbal input may supplant other forms of input in the educational applications of computing, but such a development, except in the special needs environment, is likely to be some years away.

Typing programs into the computer each time it is to be executed would be laborious and wasteful when it can be stored permanently elsewhere. Errors that might interfere later with the execution of the program can then be eliminated in advance, thus not tying up the computer unnecessarily. And although primary memory capacities of computers may be continually expanding, they are intended as working spaces and are neither suited nor intended to serve as permanent storage.

FLOPPIES, CARTRIDGES, AND CASSETTES   A common form of permanent, or "auxiliary," memory presently used in education is floppy diskettes. These flexible plastic disks, held in square protective plastic casings, contain a number of concentric tracks in which the bits and bytes of software are magnetically stored. A popular alternative to floppies is represented by some computers that are designed so that additional RAM or ROM memory can be plugged in. ROM cartridges, also referred to as ROM-packs, grew out of game programs, but other prepared material can just as easily be written. The contents of ROM cartridges are almost impossible to damage short of physical abuse. RAM cartridges provide additional working memory. A third storage medium, cassette tape, was quite prevalent when computers first entered schools, but has declined in popularity over the years.

If your school uses floppy disks, you know that a rather essential piece of equipment is the disk drive. It is the mechanism with a slot into which the disk is inserted. A specially designed magnetic head moves down close to the disk when the door to the slot is shut. When activated, the disk spins, and the drive mechanism causes the head either to read data from the disk's tracks into the primary memory or to write data onto its tracks. These data are then available for processing but are stored permanently until needed.

Disk drives and cassette players are electro-mechanical rather than electronic, and thus have moving parts. For this reason, sending information to and from them is slow compared with the speed of operation within the CPU itself. However, they more than compensate for their slowness by having large memories. Floppy disks and matching drives are manufactured for 3 1/2-inch, 5 1/4-inch, and 8-inch sizes and can store data on one or both sides. The capacities of floppy disks range from 100K (K stands for kilobyte, which equals 1,024 bytes) to over 1 megabyte (a megabyte is 1 million bytes). Cassette storage is less expensive than disk storage, but it is slower, and all searches for filed information have to follow the tape along its length until the information is found. This can take considerable time, especially if a file is at the far end of a tape. In contrast, the search process with floppy disks is very rapid because the head on the disk drive can move directly to any track on a disk without having to follow a particular pathway. Thus disk information is accessed randomly, while cassette information is accessed sequentially.

HARD DISKS AND OPTICAL DISCS   Two other forms of disk storage are gradually making their way into schools. One is the hard disk; the other is optical disc. A hard disk is housed in a sealed case with the drive machinery. While hard disks are usually more expensive than individual disk drives for floppy diskettes, one hard disk of 5, 10, or 20 megabytes can serve the storage needs of a fully equipped laboratory of school computers. Moreover, the sealed unit is not subject to the servicing needs—not to mention tampering and damage—that can occur when every computer in a room is equipped with one or more separate disk drives. The storage capacity of a hard disk is many times that of the conventional 5 ¼-inch floppy diskette, and therefore, many programs can be stored on it.

Optical disc technology is advancing slowly, from its commercial beginnings in the form of videodiscs carrying full-length movies. However, the educational potential is immense, particularly since one disc can hold information equivalent to 5,000 floppy disks or, in the case of videodiscs, over 100,000 visual slides. Videodiscs can also store both print information and pictures, and can carry one or more sound tracks. As yet, educators have barely begun to make use of the opportunities for interactive instruction and the storage of images and sound that exist with optical discs, although that can be expected to change in the fairly near future.

SOFTSTRIPS   One additional storage medium and device bears mentioning, since it too is likely to find its way into the schools: *softstrips.* In a manner similar to the UPC markings on grocery store items, complete software programs can be represented by patterns of black and white

This videodisc player reads full-motion video and/or stills from a 12-inch disc that looks like a silver record. With interactive video, a computer controls the video sequence based on the user's input. *(Courtesy of Pioneer Communications of America, Inc.)*

markings printed on regular paper. Using a softstrip scanning device, a program so displayed on paper can be read directly into the primary memory of your computer. We can imagine, then, the teacher's guide for an American history textbook having one or more end-of-chapter activities including a program printed on the same page as the other activities, ready to be scanned and run.

GRAPHICS DEVICES Graphic images are often entered into a computer by means of the keyboard, in the same way that verbal and quantitative data are input. However, they can also be entered using a graphics pad that enables a person to draw and "paint" designs much more rapidly than would be possible were they to enter information in the conventional way. A graphics pad is usually in the form of a sheet of plastic in which is embedded a wire grid that corresponds with the spaces available on the monitor. A user enters lines, shapes, and colors by way of a stylus. These images are typically displayed as output on the CRT screen, which permits the user to add to and modify artwork as it is executed. Completed programs for all these devices are typically stored on floppy diskettes, although tape cassettes may also be used. Other graphics input devices are also to be found, including joystick, paddle, mouse, and light pen.

JOYSTICK, PADDLE, MOUSE, LIGHT PEN, AND TOUCH SCREEN Joysticks and paddles evolved from arcade and home computer games, where

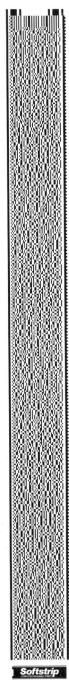

This Softstrip contains data that can be read directly into a computer using a special reader. *(Courtesy of Cauzin Systems, Inc., Waterbury, Connecticut.)*

players needed a simple method of moving the flashing light (cursor) that marks where the user is working on the screen. A joystick is a small lever in a box that moves easily in all directions. The action of the lever causes the cursor to move around the screen. Paddles consist of one or two small levers or buttons housed in small plastic cases. By activating them, the cursor is again moved around on the screen. More recently the light pen and mouse have appeared. A mouse consists of a small boxlike shape that fits easily in the hand. As the mouse is moved around on a flat surface, it transmits its location to the CPU by means of a beam of light or a rotating ball, which in turn records the track it has taken on the CRT screen. A light pen resembles a regular pen and does very much the same thing as a mouse except the input is determined by moving the light pen over the surface of the CRT screen to establish the location of lines and shapes. As we saw from the first chapter, screens that sense the location of our touch send our queries as input to the computer and display, in return, the location of onions in a grocery store or the whereabouts of a book in the library.

MODEM   Input can also be vastly expanded beyond the capabilities of a computer work station. Telephone linkages may tap information stored in large computers located some distance away by means of modems or "modulator-demodulators." A modem consists of a small attachment to the computer—sometimes in the form of a telephone—that translates impulses generated by the computer, so that they can be carried over

Joystick.   *(Courtesy of Apple Computer, Inc.)*

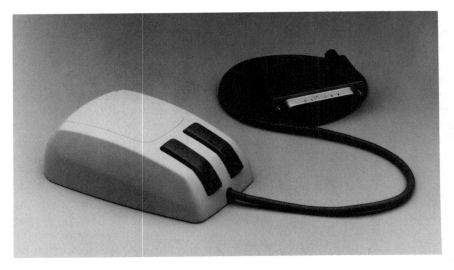

When the mouse is rolled on a tabletop, a cursor moves around the computer screen. Pressing a button on the mouse activates the function pointed to by the cursor. *(Courtesy of Microsoft Corporation.)*

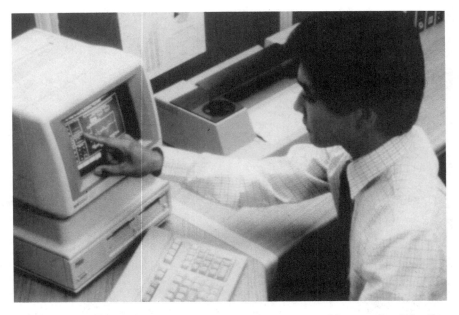

Equipped with a touch screen, a computer can operate with a touch of the finger. *(Photo courtesy of Hewlett-Packard Company.)*

telephone lines to another computer. As we mentioned in Chapter 2, people at two computers some distance from each other may be linked in this way. On other occasions, people use modems to gather information from the memories of large computers. The desired information may then be transmitted to the auxiliary memory of the microcomputer—the memory capacity of a hard disk is usually needed for this to be worthwhile. This is called *downloading*. One benefit of downloading is that it overcomes delays resulting from heavy use of large storage units as well as cutting the costs of repeatedly having to access a large computer data base. But unless a school computer is connected to a hard disk, downloading information from a large computer is usually not practical, because of the small memory available in RAM or in floppy disk memory. Some data bases, on the other hand, provide information such as bibliographical information that does not require very much memory and is practical to access even with a floppy diskette.

Modems can also be used when students from widely separated schools want to confer with each other about work in progress or want to share finished products, such as graphic images, musical compositions, or plays they have written. Teachers can also use modems to communicate with distant colleagues about ways of improving teaching.

This modem is designed to be installed completely inside a microcomputer. External modems are also available. *(Courtesy of Hayes Microcomputer Products, Inc.)*

Getting Information Out of the Computer: Output

Now that we have some ideas about how the computer receives information, we now consider how it communicates with users after it has finished its internal tasks as directed by the application software.

Output

Computer output is the reason for using a computer: it provides the solution to a problem the computer was asked to solve. The results may be numeric as in mathematical problem solving or verbal as in creative writing. They may also be visually artistic or musical. But all are the products of the action taken in the CPU on data entered into the computer as input.

Output Devices for School Computing

CATHODE RAY TUBE   Just as the keyboard is the most familiar input device, the most familiar output device is the cathode ray tube (CRT). A CRT is a vacuum tube that displays characters and pictures as a consequence of being bombarded with electrons. Some CRTs display color images while others are monochromatic. The number of points of light on a CRT that will illuminate—called *picture elements* (or *pixels*)—varies considerably and affects the legibility and clarity of the images. Other names used for a CRT are video display terminal and monitor. An ordinary television set can also be used in this way if a device called an RF modulator is attached to override the television tuner. Screen output is often described as *soft copy* because it is transient.

PRINTERS   Whatever is seen on the screen can also be shown as output using a printer and paper. Output that has been printed on paper is called *hard copy*. A number of different technological approaches have been applied to printers generally, producing thermal printers, ink jet printers, hot wire printers, laser printers, dot matrix impact printers, and full-character impact printers. Most school printers are of the type known as dot matrix; that is, the characters are created through the impact of dots arranged in the form of letters and numbers. Dot matrix printers operate very rapidly and can produce up to 200 characters per second (cps), although most range between 80 and 120 cps. They can also print black and white pictures from graphic designs that have been composed on the computer. School printers are usually restricted to output devices only. They print letters, essays, and research papers; show the results of calculations; display musical notation; and print pictures.

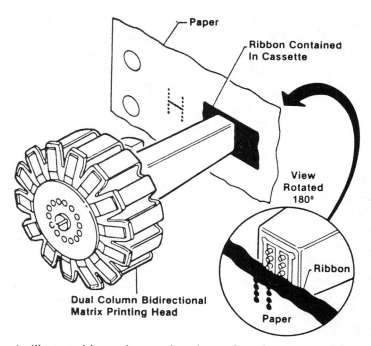

Paper

Ribbon Contained In Cassette

View Rotated 180°

Ribbon

Paper

Dual Column Bidirectional Matrix Printing Head

As illustrated here, dot-matrix printers form letters out of dots produced by pins that strike the ribbon and paper. *(Gary B. Shelly & Thomas J. Cashman,* Introduction to Computers and Data Processing: Transparency Masters, *Ana-heim Publishing Co. (PWS-Kent Publishing Company), © 1980, p. T56. Reprinted by permission.)*

Another type of printer often used in offices and schools might be called full-character impact printers, since they form letters and numbers not as a collection of dots but as completely formed characters striking an inked ribbon, like a typewriter. Some of this type are called daisy-wheel printers with the letters located at the ends of petal-like stems that radiate from a central disk. Others place the characters on a kind of thimble. The quality of the letter forms is superior to those on a dot matrix printer, but full-character printers are only about one third as fast as the dot matrix type. They are also more expensive.

PLOTTERS   Plotters make hard copy of graphic images by drawing lines resulting from following program instructions that may have been input originally either with programs in computer language code or more directly by a software program—with or without the help of a mechanical device. A plotter consists of a mechanical action where one or more colored pens move in response to coded instructions from a program. Plot-

Daisy-wheel printers produce letter-quality documents by employing a rotating wheel with fully-formed characters at the tips of its "petals." *(Photo courtesy of Qume Corporation, San Jose, California.)*

Laser printers are expensive and are typically used for desktop publishing. *(Courtesy of Apple Computer, Inc.)*

Dot-matrix printers like this one are widely used in schools. *(Courtesy of Epson America, Inc.)*

ters are manufactured in a wide range of prices and qualities. The major drawback for school use at the moment other than cost is the slow speed of operation.

MIXING INPUT AND OUTPUT Input and output devices may be housed in the same package. A cathode ray tube is used primarily for output, although when a light pen or a person's finger is used on the surface of a CRT, it functions as an input device. Similarly, input can occur through a printer when instructions are typed to it rather than to a CRT.

Summary: Hardware and Software in Action

In Chapter 4 we have brought the discussion begun in Chapter 3 full circle. Both system software and applications software put the hardware through its paces, the former quite invisible to the user, the latter quite important to the user's goals. In examining computer languages briefly, we sought to demonstrate how the software makes the hardware do our bidding. We went a step further by considering software storage media

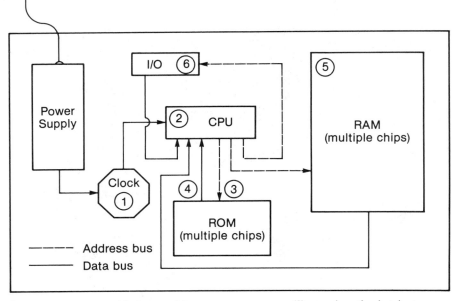

Computer system with internal bootstrap program, illustrating the intricate choreography involving hardware and software. When the computer's power supply is turned on, the internal quartz clock [1] begins to emit regular electrical pulses, several million per second, that regulate every step in the computer's operation. Within a single pulse, all the registers (temporary storage circuits) are cleared [2]. With another clock pulse, one of the registers is loaded with a preset memory address in ROM, where the CPU will find the first instruction for the bootstrap program. In successive clock pulses, a message is sent along an address bus [3] to the particular address in ROM, and the contents of that address (one bootstrap instruction) are transmitted back to the CPU via a data bus [4], where each instruction is executed. These last two steps are repeated until the entire bootstrap program has been executed.

Part of the bootstrap program runs a check on each memory address within RAM [5]. The CPU is instructed to send a value to each RAM address; then each address is instructed to return that value to the CPU. If both values match, that address is judged to be in working order. This is repeated for every address in RAM. In a computer with 64 kilobytes (64 KB) of RAM storage, this check would be run on 65,536 times eight addresses (1 K = 1,024 bits; 1 byte = 8 bits). Another part of the bootstrap program checks the input/output ports [6], in a manner similar to the RAM check.

When the bootstrap program is completed, a message is sent to another portion of ROM to retrieve the first instruction of the next program, which might be a high-level language like BASIC or perhaps an applications program that was provided internally by the manufacturer. When ready for user input, a prompt and cursor appear on the monitor, only seconds after the computer was first powered up.

and devices, demonstrating how information (ultimately divisible into zeros and ones) enters the computer and how information exits and is displayed for our use.

What is difficult to portray in all this is the dynamic interaction of hardware and software in a computer system. Thus, in concluding this chapter, we present a series of figures by which you can see the interplay of hardware and software as a microcomputer *boots,* or starts up, with a floppy disk. When working properly, the process depicted unfolds like a well-orchestrated ballet, but at incredible speeds.

More important than the elegance of this process, however, is the purpose for which it was set in motion: a teacher or student with a task to be accomplished, and a tool to assist in completing that task. In Chapter 5, we consider what some of those tasks might be.

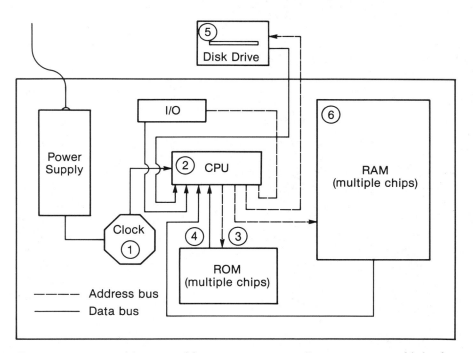

Computer system with external bootstrap program. Computers vary a bit in the bootstrap programs they use. Some follow a process closer to this figure. While much of the booting procedure is the same as in the previous figure, an instruction in ROM [steps 3 and 4] directs the computer to an external memory device like a disk drive [5]. On the disk it finds there, the computer loads into RAM [6] the program it is to use to continue booting the system. Communication between RAM and the CPU is carried out on address and data buses, just as in the first figure. When this program is completed, the computer may be directed to load and execute another "hello" program from the disk before turning control over to the user. Still, all this is accomplished in a flash.

CHAPTER 5

Computing as a Force for Educational Improvement

Introduction

Chapter 2 outlined the impact of computing on everyone's lives as well as something about what we can expect to happen in the future. Children and youth need to be prepared to live effective lives as adults in this new world and make their own contributions to it: they need to be informed about what is taking place around them, and they need to know how to use what they know to solve problems. When computing is taught in schools, the content may include general information of the kind that appears in the first two chapters. Some students may also need career counseling about opportunities in fields that are directly related to computing. Or, since the world of work is changing so dramatically, all students may need guidance in considering vocations that are not directly in computing but are in fields that are being affected by computers.

Chapters 3 and 4 were written so that teachers can learn how computers work and how hardware and software may be integrated. These chapters were also written to dispel the aura of mystery that often surrounds computers and can arouse unnecessary fears. Teachers need to be able to inform their students about what computers are capable of doing. While part of every child's experience is almost certain to require practical work on computers, this practical experience needs to be matched with knowledge about how the machines work and what their limitations are. Only in this way can young people come to recognize the problem-solving capabilities of computers. The future of computing in education continues to be uncertain, because schools have not yet integrated computing into their curriculums. But one thing is certain: computing will occupy a prominent place in schools. Just what that place will be has yet to be determined.

Over a century ago, American schools were charged with the immense task of making an immigrant nation literate in English. Problems remain with this task, but in general the goal has been achieved. A comparable task is now being thrust on the schools, one that has been made more complex by rapid changes affecting the nation and the world. The present challenge is to learn to use and to understand computers and computing, a challenge that has come about in large part by the advent of the small mass-produced personal computer during the last 15 years. This set of events has touched the lives of everyone in one way or another. An increasing proportion of jobs call for skills that have to do directly with computers, so that learning about them and knowing how to use them has become an educational necessity. Similarly, homes and recreational activities are being profoundly affected by these machines.

Harnessing computers to teach school subject matter also offers opportunities and challenges, especially at a time when students will be expected to learn more in the same period of time or less. Just as the hand-held calculator speeded up work in mathematics, so computers offer similar opportunities in subjects as different from each other as English composition, scientific experimentation, and musical composition. Because of the capability for repetition, computers are also useful in assisting students with remedial instruction. Unlike teachers, computers never tire or become bored with repetitious tasks. Such qualities are especially valuable, for example, when working with mentally handicapped students.

As recent as the development of the computer has been, it can already lay claim to an important place in the teaching and learning that goes on in schools. Schools are buying computers in ever-increasing quantities, and some reports suggest an even greater expansion in the near future. At some point in the not too distant future, therefore, computers can be expected to have assumed a very prominent place in schools, and far-reaching consequences to schooling can be expected. While some of the more distant possibilities are outlined in Chapter 8, this chapter describes educational computing as it affects teachers and students now and as it is likely to affect them over the next few years.

Three Decades of Educational Computing

A surge of interest in educational computing came during the 1960s. Much was learned from these efforts, and they influenced subsequent events. But neither the technology nor the people involved in those early projects were able to accomplish what they had hoped for. In addition, the projects were prohibitively expensive. Unlike business and industry, school needs for computing could not be clearly defined to satisfy practical daily school tasks. And not least, the use of computers in education could not demonstrate any saving of time or energy that was in any way comparable to the benefits derived by other uses.

Although the educational pioneers of the period could turn to experts in the form of programmers, there was no one from the field of education to whom they could turn for guidance. Moreover, they had no experience in calculating the costs involved in developing educational software. Many of these costs have remained high during the intervening years, but at that time, heavy programming expenditures were compounded by extremely expensive machinery costs. It was apparent then that the goal of universal computing for school classrooms would have to wait.

Part of the solution came about with the invention of the microprocessor and later the appearance of the first microcomputer. But these two technical advances did not occur until the early and mid-1970s. Most remarkable of all is the fact that some of the principal goals that the pioneers of the 1960s and 1970s hoped for are now on their way to becoming reality. Only a few years separate earlier from later enterprises in educational computing, whereas at other times in history, changes of such magnitude would have been separated by many years if not by centuries. However, rapidity of change marks our society as a whole as we explained in Chapter 2, and it seems likely that education—for probably the first time in its history—will be impelled at a rate that corresponds closely to that of the rest of society.

Prophets and Pioneers: The 1960s

Three groups of people stand out prominently among educators in this decade, each for very different reasons. They were John Kemeny, Patrick Suppes, and the team that developed PLATO. John Kemeny with Thomas Kurtz created the computer language BASIC (Beginners All-purpose Symbolic Instruction Code). It was written as an introductory computer language for students who would then move on to learn the language FORTRAN (FORmula TRANslator) or some other equally sophisticated high-level language. Unlike FORTRAN, the various components of BASIC can be pieced together to create a program, and each of the separate parts can be run independently. It is an interpreted language. A program written in FORTRAN, in contrast, must be accurate in its entirety or it will not run; it is a compiled language. Kemeny and Kurtz devised BASIC as a transitional language to help college-level beginners. The irony is that BASIC has since become the most commonly used language outside the computer science profession. It is written into the permanent memory (ROM) of most microcomputers, and it is the language used to write many educational software programs. While professionals in computing as well as many college educators consider BASIC to be an inadequate language and not well suited for education, most of the language instruction being given in teacher preservice and inservice classes is in BASIC. The outspoken protagonist for computer literacy, Arthur Luehrmann, has defended its place. In his opinion, the main problem with BASIC lies with those who write poor-quality programs with it rather than with any inherent structural weakness in the language itself.

Another prophet of the 1960s was Patrick Suppes. He began his seminal work in educational computing with quite a different perspective in mind from that of Kemeny and Kurtz. Suppes's efforts were directed at using the computer as a tool to help teach subject matter. His goal of using computers to individualize instruction for all children did not materialize during these early years—and may not for some years to come. However, Suppes's vision is as valid today as it was over 20 years ago. It continues at this time, and it is the impetus that drives many educators among the present generation.

The early work of Suppes and his colleagues is important today because it demonstrated the effectiveness of instruction by computer. A series of narrowly focused instructional programs in reading and mathematics were devised at the Institute for Mathematical Studies in the Social Studies (IMSS) at Stanford University. In 1967, Suppes also established a company, the Computer Curriculum Corporation (CCC), to deliver computerized instruction to subscribers using telephone connections to local terminals. The programs were written for groups with special needs including disadvantaged students, the handicapped, and gifted high schoolers. All the programs written under the direction of Suppes and his colleagues have been based on a painstaking analysis of the content to be taught and an equally painstaking selection of strategies for learning the content. Student users receive immediate feedback to their responses before they move ahead to the next step in a sequence. The programs also maintain records of each student's progress as the instruction advances.

Concurrent with Suppes's work at Stanford was the development of a group at the University of Illinois. A system of instruction was devised there called PLATO (Programmed Logic for Automatic Teaching Operation). The instruction was controlled by a large (mainframe) computer located on the university campus using a system of time sharing where each user communicated with it by telephone from a console consisting of a keyboard and a cathode ray tube (CRT). Over the 25 years of its existence, the PLATO system (now PLATO IV and a part of the operations of Control Data Corporation) has prepared over 7,000 hours of instruction in 150 subject areas and has a nationwide network delivery system serving school and college students.

Miniaturization: The 1970s

As we saw in Chapters 1 and 2, the decade of the 1970s was marked by the invention of the microprocessor and the production of the first microcomputer. The mass production of small, inexpensive computers made Suppes's goal much closer to realization than anyone could have imagined only a few years earlier. No longer was the purchase of a computer such an astronomical expense. The efforts of several individuals and groups stand out during this period in the evolution of educational computing. Five of the most notable events were the Solo Project at the University of Pittsburgh; the Physics Computer Development Project at the University of California at Irvine; the Minnesota Educational Computing Consortium (MECC); the M.I.T. Logo Group; together with the individual efforts of Arthur Luehrmann at the University of California.

Leadership of Project Solo was in the hands of Thomas Dwyer of the University of Pittsburgh from its inception in 1969. Dwyer's work has been directed toward giving secondary school students control over their own education from a central focus of mathematics, while reaching into other related areas. He describes his approach as "solo mode" computing, because the goal is the emancipation of students from conventional instruction by giving them the means to make decisions and solve problems on their own. One of the approaches used resembles the structure of many computer programs, that is, it is organized from the top down. Such problems are divided into their component parts together with an initial component that provides a controlling overview of the entire task.

Alfred Bork's work with the Physics Computer Development Project began in the 1970s and coincided with the period when self-contained microcomputers were first being produced in large numbers at moderate cost. Bork recognized the merits of stand-alone computers for schools and colleges, and the programs written under his direction reflect this insight. While the programs all provide instruction in science, the concepts underlying them are adaptable to other academic areas. Bork emphasizes dialogs between student and the computer-as-teacher and enhances these communications by integrating graphics into the programs. In his opinion, graphics will play an ever-increasing role in computerized instruction. And in keeping with Suppes, Bork firmly believes that all education will eventually include major computer components that are individualized and interactive, that is, students will individually engage in dialogs with computers for some part of their education. The programs that Bork has been working on include concept mastery, self-paced instruction, and testing. Although the original ones were written for college students, more recent programs are for junior high school students.

Arthur Luehrmann also came into prominence during this decade. He is best identified as an individual with a mission rather than as the initiator of any particular project. In 1972 he became associate director of the Lawrence Hall of Science at the University of California at Berkeley. Like Bork at Irvine, Luehrmann has supported teaching physics by computer, although his primary interest lies in teaching programming. He believes that computer programming is as much a basic skill for a computer-based society as the three Rs have been for a society based on print.

Luehrmann is the author of a number of influential articles that continually reassert his point of view. One written in 1972, entitled "Should the Computer Teach the Student, or Vice-Versa?" launched him into prominence as an advocate of universal education in computer programming. He distinguishes learning to program from using the computer as a means of instructing students in various school subjects. His junior high school textbook, *Computer Literacy: A Hands-On Approach,* is the latest in a series of efforts to promote the teaching of programming. A spirited exchange of articles appeared in *Mathematics Teacher,* beginning in the February 1980 issue with an article on computer literacy by David Johnson and others reporting the point of view of the Minnesota Educational Computing Consortium (MECC), founded in 1973. The conflict continues unabated between those who advocate a broad conception of computer literacy and those who interpret the need as calling for singular skills in programming.

With very much the same goal in mind, Seymour Papert and his colleagues created a new language expressly for education at the Massachusetts Institute of Technology following a period in the late 1950s and early 1960s when Papert worked with Jean Piaget, the famous developmental psychologist, in Geneva. On his return to the United States, Papert established the M.I.T. Logo Group within the Artificial Intelligence Laboratory. While some educators question the practicality of the Logo language, given the present curricular structure of most schools, Papert and his colleagues have found many enthusiastic supporters, and the number is growing.

Like Luehrmann, Papert advocates school instruction in programming, but his primary interest lies in using the computer as a vehicle to encourage the intellectual development of children rather than for the advancement of programming as such. Similarly, he has little interest in computing as a vehicle for teaching other school subjects. As he sees the task, experience in programming calls for the kind of active involvement that characterizes the fundamentals of all learning and especially the kind of learning that encourages students to think more intently about what they are doing. The goal is for children to understand their own thought processes better. Papert has worked toward the accomplishment of these goals at M.I.T. by developing a computer-controlled vehicle—a "turtle"—that leaves a visible trace on paper and obeys a language that young children as well as adults can use to program.

Although Papert was by training a mathematician and the focus of his work is understandably mathematical, neither his concepts nor his sentiments are restricted to that subject. For the best understanding of his point of view and his contributions to educational computing his book, *Mindstorms*, should be read. It has had a profound effect upon the field of educational computing.

Learning with Computers

Textbooks, subject-matter guides, and similar materials provide the tools that teachers use to help communicate content to students. Computers are now entering the educational scene in large numbers. But unlike traditional instructional resources that are printed and are typically produced as books, computers are electronic. Chapters 3 and 4 describe the qualities that distinguish computers and computer programs from printed instructional materials, and school uses of computers should not attempt to emulate what can be done just as well by means of traditional media. Similarly, the qualities that distinguish computers from other materials should be carefully analyzed to distinguish them from those that only a teacher can do effectively. Neither books nor computers can accomplish all the goals of education. Each medium has its own strengths. Moreover, one should never lose sight of the fact that the most important resource of all in education is the human touch that a skilled teacher brings to learning.

The Computer as a Unique Instructional Medium

The value of books, films, television, and now computing is that they can extend the effectiveness of teachers. In this sense, computing seems destined to serve student learning in ways that have not been possible before, except in rare and fortunate instances where students received individual attention.

Comparisons with Other Instructional Media

As we explained in the preceding chapters, computers are most effective when used to store information and retrieve it to meet a particular need. The word "information" is not restricted here to the conventional definition, which is normally reserved for words and numbers; pictorial images and sounds can be stored just as easily. Access to computer memories, moreover, is such that information that is requested can be made available almost instantly.

However, computers are not limited to being massive files of information where rapid access is possible. As useful as these functions are, computers are built to execute a wide range of logical tasks, of which information retrieval and calculation are only among the more obvious ones. The logical functions permit users to make complex comparisons that match any that might be involved in calculating. Instructions can also be stored in computer programs that will enable them to match information a user may type in, and respond to it regarding its accuracy. A program that tests spelling can be written so that a student will be informed of the accuracy of his attempts. Such a program can also include responses that catch common errors and inform the student about them in an effort to prevent their recurrence.

Another quality of computers is that because they store information electronically, students are not as limited in their access to the information as they are when working from books. Books are divided into sections, chapters, and pages and are normally organized so that the pages will be read starting at the beginning. In contrast, information stored in a computer memory can be accessed for just what is needed at a given time without the user being exposed to any of the rest of the information held in its memeory. Finding information in a book is often clumsy by comparison. Content listings and indexes may be efficiently organized, and yet locating specific information can be slow and frustrating for students.

A well-written computer program provides needed information immediately and minimizes interference with the process of learning. This same quality opens the door on the prospect of students being able to take advantage of alternative educational directions. Instead of being confined to the linear structure of books, students can use computer programs where they can be guided to select from a number of different pathways—or branches—through a course of study that fits their particular needs and interests. Students enrolled in a home economics course that had such a program could have access to menus based on foods that originated in numbers of countries and plan unique meals from combinations of ingredients that would be difficult to put together by any other means. A somewhat different application of this same quality would permit a gifted student to progress at a pace that fits his or her capabilities. A learning disabled student, on the other hand, could also make progress through the same course of study by following an alternative sequence of instruction that is better suited to his or her disability than a standard program. Not least, the calculator function of a computer can maintain a continuous record of each student's progress in all these endeavors, thus leading to less effort by the teacher on such tasks. And because of the instant availability of information the likelihood is greater for teachers to be freed to give more effective individual guidance.

The qualities of capacious memory, easy retrieval of information, and logical organization make computers extremely useful in education. Students can even engage in dialog with the computer, where both student and machine can ask for and give information. Students can also observe the consequences of selecting several different types or quantities of information from the computer memory and either comparing them or using them as the base for making calculations. When information is used in this way, a student can see the results of numbers of trials quickly and easily. Moreover, if access to these combinations of possibilities is made randomly, a program becomes almost like a computer game, and this quality has captivated the imagination of a whole generation. Thus the best uses of computing in education exploits what the machine is best at doing: providing immediate feedback, engaging the student's active participation in learning, catering to the student's individual needs, and allowing interaction between student and instructional material. Each of these constitutes one criterion for evaluating software, a subject to be addressed in Chapter 7.

Computer Assisted Instruction

Whenever a computer program is used as the direct means of instructing students, the students are engaging in computer assisted instruction (CAI). The content to be learned is recorded for permanent storage in one of several forms—a soft ("floppy") diskette, a tape cassette, a hard disk, or the memory of a large computer.

CAI programs usually present material through a sequence of frames or screens of information on a monitor. The earlier use of linear programs restricted student individuality and satisfaction. More recent programs provide alternative pathways, or branching; thus, better-informed students do not have to go through the same sequence of frames as a less well-informed or less able student. In this way, a student need only see the number of frames needed to cover the material.

In traditionally organized schools many classroom tasks are normally handled by means of notebook exercises taken from the chalkboard, dittoed handouts, or textbook exercises. Good CAI programs not only present information and ask questions, but incorrect answers lead to instant feedback followed by the same questions being displayed again. Clues to correct answers may also be provided in the event of several incorrect answers.

Most CAI programs—especially those on floppy diskettes—consist of relatively small segments of supplementary instruction rather then complete courses. This form is often called *adjunct* CAI. Programs of the kind made available through the PLATO system consist of entire courses and replace traditional delivery by a teacher. Such courses are called *primary* CAI.

Computer assisted instruction developed during the 1960s in university centers such as Stanford, Illinois, Dartmouth, Iowa, and Florida State, and also in a handful of school districts of which the Chicago City Schools Project was a notable example. It owes its origins to the teaching machines and programmed instruction that began in the first half of this century at the hands of various individuals, most notably B. F. Skinner, the Harvard psychologist. Programmed instruction and teaching machines failed partly because of high costs and partly because of unreliable equipment. More importantly for this discussion, they failed because of their inflexibility. Programs presented instruction in a single track regardless of the need of a user and hence were much inferior to traditional methods of teaching, where skilled teachers could respond to classroom circumstances as the need arose.

In recent years the quality of CAI programs has advanced immeasurably, and as teachers become better judges of such programs, it can be expected to improve even more. One thing seems highly likely, however: students who are exposed to CAI will become more actively involved in learning than those whose experience is limited to traditional classroom practices. The wise use of computers also holds out the potential for releasing teachers from many of the traditional chores associated with teaching, so that they can attend to a broader spectrum of individual needs of their students than was possible formerly.

Drill and Practice

The most common type of CAI program is drill and practice. It consists of exercises that take students through material to which they have already been introduced until they reach a point where proficiency has reached a satisfactory level. Mathematical problems and spelling lend themselves particularly well to drill-and-practice programs. Unlike conventional textbook instruction, drill-and-practice programs have the potential for offering students various pathways through a unit, so that they need not go through all of a program unless it is necessary. Alternatively, students may be given simple or complex tasks over the same content to match their abilities.

One of the benefits of drill and practice—as with all CAI material—is that students may work independently of each other and at their own speeds. They may also repeat any or all of the instruction as often as they need to. A criticism sometimes leveled at drill-and-practice instruction is that the choices of subjects are too often trivial or that the content duplicates what can be done at least as well in conventional classrooms. Another criticism about drill-and-practice programs is that students have no opportunity for input; the program makes no provision for them to introduce their own ideas other than answers to questions. Guidance in evaluating quality programs is given in Chapter 7 that should help in avoiding the purchase of unsatisfactory materials.

Tutorial Instruction

Throughout history, the parents of privileged children have traditionally employed tutors to educate them. A single instructor for every student is beyond the means of most families, however, and until the present time such a thought was far beyond the means of any society as a whole. The computer can change all that. It has opened the door to a situation where all students may soon enjoy individual instruction for at least part of their education. Tutorial CAI typically follows a pattern of introducing material that is new to a student. The new material builds cumulatively, and the student is tested periodically throughout the presentation to ensure that the content has been fully understood. As with drill-and-practice programs, effective tutorials steer students through the content to be learned in small units that are governed by the area of a monitor screen. At best, tutorial CAI is a stimulating learning experience. At worst it imitates a book by simply presenting "pages" of text for students to read.

The flexibility of tutorial programs may not compare with the alternatives that can be introduced by a highly skilled teacher to a single student. Yet, they do permit individual students in a class to pursue their own unique studies simultaneously. Also, given the different needs and abilities of students, the presence of such programs offers the possibility of students pursuing special subject matter at their own speeds and in ways that are not possible otherwise, however talented a classroom teacher happens to be. Once again, a teacher's unique qualities can also be freed by this means to enable him or her to serve as an individual counselor to students who need special assistance.

Simulation

Simulation programs present reasonable imitations of real events without requiring students to participate in the real situations themselves. Simulations also make possible experiences that would not otherwise be open to students. Such programs range over topics such as the human circulatory system, physical changes that occur under conditions of heat and pressure, economic variables affecting society, demographic changes, and game strategies, to name only a few.

Programs in this category call for students to engage in making decisions where they can test hypotheses. Students are presented with information that they can alter in order to observe the consequences of their decisions. Simulation programs cannot replace direct experience, but they do permit students to see the real and hypothetical results of decisions that would otherwise not be possible for any but a fortunate few. If a problem exists with CAI simulations, it is the need to restrict the number of variables that are used. Complexity and intricacy may delight computer programmers and well-informed adults generally, but effective instruction requires that programs for children and young people be carefully controlled for complexity. The purpose of any CAI program is always to provide effective instruction. The kinds of learning where simulation is particularly fitting include mastery learning, learning new content, and advancing student inquiry skills. Optimum effectiveness occurs, however, when these and other forms of CAI are combined with conventional teaching.

While simulation offers very considerable educational benefits of a kind that cannot be matched by other means—computing or otherwise—good programs are not yet so plentiful that we can say that the potential has been more than scratched. Furthermore, the cost of developing simulation programs is high, and few authors possess the ability to design creative ones. Nonetheless, CAI simulations hold out the prospect of making unique educational contributions in the future: they harness instruction in such a way that has no parallel elsewhere.

Problem Solving

This category of CAI program requires students to become actively engaged in solving problems, so that they develop skills that may transfer to problems outside the classroom. Computer programs are admirable for this kind of task, because unlike similar problems in print, they can be modified for each attempt. In this way, each attempt becomes a variation of the original problem and not a repetition.

Many problem-solving programs are written as logical games; in fact, some educators describe them as "instructional games." This game format, however, is very different from the fantasy games distributed to the home entertainment market. Other problem-solving programs are written as adventures that occur in imaginary worlds or present exciting situations that must be mastered. Some of the more innovative programs are designed to teach computer languages, while others use a computer language, such as Logo, to enable students to create their own problems as well as the solutions.

In order to solve the problems, students normally have to analyze the conditions that are presented for information that may be useful. They must then decide on a plan of action. Finally, they test their hypothesis. Throughout this process, teachers can encourage students to discuss what they observe and develop generalizations that will be useful for solving other problems of a similar kind.

Student abilities in problem solving take considerable time to mature, so that sets of programs often include a progression from simple experiences to those that are more complex. Good problem-solving games have been slow in appearing because of the time and skill needed to create them, but as CAI expands, more high quality products can be expected.

CAI with Computer Tools

Although CAI is conventionally restricted to these categories, important learning occurs from the use of such computer tools as word processing, spreadsheet, and filing programs. Word processors enable students to rework written language continually without the tiresome task of rewriting an entire passage. In addition, as students gain facility with a word processing program, their keyboard skills advance. Spreadsheet programs teach students the interrelatedness of numbers and also the practicality of mathematical concepts in daily life. And filing systems teach such skills as classifying and paraphrasing information.

CAI: A Summary

These categories of CAI might suggest that they cannot be used in combination, however, the fact is that they can and should be. And as indicated above, other computer programs may function as computer assisted instruction, even though not originally thought of that way. The important issue is that CAI has demonstrated its potential for education. Compared with traditional school instruction, CAI shows gains over teacher-directed learning by approximately 10 percent. However, the greatest gains are reported when teachers and computers are used together. When this percentage of gain is matched with the costs of education where traditional expenditures are increasing annually at 13 percent and the annual decrease of CAI instruction is 5 percent, the use of computers is likely to become increasingly attractive (Atkinson, 1984). In addition, the quality of CAI materials is continually improving, whereas traditional instruction has little likelihood of any comparable gain. The situation alters even more when to this information is added the comparison of personal attention given to students who work on computers compared with those working in traditional classrooms. During a typical lesson period, a teacher can give a minute or two of personal attention at best to a student compared with the potential for undivided attention when a student is working at a computer.

Computer Managed Instruction

While the potential for direct instruction by computer is increasingly making itself felt, progress is also being made in another area where the computer serves as a tool for organizing instruction. Computer managed instruction (CMI) provides a system for organizing the means of instruction rather than being the actual delivery system. Without some form of management individualized education is too unwieldly to be practical except for very small classes. And yet, some of the greatest potential for computer-based education lies with individualization.

Compared with job training schools and education schools operated by the military, elementary and secondary schools have barely begun to use CMI systems. This is partly due to the extreme diversity among public and private schools, and to the complexity of their educational programs. However, the scarcity of funds and the distrust of electronic technology by educators have also played their parts in slowing down the process of adopting CAI and especially the more comprehensive mechanisms of CMI.

Computer managed instruction has many component parts, each of which performs different functions. Teachers who use CMI systems may never need to know the details of how they are designed, but some knowledge of what they can do enables a person to understand the labor-saving services that such programs can provide. For convenience, a simplified statement is shown here that describes three clusters of components. The first cluster consists of "Tests and Records," the second is "Instructional Guidance," and the third is "Resource Availability."

Tests and Records

Schools maintain records in their files of all children enrolled there. These records include class rosters and academic histories. Special disabilities will also be noted together with information about special aptitudes such as giftedness. This information may be useful to a teacher from time to time, but in the course of a semester or grading period, a teacher needs to maintain a record of such items as the results of diagnostic testing, a list of all the scores made on tests taken during the course, as well as observations by the teacher about a student's general ability and interest in a given subject. Particularly in an individualized program teachers need immediate access to information about the tasks that have already been chosen and completed during a particular course. Armed with this information, a teacher has a much clearer understanding of his or her students and their needs, aptitudes, and intelligence.

Instructional Guidance

Although teachers of individualized courses need to maintain adequate records of what has gone on during the course, they also need some source of information about the choices of assignments that are open to students for the remainder of a course. In some instances, students may need remedial counseling and have to go back over material they were supposed to have learned earlier. In other situations teachers may need to direct students to assignments that leapfrog part of the regular course because in their judgment a student needs additional challenge. All teachers engage in this kind of decision making as part of their daily work, and yet it would be impossible for a teacher to make that task a continuous part of his or her daily work with every child in a class of thirty. In sum, selecting options for individual students requires that there be a ready source of alternatives that teachers could not hold in their minds for any period of time. A CMI program enables a teacher to have access to this kind of information as part of an organizational system serving a course.

Guidance information may also be set up in such a way that students could call in for a list of the options that are open at that point in the course. The teacher might then assume a different role than is customary in a conventional classroom and become a guide and helper rather than director and disciplinarian.

Resource Availability

Managing instruction requires that an instructor—or a student—be informed about the availability and location of the material needed for any of the pathways through a particular course. In a given assignment, for example, a student may need photographs of people dressed in the national costume of Colombia. Another student may need a clip from a videotape showing the vascular system of the human body. A music student may need a metronome, and so on. In each instance, a teacher should be able to provide the item when needed for the instruction to be effective. A CMI program has this kind of information on file, so that a teacher knows where an item is stored and whether it is available for use. Instructional resources can be indexed with lesson materials and with the lesson information itself.

A computer management system may use each of the three types of components more or less equally. Alternatively, some CMI systems are restricted to clerical tasks such as grading tests or reporting student progress.

Hybrid Strategies

Computer assisted instruction (CAI) is by far the best established application of computing in education. Computer managed instruction (CMI) offers many opportunities for use in education, although as we have explained already, comparatively little has yet been realized in public school instruction. CMI programs such as student records, gradebooks, tests, and the like provide valuable information to teachers, but one has to turn to other agencies that engage in teaching and training to discover what is taking place in CMI. Given what has already been discovered about both CAI and CMI, computers can be expected to be increasingly influential in education. However, it would be unrealistic to expect instruction to remain separate from the management of instruction. Individualized programs, in particular, will benefit immeasurably from incorporating both management and instruction to create hybrid systems.

Direct instruction by computer can supplement what a teacher does or it can comprise an entire course. In most learning situations, however, instructors also need to collect data about student progress. By one means or another they also have to know what materials will be needed in order to execute a particular task. In effect, computer-based education (CBE) is on many occasions already a combination of CAI and CMI. We shall discuss this trend in some depth in Chapter 8, but the union has already occurred and needs to be acknowledged. If nothing else, teachers should at least be aware that CAI and CMI comprise two components of the same enterprise.

Learning About Computers

No one doubts that computers are having a profound impact on the lives of everyone and will have an increasing effect with the passage of time. As we indicated in Chapter 2, in just a few years computers have become integral parts of telephones, microwave ovens, wrist watches, and a host of other everyday articles. Many of them require users to learn to operate them. Digital remote control units are becoming increasingly common on television sets, while microwave ovens have programmable control panels for cooking various dishes. And finally, digital telephone transmission is in use everywhere. The inner workings of these instruments and appliances are the domain of the engineer and the service technician, but all people need to have some understanding of how to operate them. The same is true for computers—especially for teachers.

"Computer literacy" suggests a need for a deeper understanding of computers than merely activating responses by pressing a few prescribed keys. It implies that people need to know something about how these machines work, how they contribute to society, and how society is being changed by them. This level of knowing is not generally expected with other machines, even those we operate, such as automobiles. The difference is that computers are recognized as being as great a social force as the automobile, and yet far more flexible than an automobile in the ways they can be used. Moreover, teachers may need a special kind of computer literacy that differs from the needs of the general public or manufacturing engineers or computer scientists. First, however, a case must be made for the general need to understand computers. Only then will the unique needs of teachers be identifiable.

Literacy in our native language is accepted without question after more than a century of effort in the schools. Few nations function well today without a population that is literate, that is, possessing minimal competency with verbal and quantifying skills, to which most educators add a sense of cultural identity. At the most basic level, verbal and mathematical skills are fundamental intellectual tools that all people need in order to conduct the affairs of the modern world. At the highest levels of operation these same skills provide the foundation for the kind of conceptual thinking and creative expression that characterize advanced cultures.

Primary responsibility for instructing in these basic skills rests with teachers. And children make use of these skills when learning content of the other subjects in the school curriculum. Until the early 19th century, however, these tool skills that we now accept without question had never been thought of as essential for any but a handful of leaders, intellectuals, artists, and specialized artisans. The advent of computers has now added a new dimension to communication and problem solving, one that has only recently begun to be addressed seriously—hence the present concern with computer literacy.

The fundamental structure of all computers lies in mathematical logic, which is beyond the needs and abilities of many people. As we saw in Chapter 4, computer languages translate the basic machine operations into forms that approximate human language. But instead of replicating either everyday verbal language or traditional quantification, these languages cause computers to become intellectual problem-solving machines that people with normal abilities can use very effectively. Not only can computers manipulate words and numbers; they can also manipulate images and sounds. The traditional definition of basic intellectual skills has been restricted to words and numbers, but that is now beginning to change. The advent of digital computers and higher-level languages has introduced logical systems that address the organizing and manipulating of the broadest possible range of ideas and information. Visual and auditory data, for example, have long been recognized as sources of information in their own right, but they could not be communicated satisfactorily through the medium of print. The digital structure of the computer now enables both sounds and images to be used as effectively as letters and numbers. For this reason, all facets of life, including education, can be expected to embrace these forms of information handling more than ever before.

This is not to suggest that all people will become computer programmers any more than all literate people should be expected to become novelists or mathematicians. The addition of facility and understanding of computers to our communication and problem-solving capabilities is so fundamental, however, that some knowledge of computing is rapidly becoming as necessary for all people as reading and writing. Books contain useful knowledge that can be learned, but it cannot be tapped unless a person can read. Computers make knowledge accessible in ways that transcend the qualities of books, but just as competence in reading and writing requires the experience of doing it, children and young people need to develop a working knowledge of this new medium. These skills and understandings are thus a part of the general education that everyone needs.

The swing from manufacturing to knowledge-based industries is well under way in all parts of the nation, and it can be expected to spread. Children and youth need to be aware of what faces them and to feel prepared to live in a very different environment from their parents. Everyone in the labor force will need skills that a generation ago did not exist, and the schools are the social institutions that can accept this task, much as it accepted a similar task over a century ago. If a problem exists, it is that the need for literacy in the common language of English was clearly evident a century ago, whereas a corresponding need for computer literacy may be less obvious to many people today.

Various authors have written about their interpretations of what is meant by computer literacy when translated into the educational needs of all people. As we have seen, Arthur Luehrmann is quite uncompromising in his interpretation. For him, literacy means learning how to use a computer to solve problems by way of programming. For Luehrmann, the goal of literacy is so clearly a matter of expertise in programming that he considers all broader definitions as "computer awareness." For him the only road to understanding is by way of performance at a machine. As such, programming belongs in the school curriculum for all students much as do mathematics and English.

In contrast, numbers of educators acknowledge the need for students to have sufficient programming experience to know how to use a high-level language to solve simple problems. However, they believe that most of the time, people will use professionally written programs for their specific daily needs and that programming as such will be done increasingly by professional programmers. Thus they advocate a broader definition of computer literacy than does Luehrmann and those that support his point of view. They focus attention on developing skills in word processing and calculator spreadsheet programs that also solve problems, that is, problems people encounter in their lives. A particularly well-developed statement of this point of view has been prepared by the Minnesota Educational Computing Consortium (MECC). It includes skill in programming, but it also identifies knowledge about how computers work as well as knowledge of the kinds of software programs that are available. Above all, in the view of the consortium, an important goal is to help people learn not to be intimidated by computers.

The issue is far from settled, and debate can be expected to continue for some time to come. Just because of this conflict, and the fuzzy thinking and loose terminology associated with it, teachers need to develop their own working definition of computer literacy, that is, an explanation that serves their interpretation of the general purposes of education.

In some ways, expertise in programming may not be any greater for classroom teachers than it is for the general public. And yet an increasing number of children can be expected to have acquired advanced programming skills, far in excess of present general levels. Children are growing up with computers in ways that their parents (and their teachers) have not done—not to mention their elder brothers and sisters. Consequently, if teachers hope to provide useful guidance to students, they need to advance their own computing abilities. The computer opens the door to expanded learning in all areas of the curriculum, and if teachers are able to make full use of these machines, they are likely to become more effective in the classroom. Thus, teachers can expect to feel pressures to demonstrate a higher level of understanding of computing than is expected of members of the lay public. And this expectation is likely to be even higher as computing applies to a teacher's special area. Art teachers, for example, may find that they have to be moderately proficient in computer graphics, so that they can help students understand how programming routines can be used to generate artistic compositions.

Where teachers become involved in the development of software, programming skills may take on more significance. Some may write small programs to fit particular classroom needs. With anything more ambitious, contributors would most likely be team members whose particular expertise would lie in their grasp of subject matter and student behavior, while artists and programmers would make their own unique contributions.

Some measure of programming, then, can be expected to continue to occupy an important place in the preparation of teachers if they are to be computer literate. But knowledge about software availability and its quality can also be expected to become even more important for every teacher. Just as teachers need to be skilled in reviewing books, recordings, and films, they need to be skilled in reviewing computer software they hope to use in their classrooms. In addition, teachers will probably need skill in one or more of the authoring language programs that permit the writing of lessons and the drawing of maps and charts without having to go through the time-consuming task of actually becoming proficient in a formal computing language. This topic and others related to it, however, are more appropriately discussed in Chapter 8, where we anticipate conditions that are likely to affect readers as their careers unfold. However, we should not expect any general agreements to surface in the near future.

Computer Literacy Curricula: K–12

While computer literacy is far from being defined satisfactorily for most educators, teachers need something more than theoretical arguments to guide them if they are to involve their students effectively with computers. They need to know approximately what to teach at any given grade level, so that they do not omit important skills and information and also do not duplicate material unnecessarily.

As a consequence of this need, several computer educators have come to the aid of teachers. Two of them, Beverly Hunter and Gary Bitter, wrote down their ideas in the early 1980s when microcomputers were first being purchased in large numbers for school use. They spelled out programs that spanned all—or at least substantial ranges—of school grades. Because they were among the first to do so, they influenced many of the computer literacy curriculums that have been written since. Beverly Hunter prepared a curriculum for grades one through eight, while Gary Bitter prepared one for a kindergarten through twelfth grade curriculum. Since both Bitter's and Hunter's models remain prominent, we end this chapter with a brief review of each of them, together with some of the variations that have emerged in recent years as a consequence of changes that could only have materialized as computer-based education has evolved.

The Bitter Curriculum

Bitter divides computer literacy into two parts. One of them he calls "computer awareness," which he defines primarily as information about computers and computing. It includes conventional methods and materials about the ways in which computers treat variables and mathematical functions, the value of loops and arrays, and how algorithms are written. In his view, computer awareness also includes developing keyboarding skills using either fingering charts or typewriters. However, the main thrust of computer awareness in Bitter's curriculum lies in the information about computers that students learn as distinct from the act of programming. As such it includes the kinds of applications that computing is increasingly making in our daily lives, the social impact of computing, the introduction of data bases, the history of computing, elementary logic, and artificial intelligence.

The other component of Bitter's concept of computer literacy is programming. He proposes starting children out with the language of Logo in the second grade. By the fourth grade he introduces students to the language of BASIC. From this point on, BASIC becomes the core of the programming curriculum through the ninth grade, although Bitter believes that students should have mastered the basic skills of programming by the seventh grade and after that be using them to solve algorithms and produce images and sounds. In the ninth grade he introduces the language of Pilot and follows this in grades ten through twelve with the language of Pascal.

Appendix G provides a general overview of the entire curriculum and indicates the topics that Bitter proposes for each grade level. For a more comprehensive understanding of the curriculum, readers should go to his series of articles (1982–1983). There Bitter defines and provides objectives for each topic. He also names the subject areas he believes are most appropriate for helping to achieve each objective because he is strongly committed to integrating computer literacy into the fabric of the established subject areas rather than allowing it to develop in isolation. Finally, he suggests various activities that he believes are suited to achieving each objective. Each category, however, is purposely left open-ended to encourage teachers to make decisions that suit their particular circumstances.

The Hunter Curriculum

Beverly Hunter provided a different view of a computer literacy curriculum in her book (1983). It is a rich source of activities and lessons that integrate computer learning experiences within the traditional kindergarten through eighth grade curriculum, founded on six strands constituting her computer literacy scope and sequence. These include using and developing procedures, using computer programs, fundamental concepts about computers, computer applications, impact of computers on society, and writing computer programs. As you can see, Hunter conceives of computer literacy broadly, beyond an identification of computer literacy exclusively with programming.

Each of the six strands within particular grade levels (K–2, 3–4, 5–6, 7–8) is represented by a lesson or activity, which is also developed within the context of a traditional content area (mathematics, social studies, language arts, science). Each lesson or activity typically consists of a statement of objectives, prerequisites, materials to be used, time for the activity, teacher preparation, procedures for presenting the activity, and related activities (see Appendix G).

References

ANDERSON, RONALD E., KLASSEN, DANIEL L., & JOHNSON, DAVID C. "In Defense of a Comprehensive View of Computer Literacy—A Reply to Luehrmann," *Mathematics Teacher* 74 (December 1981), pp. 687–690.

ATKINSON, MARTHA. "Computer-Assisted Instruction: Current State of the Art," *Computers in the Schools* 1, no. 1 (September 1984).

BITTER, GARY G. Series on K-12 computer literacy. *Electronic Learning*, September 1982–February 1983.

HUNTER, BEVERLY. *My Students Use Computers*. Reston, VA: Reston Publishing Company, 1983.

JOHNSON, DAVID C., ANDERSON, RONALD E., HANSEN, THOMAS P. & KLASSEN, DANIEL L. "Computer Literacy—What Is It?" *Mathematics Teacher* 73 (February 1980), pp. 91–96.

LUEHRMANN, ARTHUR. "Computer Literacy—What Should It Be?" *Mathematics Teacher* 74 (December 1981), pp. 682–686.

LUEHRMANN, ARTHUR. "Should the Computer Teach the Student, or Vice-Versa?" *American Federation of Information Processing Societies 1972 Spring Joint Computer Conference Proceedings* 40 (1972).

PAPERT, SEYMOUR. *Mindstorms*. New York: Basic Books, 1980.

CHAPTER 6

Practical Applications of Computers in Education

Introduction

While it may be useful to understand how computers work and to learn in general about the ways in which computers may be used in education, most people who plan on becoming teachers have a clear idea of the age range of the students they want to teach. Future secondary teachers, for example, will be spending considerable time and effort learning the specific subject matter they will teach. A general textbook on the topic of computers in education, therefore, is unlikely to be judged very relevant unless a reader happens to be among that small group of individuals who plan on becoming specialists in educational computing. For these reasons, this chapter includes information specific to the different ways in which computers may be used in elementary and secondary schools. And since school curriculums are typically broken into subject areas, some of the typical applications of computers in each of these areas are also discussed.

This organization is designed to help current and future elementary teachers develop an appreciation for computer-based education as it applies to classes of younger children. Secondary teachers will naturally be drawn to the applications that apply to the subjects in which they will specialize. However, many prospective secondary teachers are also likely to have one or more minor teaching areas, so they may benefit from studying the ways in which computers may be used in those areas as well. Moreover, future elementary teachers often have a particular interest in one subject and may even be working toward a special teaching qualification in that area. For these people, some of the special subject overviews will be of interest. Not least, the reviews of how computing may be used in the various subject areas will provide insights into computing as it applies across the entire curriculum, subject by subject. All too often—especially among secondary specialists—teachers have little sense of the breadth of content represented by the total school curriculum, not to mention similarities and differences among the ways in which computers may serve the various areas.

After examining computing within discrete subject areas, we tackle issues surrounding the teaching of programming: for what purposes should programming be taught, how should it be taught, and what language should be taught. These issues are very much related to the question of computer literacy developed in the previous chapter, but the rationale for teaching programming in particular is explored in considerable depth in this chapter.

Finally, the chapter would not be complete without some discussion of the place of computer science. For this reason, a review of the kinds of topics likely to be found in a computer science curriculum is included. For further discussions of computer science, as well as computer programming, the reader is directed to Appendices B and C, where programming texts and a computer science course outline are presented, respectively.

To begin, however, we take a look at how computers are used, and can be used, in a number of key curriculum areas.

Computer Use in the Subject Areas

Computers in Reading and Language Arts

Drill and tutorial software is quite readily available today for reading and language arts, particularly in providing instruction and reinforcement in spelling, grammar, vocabulary, and reading comprehension. Students preparing for the verbal component of the Scholastic Aptitude Test (SAT) can select from a number of preparation programs, some of which claim to improve performance significantly. Beyond simple drill and practice, increasing numbers of computer-based tools are appearing. For those who wish to increase their reading speed, speed reading programs are available. Teachers who wish to gauge the reading level required by their students' texts can run the full range of readability tests via computer.

Once we move out of CAI applications, the involvement of computer technology in language arts and reading deepens and broadens considerably. One area to which this particularly applies is journalism and the influence of evolving and expanding information technologies. Instantaneous, long-distance information transmission and retrieval redefine the concept of journalism, as is evident in the growth of teletext and videotex systems. To the extent that addressing information and its manipulation is a part of the language arts curriculum, so must the curriculum attend to telecommunications technology and its practical uses in the current and future experiences of students.

Composition is another area of the language arts curriculum to which computer technology has been applied. A rather interesting application of the technology has been in writing style. Given a written passage, the program will indicate whether you've used too many complex sentences (or too many simple sentences) and whether you use passive voice too much. A healthy skepticism exists about how much of the critiquing task a computer can realisitically accomplish, not to mention its desirability when the unique style of history's greatest authors "fail" the computer's assessments. On the other hand, consider the fact that one U.S. government agency has altered its internal word processing system so that it automatically replaces jargon with a series of Xs, forcing the author to de-jargonize his or her writing before it reaches the public's eyes.

The use of word processors for writing has enjoyed considerable support in the language arts curriculum. Several advantages flow from the use of the computer as a writing tool. Students who are reluctant writers because they possess poor motor skills, and thus illegible writing, can overcome that obstacle, relying on the computer and printer to produce visually pleasing products. Revisions are easily made and encourage the production of successively improved drafts. Perhaps most important, well-designed word processors used skillfully by the teacher can strengthen student understanding of writing as a process. Indeed, a number of word processors for education have been explicitly designed to support the writing process. They initiate the process at the prewriting stage by aiding the student in generating and organizing ideas; they allow for greater student ease in composing and especially in revising; and they provide motivation in sharing students' writing due to the visual quality of the final product.

Computers in Mathematics and Geometry

Mathematics education has been a natural focus for computer-based education from the very outset. And if a visitor to a secondary school is in doubt about where to find the computers, the most likely place to look is in the mathematics department. This is due partly to the historically close relationships that have existed between mathematics and computing as a consequence of the ways in which computers work as well as with the natural ease with which computers solve mathematical problems. Moreover, the logic structure of computer language also has an affinity with procedures that are integral to mathematics. It is no wonder, then, that mathematics teachers were among the first to begin using computers in schools. It should come as no surprise, therefore, to learn that as long ago as 1977, the National Council of Supervisors of Mathematics declared computer literacy to be one of ten basic mathematical skills (Suydam, 1984). Computing permits students to approach mathematics as algorithmic problem solving (see the section on programming later in this chapter). Numbers of mathematics educators foresee algorithms to be important objects of study in their own right and also to be useful in organizing all forms of knowledge (Grady and Gawronski, 1983).

Although microcomputers and mathematics enjoy a natural bond, the relationship has been a mixed blessing. The effects of the information revolution are being felt everywhere, and nowhere quite so powerfully as in the teaching of mathematics. Pocket calculators rapidly undermined traditional paper-and-pencil computation, and almost overnight slide rules and trigonometry tables became obsolete. Numbers of mathematics teachers have been reluctant to make the transition to allow calculators and computers become the primary computational tools in schools, just as some critics believe they are reluctant to admit practical applications of mathematics from the world outside school into the classroom (Maier, 1983). Others declare that students should not waste their time developing obsolete pencil-and-paper skills (Usiskin, 1984). They consider such practices to be futile when it is clear that calculators and computers are destined to become the primary computational tools (Maier, 1983).

In sum, the traditional mission of school mathematics—of teaching basic arithmetic skills—is now facing the prospect of becoming a method of using numeric reasoning to solve problems rather than one of focusing on the mastery of content as defined by school curriculums. What is emerging is the development of methods of logical thinking, where students use computers as partners in solving nonroutine problems and especially those problems where the consequences of actions are revealed (Piele, 1983). Efforts toward this end are occurring at the Harvard Graduate School of Education, for example, where new ways of teaching algebra and geometry using microcomputers are being studied.

Nonetheless, the majority of elementary and secondary mathematics problem-solving CAI programs that have been published support the conventional mathematics curriculum. Some of them use stories, clue words, and word problems as well as mathematical scoring games and decision tree strategies. Linear and nonlinear algebra tutorials and drill programs are also available to facilitate individual learning. Computer programs are also available for use with geometry. For example, younger children may learn points on a plane and construction of parallel and perpendicular lines and areas, as well as experiments that help them learn geometric shapes. Graphics are used with considerable effectiveness in some programs, such as those that illustrate changes in geometric figures when acted on in particular ways.

Of course, the programming language Logo comes to mind immediately when discussing the development of geometric understanding through graphics. Logo is also seen as a means for helping children develop logical problem-solving skills, through children's efforts to "teach" the turtle how to create a particular picture.

Computers in Social Studies

The major focus of social studies education is the development of effective citizens capable of reasoned decision making based on a keen ability to find, assess, and apply information from and about their social environment. While computer technology can aid in transmitting facts and figures, many social studies educators are directing primary attention to the computer as an information-processing and problem-solving tool (Diem, 1983; Braun, 1986; Budin, Kendall, and Lengel, 1986; Rooze and Northup, 1986).

Understanding social processes and phenomena is essential to effective citizenship, and the computer's ability to simulate complex processes lends itself well to this goal of social studies education. Simulations allow students to learn how social systems work and to experience (albeit artificially) the consequences of their actions within these systems (Martorella, 1984; White, 1984). Since reasoned decision making also demands well-developed skills in finding information that is necessary and relevant to the issue at hand, many social studies educators are embracing the use of computerized data bases to develop and polish information skills (White, 1985).

In the case of both simulations and data bases, schools so equipped can engage students in long-distance simulation gaming and information retrieval via modem. A fascinating example of the former is a simulation developed by Tom Snyder Productions called *The Other Side*. It is an international conflict resolution simulation involving two major powers who must coexist in a world of limited resources. While the simulation can be used within a single classroom, communications software is included on the same disk as the simulation, so that a school in San Diego can be linked by modem to a school in Houston in a mutual effort to "win" the game by averting conflict. The simulation's producers have initiated The Other Side clubs to facilitate interschool participation.

Spreadsheet programs allow students to perform calculations on rows and columns of numbers; those numbers can be election results or Dow Jones averages or other data relevant to social studies topics (Martorella, 1984).

Map and globe skills are fundamental to many topics within the social studies curriculum, and here we can exploit the graphics capability of computers. Tutorial programs can help support the development of basic map-reading skills, and simulations using maps can encourage stu-

A team of young diplomats enters its decisions and will await a response from "The Other Side." *(Courtesy of Tom Snyder Productions, Inc., Cambridge, Massachusetts.)*

dents to draw inferences from geographical data contained in computer-generated maps.

Since surveys and questionnaires are tools that social scientists use in their work, they are also applicable to school social studies. Software that allows students to enter and analyze survey data quickly has a twofold impact. First, it allows students to focus on data analysis rather than on the laborious mechanics of manual survey analysis. Second, it demonstrates one way social scientists use technology as a tool in their work.

Illuminating how computers are used by various sectors of society leads to a final thought. The social studies curriculum bears a special responsibility to address the legal and ethical issues surrounding the use and abuse of technology generally, and computers specifically. This is particularly applicable to government's use of computers, since the consequences of government misuse of technology can have a profound impact on our lives as citizens.

Computers in Science Education

The literature of science includes important information, but the heart of science education of necessity involves firsthand experience with materials and events. Ironically, however, school science laboratories are becoming increasingly expensive to install and maintain, and as a consequence many are being eliminated. To fill the need for direct experience, computers are being used increasingly to satisfy some of the learning that has traditionally been undertaken in laboratories.

As with all subject areas, much science software has been restricted to instructing students by means of text and graphics, much as occurs in books. The only advantage to using computers lies primarily in self-pacing, together with the periodic tests and immediate feedback on performance embedded in the better programs. Some programs, however, teach the content through a process of questioning—the Socratic method— rather than telling students information (Bork, 1985). Interactive programs of this kind are self-pacing and are particularly effective with student populations where rates of learning differ widely. Some of the more effective uses of computers in science teaching, however, show themselves through simulation programs and through the use of electronic sensing devices linked to computers that record actual information.

Simulation can be particularly valuable in science instruction when it enables students to manipulate information in ways that closely resemble experiences that occur when real data are used. For example, programs for science teaching are available that enable students to practice calculating the epicenters of imaginary earthquakes in various geographic locations. Similar programs have also been written that enable students to apply their knowledge in such diverse areas of science as vaporization, thermodynamics, optics, and osmosis. Viral invasions of the body, together with the responses of the immune system also lend themselves to simulation. Learning may also occur as a student manipulates the viral and defense variables in ways that permit a hypothetical person to recover quickly or slowly—or not at all. In others, students may manipulate genetic variables and observe changes that occur in the natural world that would be either too time-consuming or wholly impractical for consideration in school.

Some scientists express concern about these approaches to learning, because scientific experimentation rarely comes in the neat, tidy packages represented in computer simulations. Yet, the universal presence of computers in research laboratories has quieted some of these critics (Mace, 1984). Science educators, however, have acknowledged the value of modeling, because only by such means can hard-to-grasp concepts such as enormous time spans, massive physical changes, cross-sectional analyses, weather studies, and astronomical observations be communicated to students (Fazio and Beventy, 1983).

Of recent interest to science teachers is the microcomputer-based laboratory (MBL). The name was coined by Robert F. Tinker, who is director of Technical Education Research Centers, and describes a method that gathers and displays actual data directly from the environment. Some

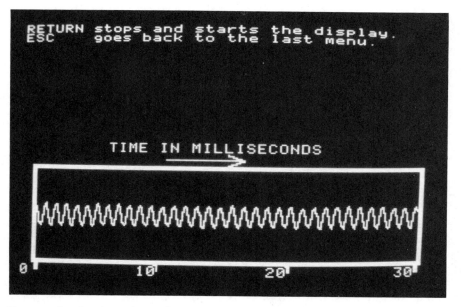

Young scientists investigate the sound waves created by a ukulele. Segments of the waves can be stored, displayed, and studied on the computer screen. *(Phinney Morrison, Photographer; Courtesy of Technical Education Research Centers (TERC), Cambridge, Massachusetts.)*

science educators see MBL as one means of bridging the gap between classroom theory and laboratory reality (Graef, 1983). An MBL consists of one or more sensors that measure phenomena such as light or heat interfaced with a microcomputer. The sensors respond to the environment and transmit it to the computer where it is converted to digital information, while the output appears as a graphic or alphanumeric display. So, while an MBL is computer driven, the data it collects are derived from responses to actual conditions.

Computers in the Visual Arts

Art teachers have been relatively slow in putting computers to use in their art rooms. For some, any thought of using electronic machinery is alien to the creative qualities that characterize art. For others, the abstract mathematical base of computing has led to the conclusion that computing has little significance for their subject. Others have concluded that graphics in particular is still at too primitive a level for it to be worth serious consideration in the art curriculum. However, after a slow start, art teachers are gradually taking advantage of this new medium, though computing is taking on a different form from that commonly found in the conventional academic subjects or in classes on learning how to program, where information is to be learned and remembered (Hubbard and Linehan, 1983). Much of the software for these areas addresses practice and mastery of facts and tool skills.

In contrast, very little instructional software has been written for art instruction. This is partly because school art programs are not as clearly prescribed as those for academic areas. There are few textbooks in art and no well-defined state or national requirements for art teachers to meet that might have given software publishers a guide about what to produce. As a consequence, the primary source of programs for art teachers to use consists of graphics packages that derive mainly from computer games and from inexpensive versions of industrial and commercial digitizing tablets that are as likely to be sold for home consumption as for classroom use.

Consequently, the artistic use of computers has been as a tool—much as word processing is to language composition—where students put the capabilities of the software program to use for some expressive, communicative end. At worst, students in art classes receive no guidance and doodle aimlessly on a screen instead of on paper. At best, they are guided toward an understanding of the unique qualities that distinguish computer graphics from other graphic media, and also to distinguish the merits of one program of graphics software over another. Some art teachers photograph the finished images directly from monitor screens, while others make hard-copy printouts of their work in color or in black and white on paper using dot matrix printers.

What looks like a photograph of real objects is actually the product of an artist's imagination and advanced computer graphics. *(Courtesy of AT&T)*

In addition to programs that permit students to create purely graphic images, numbers of commercial programs provide sets of alphabets (fonts) for lettering design. Some programs also permit the user to design and construct a unique alphabet or a set of shapes (shape tables) that may be used repeatedly when creating images. Others make possible the drawing of mirror images, inversions, enlargements, and reductions. Relatively inexpensive programs are also available that, when connected with a video camera, display digitized images on the screen. As with any image that can be displayed and recorded, such pictures can be modified, thus making them candidates for creative expression. Most inviting of all, perhaps, are those programs that permit students to animate their graphic images, although such programs usually call for a level of maturity not normally associated with secondary students. The more exotic the equipment, however, the more expensive it usually is, and the less likely a school will have the funds to purchase it. For this reason, art teachers can only expect to work with camera-driven digitizing programs if the school already owns a video camera, while only the least expensive tablets are likely to be available in most schools.

Computers in Foreign Language Education

In some respects, computer applications in foreign language education resemble those in other subject areas. A body of knowledge exists that students must acquire, and the computer can help transmit and reinforce. Grammar and vocabulary come to mind in particular. The use of CAI to this end frees the teacher to spend more time on building communication skills. Knowledge of the culture within which the language is spoken is another important element of foreign language instruction. Here, interactive video holds real promise. Through it students can experience language within a cultural context that involves native speakers in native environments in a way that is visually and auditorially rich.

With regard to foreign language skills, word processors can enhance the writing of the language, while reading skills can be honed through programs that move students away from word-by-word translation to more useful reading strategies.

Beyond these rather straightforward instances, computer technology faces some real challenges when applied to foreign language education, specifically in the areas of listening and speaking skills. Using computers to develop listening skills in a foreign language requires voice synthesis systems capable of clear pronunciation. While mediocre voice production in one's native language can be decoded and understood with little difficulty, such is not the case when learning a foreign language. However, the quality of voice synthesis has improved and will continue to improve. Coupled with the use of random access audio disks, the computer can assist in the refinement of listening skills.

Speaking-skill development is similarly challenging for computer technology, given the limitations thus far in voice recognition, the flip side of voice production. An added limitation is the ability of the technology to accept and process "natural-language" user responses—in short, the ability to carry on an open-ended conversation. (By the way, this limitation holds regardless of whether the student is typing in an open-ended response or verbalizing such a response.) Considerable computer power and memory are required here. It must be said, though, that both power and memory are increasing steadily, boding well for advances in this area of foreign language education as well.

Computers in Music

In the judgment of numbers of influential music educators, much music teaching in schools remains at the level it was a century ago (Upitis, 1983). Elementary classroom teachers spend most of their time teaching songs by rote. Only a very few of them have learned to play an instrument satisfactorily, and fewer still can create music structures. As a consequence, most music education programs fail to provide challenging and inspiring musical environments. At the same time, however, leaders in the field are proposing that children should be doing more than interpreting the work of others (Slind, 1971). They believe that children should be given opportunities to develop their own musical ideas as they do in written English or artistic creation.

In the opinions of some music educators, the principal advance has been the invention of the microcomputer synthesizer. Unlike most CAI software, a synthesizer does not carry explicit pedagogical content. Instead it fulfills much the same "tool" function as a word processor does for written language or a graphics package does for art. A music synthesizer permits a user possessing only modest knowledge of music to choose sounds from a range of possibilities and "play" them. Because electronic sounds may be organized in any way, students can create their own music without first having mastered an instrument.

Although music education has usually included some theory, the main thrust has traditionally been directed at performing music composed by someone else. These interpretive activities will undoubtedly persist in music teaching and should do so, but the availability of compositional programming software and synthesizers makes the possibility of transforming music teaching so that students may compose their own music. Moreover, these student experiences will receive immediate feedback on the actual instrument they are composing for, unlike the experience of the traditional composer, who hears a piece of music only on a piano until it is actually performed. Students may also edit their compositions and make any deletions, repetitions, and alterations of key or time as easily as editing with a word processor. Finished compositions may then be saved as permanent file entries on diskettes and replayed at will.

More advanced students may discover that synthesizer sounds are too limited for their needs, and they may prefer to work at a piano, especially if they are orchestrating or analyzing musical content. On the other hand, computer-synthesized music—much like computer graphics—can rightfully be considered an art form in its own right, and students may prefer working on a synthesizer throughout their school years and beyond.

Computers in Business Education

While computers have affected all walks of life, nowhere has this effect been so obvious as in the American office. Offices no longer look the same as they did even 5 years ago. High school graduates who find office jobs soon discover that their workplaces are equipped with computers and related electronic equipment, where communications and record keeping of all kinds are moving toward a paperlessness that might have been thought of as science fiction only a few years ago. The changes first affected secretaries and accountants probably more than any others, and this is reflected in school business instruction, though the influence of electronics has since been extending into just about every sphere of office life and even into the middle levels of management.

Typing skills continue to dominate school business curriculums, because knowledge and skill at the keyboard remains a foundational skill: it is applicable to conventional typing as well as to word processing and other office tasks that have become electronic. And yet keyboard instruction is now entering the school curriculum at all levels and in all subjects. One educational researcher, Robert Gagné, describes the lack of keyboard skills as one of the biggest bottlenecks to introducing computers generally into schools. As a consequence of such conclusions, keyboard instruction is now occurring in numbers of elementary schools. Were typing to become universal in elementary education, students might have little need to enroll in secondary school typing classes unless to learn business layout needs.

The professional associations representing business educators understandably declare that the best place for learning keyboarding is the business classroom, with specially trained business teachers in charge (Grady and Gawronski, 1983). And some might go so far as to claim that all computer studies in school belong in the business curriculum rather than under the wing of subjects such as mathematics. But given the dynamics of American education, any restrictions of this kind would be impossible to impose.

Leaving the keyboarding problem to one side, perhaps the greatest impetus for using computers in business education is the demand that students learn how to handle the specialized office machinery of the computerized business world. High school graduates need to be able to participate in the networking of information and teleconferencing with other offices and other businesses through modems and telephone-satellite linkages (Egatz, 1984) as well as manipulate information through interactive video (Titen, 1983). More than ever before, students need to be prepared for jobs where they analyze, synthesize, and manage information rather than transcribe it (McMullen, 1984). Responsibility for training workers to engage in these tasks will fall in part to the organizations that need these skills. On the other hand, past history shows that business and industry expect schools to share the responsibility for preparing people for the world of work.

Although word processing is almost always seen as part of the business curriculum, some business educators (Stagg, 1984) include more specific competencies that correspond with the needs of the electronic office such as inputting, storing, and outputting documents from handwritten or dictated sources. Other business educators include locating and revising previously stored documents, coding documents, logging daily outputs, and developing procedures for using forms typically found in automated offices. Others have defined the tasks somewhat differently where students initially develop competence on regular typewriters and from there progress to word processing and general computer literacy. Students may also need familiarity with spelling dictionaries, mail merge programs, long documents, and use of a library account to pull selected documents to a screen.

The teaching of typing will almost certainly continue to be challenged by school programs in computer literacy and written composition, but instruction in accounting and business management is likely to remain the domain of business teachers. And a number of simulation programs have been published to instruct students in banking and economics, company management, and business strategies; they offer excellent opportunities for engaging kinds of student participation that have not been possible before. Thus, while business teachers may resent the inroads being made by other subject-matter specialists into what formerly was their exclusive domain, the transformational changes in offices are likely to consume any additional time that may be liberated by the decline in responsibility for typing.

In addition, just as the hand calculator terminated the usefulness of slide rules, so growth and miniaturization have led to the development of ever more portable dictating machines and to the continued decline in teaching shorthand. Moreover, linkages between business and vocational education have also occurred, where computers are interfaced with cash registers for point-of-sale inventory control to bring work from the outside world into the school (Titen, 1983). This is not to suggest that business teachers are all equally willing to use computers. Numbers of them are opposed to any use of microcomputers (Nigor, 1984), and others maintain that shorthand continues to be necessary. On the other hand, office productivity increased only 4 percent during the 1970s compared with an 85 percent increase in factory productivity during the same period. Consequently, the labor intensiveness of offices is being challenged by the increasing presence of computers that are purchased for the express purpose of increasing productivity.

Computers in Home Economics

Home economics comprises a broad range of subjects, from nutrition to child care to clothing design to household budgeting to health care to family living to interior design. The opportunities to use computers as tools in this diverse field are legion. In fact, interest in the use of computing in home economics began as long ago as 1972. In 1984 a study of 500 secondary home economics teachers nationwide (Burkhart, Muller, and O'Neil, 1984) revealed that well over half were using computers, and another 31 percent expected to do so in the near future. The study showed that computers were being used for quizzes, drill, and review, together with some administrative uses, such as grade records and examinations. At that time the main software use was in food and nutrition, clothing, and housing, while lesser uses were made of programs dealing with energy, child development, consumer education, career education, and money management.

The range of materials has increased since this study was made, though the number of programs remains quite modest compared with areas such as mathematics and social studies. Several programs calculate the nutrient content of foods and display such analyses as proteins, fats, carbohydrates, and calcium, as well as vitamins. Others present meals typically found in school cafeterias, and by means of interactive programming steer students toward wise dietary choices. And some programs make comparisons between the dietary needs of different people. In addition to software written expressly for school use, numbers of programs written for the home market are suitable for students. These include recipes for a wide range of dishes, together with planning guides to help prepare entire meals.

Home economics teachers may also use computers to prepare students for life after graduation, with software on such topics as how to handle household accounting, annual utility costs, and personal budgeting. Other programs may be used to help students estimate the kind of housing they can afford on a given income. Miscellaneous topics are also addressed by programs that present students with the decision about whether or not to smoke, issues about urban welfare, and guidance on infant care. Recent research by Richard Feinberg and Kathy Walton (1983) extended the work of Sherry Turkle with a study where students revealed a greater willingness to respond to intimate questions when the question was posed by a computer than by another person. While the results may be applied to numbers of situations. Feinberg and Walton related them specifically to consumer and family-oriented applications.

Familiar tool programs including word processing, filing systems, graphics, and spreadsheets also lend themselves to home economics education. Students and teachers can compile their own recipe collections, design and print menus, design interiors, maintain inventories of foods and appliances, and much more. In fact, Dr. Zoe Ann Holmes of the College of Home Economics at Oregon State University suggests that as sophisticated software becomes increasingly available, computer technology can make the home "a learning center in an effective, efficient way" (personal correspondence).

Computers in Vocational Education

Unlike most areas in the curriculum, vocational education is intended to prepare students for work in recognized occupations. Although it may include areas such as business education and home economics, we have chosen to keep them separate from each other. Thus, vocational education here refers primarily to trade and industry programs and to vocational agriculture, with some mention of marketing and health occupations.

The very considerable growth in efficiency in manufacturing over the last 15 years can be attributed in large measure to advances in computing. It is only to be expected, therefore, that schools are incorporating those features of these changes into their vocational programs. Whereas vocational education in the recent past focused on drafting and working with wood, metal, and internal combustion engines, a swing is now underway toward incorporating electronics and computer-based devices. For example, computer-aided design (CAD) is beginning to take over from conventional drafting, so that students may now be learning to work with computers linked to digitizing tablets or similar devices rather than with drawing boards and T-squares. And as the cost of this electronic equipment decreases, schools will continue to change over to equipment that corresponds with that to be found in industry. In fact, it may well be that traditional drafting instruction will eventually seem as quaint as using a slide rule. Moreover, admission to technical colleges and similar institutions increasingly requires high school computer experiences in order for applications to be considered.

In more traditional vocational education settings, however, tutorials are being used for tasks such as reading micrometers, learning welding techniques, and auto-mechanics safety, thus freeing instructors to work more closely with students.

Vocational education for the printing trades and commercial layout are also being affected by computers. "Desktop publishing" is a prime example of this. For some years, publishers have been using fonts of type from electronic storage rather than casting them in metal, but only during the last few years have these capabilities been possible with microcomputers. The same is true for pictures of every conceivable kind, so that paste-up work for advertising is being done increasingly by electronic means without reliance on clip books or original art. Numbers of microcomputer programs enable students to learn how to manipulate lettering and layout, so that students who plan to enter this kind of work on graduation will only need to be made familiar with the particular characteristics of the machines they eventually work on.

Building trades instruction not only includes electronic drafting methods; it also includes special programs that permit building specifications to be entered. Thus the process of materials costing of jobs—even to the inclusion of labor costs—can be executed at electronic speeds with the help of specialized software, and modifications to original specifications can be made instantaneously. Regardless of whether students become independent craftsmen or work for construction companies, the issue remains the same: skill and knowledge of computer programs is invaluable for people entering these occupations.

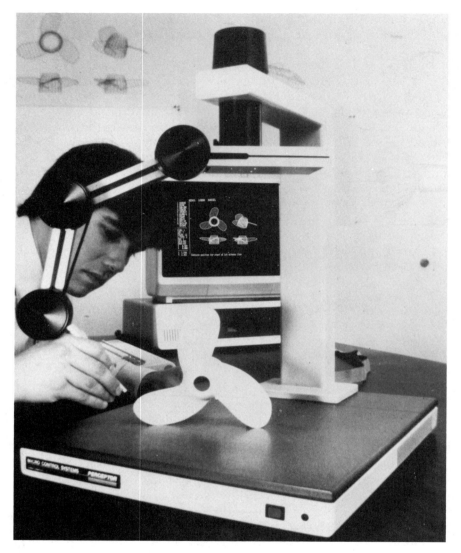

A three-dimensional electro-mechanical digitizer, used to convert a three-dimensional object (like this propeller) into a computer model, which can then be revised or redesigned. *(Courtesy of Micro Control Systems, Inc.)*

In another area, computers are causing agriculture to experience yet another upheaval. The demise of the family farm is now being followed by the impact of computers. So powerful has this trend been that in numbers of farm communities parents are insisting that computing be required throughout the local school systems—and not just for those

The study of robotics is growing in the precollege curriculum, and the use of devices like the one pictured here is increasing. *(Courtesy of General Robotics Corporation.)*

intent on careers in farming. Two major approaches to computers occur in vocational agriculture. One is to teach students to write the kinds of programs for themselves that fully meet their unique needs, while the other is to teach them to become competent in the selection and use of selected software programs that have been designed to help farmers. These include dairy automation and quality control, planting schedules and alternatives subject to weather and economic conditions, fertilization, and the like.

Vocational education also includes marketing and distributive education as well as health education. Computer software includes simulation programs that monitor warehouse inventories, generate sales price/cost margin reports, make hotel reservations, and use point-of-sale systems— just to name a few. In some instances, marketing and distributive education students may learn to use spreadsheet software, while others learn to use data-base management. Much health care training typically occurs on the job at present, but school participation is on the increase as employers want incoming employees to have some introduction to computers and relevant software while still in school. School instruction in health care may include preparing patient records, using standardized patient care plans, and becoming familiar with reading video displays on terminals.

Computers in Physical Education and Dance

The most influential applications of computing in physical education and dance have been in the uses of software to maintain records easily and more efficiently than in the past. Coaches and teachers continually evaluate student physique, monitor training programs, and maintain records of sports performance. And nutrition software compares analyses among foods in order to determine suitable dietary regimens.

Complex and constantly changing relationships may also be monitored and modified. Scheduling of many kinds is a constant concern for coaching staff. It includes arranging sports meets, and also recording team draws, round robins, single and double eliminations, and seeding options. All these tasks lend themselves to resolutions by computer, thus freeing staff for other duties—while at the same minimizing errors. Computer software can also enable staffs to maintain control of reservations for sports events and equipment, inventories of uniforms and equipment, not to mention budget and general accounting responsibilities.

Instructional software also facilitates CAI needs relative to definitions, rules, concepts, principles, and strategies that apply to various dimensions of physical fitness. Similar materials are available for volleyball, bowling, basketball, and football. Software instruction is also available for cardiovascular resuscitation (CPR). For all this, however, it is not yet clear whether computer applications have been found by teachers and coaches to be useful alternatives to traditional methods, compared with the value of electronic record keeping and administrative applications. For example, some simulation problems based on actual performance may prove to be more flexible and appealing than printed materials, while basketball statistics may not offer any advance over conventional forms. Moreover, reports in the professional literature indicate considerable inhibition and resistence to using computers. This is reinforced by the very few examples of software that have been published compared with the mass of materials available for mathematics and language instruction.

While dance is not found generally in American schools, it does exist in numbers of school curriculums. Once again, little software has been written for dance education, although some is available for social dancing, and some of it makes use of animated figures to help teach dance movements. A program has also been developed that computerizes the Laban Movement Analysis (LMA) and permits the presentation of dance movements in graphic form that is quicker to produce and more precise than anything handwritten. Such a program may be useful in some school settings, though again it seems more likely to be used in the professional training of dancers and choreographers than in elementary and secondary schools. The same may be true of a program that provides a computerized behavioral profile of dance teachers. Also for more serious students, computer programs exist that permit drawn graphic overlays to be placed over videotape or film displays to help with the teaching and refinement of dance movements. A drawback for school use, however, is that such programs require electronic equipment with greater capabilities than that typically found in schools.

Computers in Special Education

The field of special education addresses an extraordinarily broad range of educational needs, from mildly learning disabled to profoundly mentally or physically handicapped. Nonetheless, special education professionals have found powerful ways to meet the needs of their students via computer technology: through computer assisted and computer managed instruction, and through the development of adaptive and assistive devices.

The capability of the computer to deliver instruction, to maintain ongoing records of student responses, to provide diagnostic information by evaluating patterns of responses, and even to propose avenues of remediation serve to assist the special education teacher in shaping instruction that best addresses an individual student's unique learning needs. The whole area of computer managed instruction (CMI) thus holds tremendous promise if the management software is skillfully designed and implemented. Further development of expert systems (see Chapter 2) may also allow deeper analysis of learner needs and more effective remediation. Coupled with interactive video, the computer can continue to serve as an important instructional resource for students and teachers.

Combining CMI applications with data-management programs and report generators further assists the teacher in tracking the progress of individual students. The development of individual education plans (IEPs) with the help of computers will continue to produce more finely tuned strategies and, ultimately, greater success for the special education student. Thus, the computer becomes an aid to the teachers as well as an instructional resource for students.

The technology is also contributing to increasing the mobility and sense of control for many physically handicapped students. New sophisticated adaptive devices serve to increase both the ease with which handicapped students can gain access to computer technology and can also accomplish everyday tasks without having to rely on others for assistance. For example, blind students can place a book on what looks like a copying machine and then listen as the Kurzweil Reading Machine "reads" the book through synthesized speech. The same student could finish a word processing assignment by having the text outputted to a Braille printer. Other adaptive and assistive devices include oversized keyboards, touch screens, photo sensitive relays, mouth and head sticks, voice synthesizers, and even devices that respond only to eyebrow twitches. Consider also the many ways that computer technology can control appliances in the home, direct wheelchairs by voice command, and the like. In this context, then, the computer serves as a personal aid for handicapped students.

Teaching and Learning a Programming Language

Why Teach Programming: Two Reasons

Controversy continues to swirl around the issue of what emphasis should be placed on teaching and learning a programming language. From the teacher's perspective, an exposure to the fundamentals of programming should be part of a general introductory computer literacy experience provided through inservice and staff development. Since few teachers will develop a commitment to producing software for their own classes, the prime rationale for deeper involvement by teachers in programming is to develop enough proficiency to teach programming to their students. But again, only a small minority of teachers will be so engaged. Assuming, however, that you are one of the those who will be teaching programming, a fundamental question remains: Why are students learning to program?

Perhaps the strongest rationale for teaching programming to all students is the positive effect programming may have on the development of problem-solving skills, which will be discussed in some detail. A second rationale would support the teaching of programming to a specialized audience: those high school students anticipating college study of computer science who wish to attempt advanced placement. Both rationales demand that the teacher's programming expertise go beyond an introductory inservice workshop. Moreover, knowledge of programming alone will be insufficient to address either rationale. In the former case, an understanding of the relationship between programming and problem solving is essential; in the latter, an understanding of programming within the larger discipline of computer science is equally necessary. One must hasten to add that these understandings are not mutually exclusive. Indeed, the first rationale is largely subsumed in the second, as the following discussion will suggest.

The presumed relationship between programming and problem solving deserves further illumination before we discuss methods of teaching programming. At the heart of the matter is the symbiotic relationship between algorithmic and heuristic problem solving.

Programming and Thinking

The act of programming a computer can help students develop problem-solving skills and is obviously imperative for those who plan on becoming professional computer scientists. Most teachers and students, on the other hand, are more likely to be described as "end users," where problem solving with a computer is not a primary interest. Nonetheless, the act of manipulating a computer by means of a high-level language—especially a language that can handle subparts of programs separately—enables a person to participate actively in the work that computers do best, which in turn leads to a fuller understanding of their operation. For example, unless told otherwise, computers act on each instruction separately and in the sequence they appear in a program. Consequently, events that occur first may be obliterated by what follows. On the other hand, instructions that appear early in a program will continue to affect everything that follows unless rescinded. Programs can also be slowed down, speeded up, and even be made to stop completely. And control of a program can be transferred to and fro from the written program to the person using the program as long as the ways in which it is done are defined quite specifically. Moreover, computer programs can be used to generate music and images as readily as they can present text or make calculations. And while the computer keyboard resembles a typewriter, that need not be permanent. All keys are assigned a meaning by a programmer, and these meanings may be altered to serve any particular need.

These capabilities and limitations deserve to be understood, though all of them boil down to two primary issues. A computer can only respond if instructions exist in a program to drive it. And while a computer is remarkably accurate and rapid in its responses to instructions, it is far less effective when it must search for alternatives among a set of possibilities, especially when the selection process is not precise or when a substantial number of alternatives is possible. Two terms are used to define the differences between precise procedures and judgments: *algorithms* and *heuristics*. Computers, and microcomputers in particular, are admirable for algorithms, because as long as the instructions—be they formulas, specific procedures, or set rules—are precise and when all the information needed is available, a computer can execute them at great speed and with unerring accuracy. When a task requires that a strategy be devised or a choice of strategy be made that may have to do with the best buy on a product (whether a car or a carpet) given the cost, durability, and compatibility with other items, a computer is likely to be ill equipped to respond.

The impetus that led to the invention of calculators and embroidery machines was the desire to reduce the tedium, slowness, and inaccuracy of this work. Human beings guide their lives by means of algorithmic thinking: they write their names, observe driving regulations, and abide by the rules of games. And numbers of critics of education are disturbed that many students today can no longer recall multiplication tables (algorithms). However, the emergence of miniature electronic computers has caused many of these tasks to be delegated. "Good" handwriting was eclipsed by the invention of the typewriter and was put to rest by the ball point pen. The advent of computing is not announcing the end of algorithmic thinking by people. Rather it is replacing low-level algorithms as well as refocusing the efforts of students and teachers on complementary (heuristic) decisions-making tasks.

All problem solving requires that first a body of knowledge exist, whether in a person's memory or in a computer memory. Problems need to be defined before they can be tackled, and this implies the presence of knowledge. It also requires that a stock of algorithms and heuristics be available that may be used to manipulate that knowledge and solve particular problems. Computer memories typically far outstrip human memories in their ability to store information. And while algorithms can be written so that computers can retrieve and manipulate this information, strategies for deciding which conclusions are most relevant, the heuristic dimension, is eminently human. And while computers can be programmed to make heuristic decisions, most of them have quite limited capabilities in this dimension of problem solving. Large computers offer greater opportunities for such possibilities, though with the growth of artificial intelligence, they are sure to become more effective. But for the purpose of this book—if not for educational computing generally—these qualities are better considered the domain of people.

Problem solving where algorithms predominate obviously belongs with computer operations. A handful of teachers can be expected to want to write their own algorithms, and when they do, teachers will need to sharpen their skills. And as computer memory has expanded, other kinds of procedural applications have evolved. Computers were discovered to be capable of handling a wide variety of algorithmic tasks beyond the original focus on mathematical computation. Grammar and conventional syntax is algorithmic, so text presentations lend themselves to computing, with the result that word processing is fast becoming universal in all jobs where the printed word is used. Similarly, the structure of music is algorithmic, and the dimensions of graphic images can be defined precisely and also assigned specific colors. But except at rudimentary levels, microcomputer programs do not lend themselves to determining whether one paragraph communicates a particular sentiment better than another. Likewise, one arrangement of colors and shapes may be superior to another, but it takes the heuristic judgment of a human being to reach that conclusion.

The heart of the issue lies not so much in declaring that computers are good only for certain tasks and people are good for other tasks. Rather, it is the recognition that both qualities are essential in an ever-increasing number of problem-solving tasks and that learning to program in a high-level language offers students the opportunity to participate actively in exploring the best mix of the two areas for given problems. Arthur Luehrmann takes the position, for example, that we miss the point of the value of computing when focusing discussion of the merits of computing on whether CAI methods are as effective as conventional schooling practices. He sees the computer as an instrument that fulfills numbers of needs, much like a piano. But a piano is not a teaching machine any more than a movie projector is a teaching machine. A piano may facilitate the solution of musical problems, however, in ways that no other instrument can. In much the same way, Luehrmann believes that a computer can solve certain kinds of problems. But that is only likely to happen if a person learns how to use it, and programming is probably the best means by which people may communicate with computers. In sum, a computer contributes its unique qualities to the kind of thinking that helps solve problems.

General Methods of Teaching a Programming Language

Given that the central purpose of teaching a programming language is as a problem-solving skill developer, the teaching methods one uses ought to facilitate the development of those skills. Some may argue that the act of programming itself transmits problem-solving skills, yet Perkins (1985) advanced an important point. He suggested that anticipated outcomes will only be achieved if the learning experience actually has the potential for producing those outcomes, *and* if the learner recognizes that potential, *and* if the learner is motivated to seize the opportunity to take advantage of the potential. If this is accurate, a teacher must lead students to recognize the problem-solving skills inherent in programming and must design experiences that will motivate students to exercise those skills. Thus, teachers of programming must understand, first, what problem solving is and, second, how to provide an environment conducive to skill development.

THE NATURE OF PROBLEM SOLVING   George Polya (1957) summarized problem solving into four fundamental steps: (1) understanding the problem, (2) devising a plan, (3) carrying out the plan, and (4) looking back. Understanding the problem requires analysis of the starting conditions, the desired end state, and the operations implied in the problem statement. Such analysis is crucial for devising the plan, since it will guide the selection and sequence of subgoals required in order to achieve the overall problem goal (the desired end state). Operationalizing and executing the plan follows, step by step through the subgoals to a generated outcome. Looking back to the problem—that is, the plan and its execution—the problem solvers assess the extent to which the outcome they have achieved matches the desired end state. If not, the process must be repeated: the problem analysis may have been faulty, the plan may have been incomplete, or the execution may have been flawed. If a desired end state is attained, looking back is still required to ensure that the solution holds for all conditions implied by the problem.

Experienced programmers may recognize in this process some striking similarities to what they do when they program. Successful programmers focus initial attention on the requirements of the problem task: what data are involved, what processes are needed, and what constraints are imposed. When devising a plan, programmers use the results of problem analysis to produce design specifications, perhaps using flowcharts and other diagrams, and then implement these specifications through appropriate data structures and algorithms. Moving to the actual coding of the program, they carry out the plan they have designed, debugging and refining by looking back at the original problem task and testing the program according to a well-conceived test plan.

TEACHING PROGRAMMING FOR PROBLEM SOLVING   Teaching programming in a manner likely to develop facility in problem solving requires teachers to attend to issues relating to, among other things, problem selection, top-down design, and structured programming.

Choosing programming tasks only on the basis of "covering" syntax will be insufficient for developing problem-solving skills. Two fundamental criteria should guide problem selection: (1) does its solution require students to apply new data structures and new algorithms? and (2) is it nontrivial? While there is some controversy concerning the latter, nontrivial problems seem particularly important in that they call on students to exercise considerable analysis and force them to break problems into smaller pieces more amenable to solution.

Selecting complex problems must be accompanied with explicit instruction in top-down design, that is, moving from high levels of generality in program design to the lowest levels, increasing in detail in the process. In breaking the problem down into smaller parts, students are producing programs that are constructed from modules, each of which can be tested and refined independently and in interaction with others.

At the lowest level of generality, students are coding the program in some computer language. The structure of the program ought to match the modularity of the design. So, teachers must provide instruction in structured programming in whatever language they are using. Some languages lend themselves to structure better than others.

Above all, teachers must make the *process* of problem solving explicit and obvious to students, must provide guidance in applying the process to numerous practice problems, and must model the process in the examples they use for instruction. This is true regardless of the age level of the student, although the content and complexity of the problems will vary greatly across grade levels.

Selecting a Programming Language

It may seem strange that the mention of a programming language was left for last. This reflects a belief that rationales for and methods of teaching programming are more important than the particular language one chooses. The range of choice is large—a veritable alphabet soup of languages from APL to UNICODE. While a surprising segment of this collection can be found in elementary and secondary schools, the dominant languages at this time boil down to three: BASIC, Logo, and Pascal. We have described these languages briefly in Chapter 4, but we consider them here in the context of teaching and learning a programming language.

BASIC   Developed by John Kemeny and Thomas Kurtz to help their students at Dartmouth learn programming, BASIC (Beginners All-purpose Symbolic Instruction Code) is the dominant programming language in schools. In as many dialects as there are computer brands, BASIC rapidly became the *lingua franca* of computer literacy programs. BASIC is a relatively easy language to learn, providing numbers of avenues for achieving the same end (whether efficient or not). Moreover, as an interpreted language, BASIC programs can be run at any stage of completion.

What makes BASIC easy also makes it less useful for developing disciplined approaches to programming and, more fundamentally, for supporting the problem-solving process described above. The language is not very useful for large, nontrivial programs, like a sophisticated word processor or data-base program. Indeed, its developers were so appalled with the versions of BASIC produced for microcomputers that they have twice revised the original BASIC. Their most recent revision produced TrueBASIC, incorporating control structures more conductive to structured programming.

LOGO   Seymour Papert wanted to give children "an object to think with" and produced the Turtle, the object playing a starring role in the Logo language. Derived from the artificial intelligence language LISP, Logo is considerably more effective than BASIC in fostering structure in programming. Logo programs are built from procedures (Logo is a "procedural" language), supporting the concept of modular design, that is, building large programs by linking together a collection of smaller modules. Each procedure can stand alone and be tested independently but can also be linked to other procedures, passing information from one procedure to another. Logo is also extensible, in that new commands can be defined by the programmer and then used like other commands already available (called "primitives" in Logo).

At first blush, it would seem that Logo would be a natural choice for the kind of complex problem solving one might see in high school or college computer science courses. But Logo suffers from an image problem: it is perceived as a language for kids only. This is partly because of an overemphasis on the Turtle graphics of Logo, to the detriment of its more powerful features. The rather broad leap required to get from the former to the latter may explain this situation in part. Nonetheless, even if Logo is relegated to the elementary classroom, it provides a potentially powerful foundation for Pascal in the high school classroom.

PASCAL   A Swiss computer scientist named Niklaus Wirth developed Pascal in the late 1960s during an attempt to improve another language, ALGOL. Like Logo, Pascal is a procedural language, conducive to modular design; Pascal also allows the passing of parameters from one procedure to another, again important for modular programming, and a fundamental concept in computer science. Unlike Logo and BASIC, Pascal is compiled rather than interpreted. One bug will prevent the entire procedure or program from running: you won't get past the compiler's error statement. This imposes a rather strict discipline on the Pascal programmer to analyze problems and design programs with care before coding.

What may seem a hindrance for writing short programs is essential for designing and executing large programs. For this and other reasons, the Educational Testing Service chose Pascal as the official language of the Advanced Placement Computer Science test it began administering in 1984.

It is possible to teach rather sophisticated programming concepts with any of these languages, though Pascal can probably take the student farther into the field of computer science that either Logo or BASIC. As this statement suggests, the choice of a programming language has a lot to do with your purposes for teaching programming and, of course, what you have available in your school. To assist in teaching programming, a wide range of textbooks has appeared in recent years (see Appendix B).

If your purpose is indeed to teach computer science, we turn now to consider recommendations for high school computer science and for certification of computer science education teachers.

Computer Science Education

While most students will encounter and learn from CAI or CMI applications in schools and most will be required to achieve a prescribed level of computer literacy, a small segment of the school population will want to specialize more narrowly on computer science as a discipline. Most of these high school students are anticipating a college major in computer science or in a field requiring a high level of expertise in computing.

Colleges and universities have long encouraged links with high schools in the development of precollege courses that are equivalent to an introductory college course. Such advanced placement or AP courses are accepted by numerous colleges in a wide variety of fields; computer science is the most recent newcomer to the AP collection.

As a guide for colleges in granting advanced placement or credit to individual students, the Educational Testing Service annually administers an AP Computer Science examination, yielding a grade (ranging from a low of 1 to a maximum of 5) that college computer science departments may use to compare individuals seeking such placement or credit. The examination assumes a body of content that is equivalent to the first year of college computer science. High school courses covering the same content usually extend over two years.

As outlined by the College Entrance Examination Board, the prime emphases in an AP computer science course are programming methodology, algorithms, and data structures. More than a programming course in Pascal, AP computer science introduces students to fundamental concepts of the computer science discipline. The course goals are as follows:

1. The student will be able to design and implement computer-based solutions to problems in several application areas.
2. The student will learn well-known algorithms and data structures.

3. The student will be able to develop and select appropriate algorithms and data structures to solve problems.
4. The student will be able to code fluently in a well-structured fashion using an accepted high-level language. (The first offerings of the AP Computer Science Examination will require knowledge of Pascal.)
5. The student will be able to identify the major hardware and software components of a computer system, their relationship to one another, and the roles of these components within the system.
6. The student will be able to recognize the ethical and social implications of computer use. (College Entrance Examination Board, 1984, pp. 7–8).

As is evident from these goals and a typical course outline presented in Appendix C, computer science education is distinctly different from general computer literacy. It is more specialized, serving a small subset of students and demanding considerable expertise on the part of the teacher. In essence, a computer science teacher ought to be able to present a college-level first-year course in computer science. The College Board argues against discouraging teachers who are currently unprepared to teach such a course from acquiring the needed knowledge and skills, either through self-instruction or additional coursework. Others have laid out rather specific competencies for teachers as prerequisites for gaining certification in computer science education.

The push to establish teacher certification guidelines for computer science has gained considerable popularity of late, though one can still observe confusion among those advocating identical standards for teachers of computer *literacy*. This mirrors the failure of some educators to make a distinction between computer literacy and computer science education. This is true of one set of recommendations for certification requirements published in the 1984 Proceedings of the Association for Educational Data Systems (AEDS) Annual Convention. The rationale statements for computer science education subsume those normally associated with the broader topic of general computer literacy. Nonetheless, they do represent an important effort to identify teacher competencies for computer science specifically. According to these guidelines, all programs in training high school computer science teachers should include a course "on the materials and methods of teaching computer science" and courses "on programming applications in both Pascal and BASIC" with at least one course of these to include Logo (Taylor and Poirot, 1984, pp. 302–303). Five required courses were recommended:

1. Introduction to Programming and Algorithm Design, including programming using a high-level language;
2. Computers and Education, including analysis of the major instructional uses of computers;

3. Computers and Society;
4. Programming Languages, including the definition and structure of languages and the comparison of languages;
5. A choice of either Introduction to Computer Systems or Microcomputer Systems and Applications. (Taylor and Poirot, 1984, p. 303)

In addition to these five, a group of electives is recommended as well:

1. Advanced Topics in Programming and Algorithm Design and Analysis;
2. Computer Assisted Instruction;
3. Introduction to File Processing;
4. Data Structures;
5. Fundamentals of Computer Organization and Digital Logic;
6. Assembly Language Programming. (Taylor and Poirot, 1984, p. 303)

Debate will continue for some time regarding the relationship between computer literacy and computer science, and the place of computer science within the central goals of general public education. For our part, as we have stated, computer science is a specialized field for a narrow range of students, whereas computer literacy is an aspect of general education required by all students.

Summary

Moving beyond the general ideas set forth in Chapter 5, we described in this chapter practical applications of computers in a variety of subject areas in the school curriculum. We recognize that books can be written (and in many cases have been written) on the use of computers within each subject area; thus, we recognize that our commentary only hints at what is happening and what is possible in the curriculum. Check the bibliography for additional information on these subject areas, or contact their respective professional organizations (see Appendix E).

We have also examined at considerable length the issue of teaching and learning programming, as well as the emergence of computer science as a (relatively) new discipline vying for a place within the secondary school curriculum. Both topics are subjects of sometimes heated debate, due to some extent on failures to distinguish between general education and specialized education in computing.

Deciding how best to incorporate computers into schools, the focus of Chapters 5 and 6, must be coupled with skillful evaluation of computer-based and computer-related materials for the maximum instructional impact to be achieved. In Chapter 7, we move the discussion in this second direction and examine the topic of software evaluation.

References

APPLE PUGET SOUND PROGRAM LIBRARY EXCHANGE. *Call-A.P.P.L.E. in Depth—All about Pascal.* Renton, WA: A.P.P.L.E., 1984. (304 Main Avenue South, Suite 300, Renton, WA 98055).

BORK, ALFRED. "Computer-Based Instruction in Physics," in Dale Peterson (ed.), *The Intelligent Schoolhouse.* Reston, VA: Reston Publishing Company, 1985, pp. 117–130.

BRAUN, JOSEPH A., JR. *Microcomputers and the Social Studies.* New York: Garland Publishing, 1986.

BUDIN, HOWARD, KENDALL, DIANE S., & LENGEL, JAMES. *Using Computers in the Social Studies.* New York: Teachers College Press, 1986.

BURKHART, AUDREY C., MULLER, ELAINE, & O'NEIL, BARBARA. "Computers in the Home Economics Classroom," *Journal of Home Economics* 77, no. 3 (1984), pp. 24–31.

COLLEGE ENTRANCE EXAMINATION BOARD. *Advanced Placement Course Description: Computer Science.* Princeton, NJ: CEEB, 1984.

DIEM, RICHARD A. (ED.) "Technology and the Social Studies" (special section), *Social Education* 47 (1983), pp. 308–343.

DIJKSTRA, EDSGER. "GOTO Statement Considered Harmful," *Communications of the Association for Computing Machinery* 11, no. 3 (March 1968), pp. 147–148.

EGATZ, LAURA B. "How Does Telecommunications Fit into the Curriculum?" *Business Education Forum* 38, no. 7 (March 1984), pp. 25–29.

FAZIO, ROSARIO P., & BEVENTY, FRANCIS J. "Everyone Wins in Group Programming," *The Science Teacher* 50, no. 7 (September 1983), pp. 56–58.

FEINBERG, RICHARD, & WALTON, KATHY. "The Computers are Coming, The Computers are Coming: A Study of Human-Computer Social Interaction," *Home Economics Research Journal* 11, no. 4 (1983), pp. 319–326.

GRADY, M. TIM, & GAWRONSKI, JANE D. (EDS.) *Computers in Curriculum and Instruction.* Arlington, VA: Association for Supervision and Curriculum Development, 1983.

GRAEF, JEAN L. "The Computer Connection: Four Approaches to Microcomputer Laboratory Interfacing," *The Science Teacher* 50, no. 4 (April 1983), pp. 42–47.

HUBBARD, GUY, & LINEHAM, THOMAS E. "Arcade Games, Mindstorms, and Art Education," *Art Education* 36, no. 3 (May 1983), pp. 18–20.

MACE, SCOTT. "Science for the Home," *InfoWorld,* July 23, 1984, pp. 34–35.

MAIER, GENE. "We Have a Choice," *Mathematics Teacher* 76, no. 6 (September 1983), pp. 386–387.

MARTORELLA, PETER. "Software: Side by Side (Six Election Simulations)," *Electronic Learning,* September 1984, pp. 63–64.

MCMULLEN, LINDA. "Is Shorthand Dead, Terminally Ill, or Just Ailing?" *Business Education Forum* 38, no. 8 (April 1984), pp. 3–7.

NIGRO, JOHH S. "Prepare for Microcomputers With or Without Hardware," *Business Education Forum* 38, no. 9 (May 1984), pp. 20–22.

PERKINS, D. N. "The Fingertip Effect: How Information-processing Technology Shapes Thinking," *Educational Researcher* 14, no. 7 (1985), pp. 11–17.

PIELE, DONALD, "Computer-Assisted Mathematics," in M. Tim Grady & Jane D.

Gawronski (eds.), *Computers in Curriculum and Instruction.* Arlington, VA: Association for Supervision and Curriculum Development, 1983.

POLYA, G. *How to Solve It,* 2d ed. New York: Doubleday, 1957.

ROOZE, GENE E., & NORTHUP, TERRY. *Using Computers to Teach Social Studies.* Littleton, CO: Libraries Unlimited, 1986.

SLIND, L. H. "A New Look at Elementary Music Education," *Canadian Music Educator* 12 (1971), pp. 3–6.

STAGG, BEVERLY. "The Automated Office: What Will You Do with It?" *Business Education Forum* 38, no. 9 (May 1984), pp. 13–15.

SUYDAM, MARILYN N. "What Research Says: Microcomputers and Mathematics Education," *School Science and Mathematics* 84, no. 4 (April 1984), pp. 337–343.

TAYLOR, HARRIET G., & POIROT, JAMES L. "The certification of high school computer science teachers," *Capitol-izing on computers in education.* Proceedings of the 1984 Association of Educational Data Systems Annual Convention. Rockville, MD: Computer Science Press, 1984.

TITEN, HAROLD. "Computer Instruction in Marketing and Distributive Education," *Business Education Forum* 38, no. 1 (October 1983), pp. 28–29.

UPITIS, RENA. "The Synthesizer: A Bridge from Reality to Ideals in Music Education," *The Computing Teacher,* August 1983, pp. 54–57.

USISKIN, ZALMAN, "The Arithmetic Curriculum is Obsolete," *Arithmetic Teacher* 30, no. 9 (May 1983), p. 2.

WHITE, CHARLES S. "PFS:File Review," *Social Education* 49 (1985), pp. 228, 230–231.

WHITE, CHARLES S. "Software: Side by Side (Six Economics Simulations)," *Electronic Learning,* September 1984, pp. 60–61.

CHAPTER 7

The Qualities of Good Software

Introduction

A fundamental question we continue to ask is "What do we anticipate teachers will actually *do* with computers?" In our judgment, given the limited time and considerable demands on teachers in school, software development by teachers is unlikely. Teachers are not expected to write their own textbooks, and we should not expect teachers to produce the computer software they need. On the other hand, we *do* expect teachers to be skilled evaluators of instructional materials, whether in the form of textbooks, supplemental materials, or nonprint media. Therefore, our assumption here is that teachers must also be skilled evaluators of com-. puter-based materials. This is the primary role that teachers now perform in the process by which curriculum materials are produced, and we anticipate no major change in this role in the near future.

Chapter 7 thus begins with a discussion of two key concepts. The first involves the attributes of computer-based materials that are largely unique to this particular medium. Within this context, we will recapitulate a number of observations we made in Chapter 5, providing some more concrete examples of things to look for in software. The second relates to the problem of linking the various types of software defined in Chapter 5 to instructional goals. From this foundation, we will examine a number of evaluation instruments and consider the criteria they identify for assessing the quality of instructional software. We will also look at some additional criteria relevant to particular software types. The chapter concludes with some hints for applying criteria to software and for approaching the evaluation task.

This detailed discussion of software evaluation is crucial if computer-based instructional materials are to increase in quality and to be implemented effectively.

Key Concepts

There is more to evaluating educational software than making marks on an evaluation form. Two overarching questions must direct your approach to software evaluation: (1) How can I exploit the computer's most powerful, and often unique, capabilities? and (2) What kind of software is best suited to my instructional goals?

Exploiting Machine Capabilities

Central to any discussion of software evaluation is a firm understanding of what it is that the computer can do well. These capabilities, examined briefly in Chapter 5, might be best viewed as potentials, since their actualization depends on the skills of the development team that produced the software: the instructional designer, the content area specialist, and the programmers. Not all these capabilities need be present in every piece of instructional software, nor are they all unique to the computer medium, but each of the features, when used appropriately, is a sign of quality. The presence of these features gives added assurance to teachers that they are using the right instructional medium, the right tool, to accomplish the intended instructional purposes.

INTERACTIVITY   We have described interactivity as a two-way communication between computer and student, a kind of dialog. When gauging the level of interactivity of software, it might be useful to visualize a continuum. Consider, for example, a computer-based multiple-choice test. One could say that merely providing "correct" and "incorrect" as feedback is evidence of interactivity, though at a minimal level. Print material can display this degree of interactivity, while computer-based materials can go considerably further and provide informative feedback for each of the distractors (incorrect choices) used in this test. That is, distractors may be incorrect for different reasons, and the feedback for each distractor can explain to students *why* their choice was wrong.

At a higher level of interactivity, the flow of the program can be altered, based on the students' "response histories" (the collection of student responses analyzed as a whole). Again using the example of the multiple-choice test, the program could vary the difficulty level of questions either to challenge able students or to avoid counterproductive frustration for less able students. Or perhaps their series of responses indicate weakness in one of the concepts tested; the program could provide additional questions on that concept. This level of interactivity suggests a fairly complex branching design, and is the hallmark of high-quality software.

IMMEDIATE FEEDBACK   We noted earlier that unlike other media, the computer can provide immediate feedback for the student. The immediacy of feedback has a strong *motivational* quality and is one of several factors that make computer-based materials so attractive to learners. The justification for withholding feedback until the conclusion of a program would have to be very compelling in order to grade a program favorably.

INDIVIDUALIZATION   Using their management and branching capabilities, computer-based materials can provide for differences in the abilities of students. The computer program can work with a student one on one and, when exploiting its interactive and management capabilities to the fullest, can carry much of the burden once carried by the teacher alone. This is the essence of what individualization is. Good software adjusts the sequence of presentation to account for the differing learning needs of students.

Individual learning is also served well by software that allows control of the program to reside with the student. That is, the program is *user-controlled*. The *student* decides when to advance to the next screen, whether to do the remedial exercise immediately after the test, whether to ask for hints or for the directions again, when to leave the program, and so on.

ACTIVE LEARNING   Good software demands that students take an active role as the program unfolds. A skillfully designed simulation exemplifies the active learning capability of the computer. Students are called upon to respond to program prompts frequently and, more important, students are required to remain mentally engaged and to perform a broad range of cognitive operations. This is possible when the program blends the right mixture of interactivity, management, and individualization. Poor software requires little more than reading endless screens of text, with student action perhaps limited to "press space bar to continue."

DEVELOPMENT OF AND ACCESS TO DATA BASES   In Chapter 5, we described how the computer can store and process large amounts of information; indeed, one could say that these functions are fundamental to the nature of the computer. Only a small leap is needed to recognize the computer's potential as a "window" to a variety of existing data bases and its use in creating new ones.

With the computer hooked up to the telephone lines by way of a modem (see Chapter 4), students can access large amounts of information stored in large computers some distance from their microcomputer or terminal. The PLATO system is an example of such an arrangement within the context of CAI; while "The Source" and "CompuServe" are examples of accessible data bases. On a smaller scale, some software provides programs that allow students to represent the data stored on the disk or tape in different ways, encouraging students to draw inferences from the information. DEMO-GRAPHICS, a population studies program from CONDUIT, exemplifies this approach to data manipulation and interpretation. Students can request certain information to be drawn from the data base and can organize and rearrange the information in a variety of ways that facilitate interpretation. Nonetheless, the ability of computers to access increasing amounts of information must be matched by the students' abilities to reorganize, represent, and interpret information if the power of this capability is to be realized. Indeed, the need for new information skills in tune with the Information Age, as we discussed in Chapter 5, is one concern expressed by those involved in the relatively young discipline called *informatics.*

The ability to access and manipulate large amounts of data is, however, only one side of the coin. Through the use of data-base management systems, students can create their own data bases. The process of data-base development helps students learn about the nature of information and the range of ways in which information can be represented. Demographic information that students collect about their own community can constitute a data base. Survey data, sports statistics for school teams, results of science experiments, and collections of famous quotations from literature are other examples of potential data bases that students might find useful to store and manipulate.

INSTRUCTIONAL MANAGEMENT   Another manifestation of the computer's information-storage expertise is represented in CMI. As we described in an earlier chapter, some of these tasks involve scoring of student work. Computer-based materials can perform some of the interpretation of student performance as well. For example, at the conclusion a drill-and-practice program on regions of the United States, the computer might display the message: "You need to work a bit on midwestern agriculture, Mary." Here the program goes beyond simply scoring Mary's performance to diagnosing a learning need and prescribing remediation. The program may even go further and actually provide remediation: "Let's take a look at the Midwest again, Mary." A branch of the program would then help the student review that area of weakness, or the student might be directed to another program or to a chapter in a workbook or text.

A well-designed management software component doesn't forget the teacher, who remains the ultimate educational decision maker and guide. The teacher must be informed frequently about the student's progress through any computer-managed cycle of instruction, test, diagnosis, remediation, and retest. At any point in the cycle, the teacher must be able to intervene effectively, armed with computer-generated data and with professional insight, to head off student frustration and instructional stagnation. The latter condition can occur when a student is allowed to languish in an endless loop of instruction and remediation on the same concept or topic for weeks on end.

Knowledge of the computer's special capabilities will help you assess whether a particular piece of software is exploiting one or more of these features adequately. We have tried in this chapter to provide more concrete examples of these capabilities, as one guide to finding high-quality educational software. This knowledge will also help you decide whether this is the proper medium to select to accomplish certain objectives, or whether a textbook or film would perform the job equally well. The choice of an appropriate instructional medium requires more information, however. Given the various types of courseware available, the teacher must understand which kind of software is most effective for accomplishing certain kinds of instructional goals.

Linking Learning Objectives and Software Types

In Chapter 5 we described several categories of computer-assisted instructional software: drill-and-practice, tutorial, simulation, and problem-solving. No single category of software can support the full range of learning objectives in one's subject area. But each type of software can support a particular and limited range of objectives. Understanding the link between software types and learning objectives can assist the teacher in making wise use of CAI. The fundamental question here is whether this kind of CAI program helps accomplish the kind of learning objective the teacher has in mind.

Let's take an example of an objective you might want to accomplish: "The student should recall three fundamental parts of atoms." Remembering information is the core of this objective; you want the student to remember specific information. Would a drill-and-practice program help students remember these generalizations, assuming you've found a program with this particular content? Yes. In fact, the primary focus of drill and practice is the reinforcement of what the student must commit to memory. Let's try another.

Suppose you want students to interpret a bar graph representing the growth of U.S. GNP over the last 50 years. Would a drill-and-practice program that requires students to recall the peak and trough years over the same period help them interpret bar graphs? No. The focus of your objective is the skill of interpretation, a very different intellectual activity from memory recall. The program you really want is one that might ask students to choose the interpretation that is supported by a graph displayed on the screen. This might be a more involved practice program or a tutorial program.

Now let's really exercise the students' minds. Suppose you have just finished a unit on archaeology and the class has learned about the methods an archaeologist uses to discover information about ancient cultures. What kind of computer program could you use that would challenge students to apply their newly acquired knowledge? A drill-and-practice program just wouldn't work, because the student would just be recalling the steps an archaeologist uses, not really applying those steps. A tutorial program isn't quite right either, since your purpose is not to provide additional instruction. How about a simulated archaeological dig? To be successful in performing such a simulation, the students would have to apply their understanding of archaeological concepts and methods of investigation.

The example of an archaeological simulation would also be appropriate for these objectives: "Students will hypothesize about the relationships among the artifacts they have found" and "Students will assemble the artifacts and hypothesize about the culture that left these traces of their existence." Here, we are asking students to analyze and synthesize information, cognitive tasks supported by some good simulations, but which are far beyond the lower-order thinking skills demanded by drill-and-practice programs.

We have seen, then, that a single type of software (drill-and-practice, tutorial, simulation) cannot help students achieve all levels of intellectual skills. Your task, then, is to be clear about the level of intellectual skills you are looking for in each of your objectives and to identify the type of software most likely to encourage students to use that skill. A match between objective and software type is not always possible, of course, and this might be a good indication that the computer is just not the right medium or tool for the job. (Of course, some enterprising teachers may want to consider writing a program of their own).

From the two broad concepts involved in assessing the appropriateness and effectiveness of computer-based materials, we move now to some of the specific criteria for identifying what is good software.

Evaluation Instruments and Criteria

In recent years, software evaluation instruments and guides have proliferated. They vary in their level of detail and breadth of applicability to available software. None is entirely adequate for the task of software evaluation, but each contributes to a fuller understanding of what constitutes quality software. In the discussion of evaluation criteria that follows, we will examine a number of common criteria identified by these instruments and guides. We will then turn our attention to additional criteria targeted at specific software types.

General Criteria

MicroSIFT's *Evaluator's Guide for Microcomputer-Based Instructional Materials* (1983) provides a useful division of evaluation criteria into three categories: content, instructional quality, and technical quality. We will use this structure to discuss some general criteria for software evaluation.

QUALITY OF CONTENT   At the most obvious level, one hopes that the content of a particular piece of software is *accurate*. The facts and all associated graphs and numbers should be error-free. The software should also be grammatically accurate. If a program contains spelling, punctuation, and usage errors, send it back! There is no excuse for such errors. They do occur, but they can only be explained as shoddy development and evaluation techniques.

Beyond mere accuracy, you'll want to be sure that the content is really relevant to your needs; that it fits well into what you're teaching, requiring only minimal effort to incorporate the software into your lesson plans. You'll never find perfect software, just as you'll never find the perfect film or textbook. But if you have to consider making major changes in the content of lessons or their objectives in order to make the software useful, you probably have the wrong piece of software.

Finally, teachers need to be as sensitive to the existence of subtle, often unintended messages transmitted in courseware content as in any other instructional medium. For example, the content should should be free from stereotyping or discrimination based on ethnic background, race, or sex.

INSTRUCTIONAL QUALITY   When you're satisfied that the content of the courseware you are evaluating is of acceptable quality, you need to establish that it conforms to fundamental principles of instructional design. One rather basic requirement is that the purpose of the courseware is explained. Somewhere, either in the software or in printed support materials, you should be able to find a statement of purpose and a list of clearly stated objectives. Poor courseware forces you and your students to guess what it intends students to be able to do after they have used it. You should be able to look at the list of objectives for the software and compare them with the objectives you have set for your lesson or unit.

The road to developing quality computer courseware, however, is littered with good intentions. It is not enough to examine the stated objectives of a program. You must decide whether the software accomplishes the objectives it claims to attain. Unless you have students actually use the software and unless you administer a test based on the objectives, only your judgment and experience can guide you when you work through the program yourself. Other teachers who have used the program with students are valuable resources for establishing the effectiveness of software, so seek them out.

Accomplishing the stated objectives requires sensitivity to an array of features that support software effectiveness. The content must be presented clearly, in a sensible, logical manner. Graphics, sound, and color should be used appropriately to highlight important information and to provide the user with cues for subsequent action. Inappropriate or gratuitous use of any of these features creates a distraction and reduces effectiveness. The screen displays should support the content to be addressed, rather than getting lost in the special effects.

Effectiveness is also in jeopardy when the style, difficulty, or reading level of the material does not match the audience for which it was intended. Good software will describe the kind of students for which it was developed and will state the prerequisite skills it assumes the students already possess before they use the software. You must judge whether these skills are realistic for the students of a given age or grade level.

Good software, like good noncomputer materials in general, is more useful if it is motivational. But flashy displays alone cannot retain student interest. Interest is maintained when the computer communicates with the child in a natural, conversational manner, and when a variety of screen presentation formats is used. Motivation is also increased if the child's creativity is challenged and if the learner is given control over the rate, sequence, and review of material. Programs should avoid delays between screens of more than two or three seconds; if this is not possible, keep the student informed about what's happening (for example, "BE PATIENT, SUZY. I'M THINKING."). The quality of feedback also enhances motivation, if it is credible and nonthreatening.

Beyond its potential motivational qualities, feedback can also support software effectiveness generally, but only if it possesses some important qualities. Feedback should be personalized and timely; it should explain and remediate; and it should direct the student to the appropriate next step in the learning sequence.

TECHNICAL QUALITY From the standpoint of technical quality, the paramount criterion to assess is whether the software works reliably. Are there bugs in the program that make it stop suddenly and inexplicably and no amount of punching of keys will let you continue? Does the program load into the computer reliably? Reliable operation is important for at least two reasons. First, an unreliable program cannot be used easily by students. Of course, even many reliably operating programs require inordinate amounts of supervision, and once again such programs should be avoided. Students should be able to use the program independently. The student should be able to access the program quickly, and the program itself should load into the computer's memory quickly. Second, an unreliable program cannot be used easily by the teacher. The teacher should not have to be a computer expert to get the program running and to keep it running.

A good piece of courseware is "classroom-friendly." That is, the program has been designed with the realities of classroom organization and management in mind. The software should be adaptable to a variety of classroom environments, including the situation where one computer is to be used in an entire class of 30 students. Some of this flexibility can be attained if comprehensive and clear support materials are provided. Yes, software evaluation does require an examination of support material; it's all part of the same package.

Given a program that is reliable, easy to use, and classroom-friendly, we must still assess whether information displays are effective. What do the screens look alike? Are the displays consistent, and are students able to respond to prompts in a consistent manner? Are screens barely readable because of text overcrowding? Is the text wordy or ambiguous? Are students presented with too many concepts at a time? Are students forced to handle large quantities of abstract, rather than concrete, information? Does the effectiveness of a screen depend on color? Does the screen scroll? That is, do lines disappear from the top of the screen as new lines appear at the bottom? They should not. Each screen should appear as a whole "page," like a book, to be replaced by the next screen. Can the sound be turned off? It is difficult to engage students in large-group instruction when one or two students at the classroom's computer produce distracting music or other sounds built into some software.

This overview of general software evaluation criteria may seem to present the teacher-evaluator with an enormous task. Yet, the fact is that the more software you view, the easier it is to separate the electronic wheat from the chaff. Each of the features of good software will appear somewhere in the collection of products you examine over time, though no single package will be perfect. Diligence in software evaluation reaps at least two important benefits. Your ultimate selection and use of software will be more likely to enhance the progress of your students. Moreover, using these general criteria to identify good software will help insure that the school's costly investment in hardware is not wasted. In the final analysis, the best of machines running the worst of software results in an inferior tool for assisting instruction.

A Special Word About Simulations

In Chapter 5, we described a simulation as a computer representation of some environment or system, either real or imaginary. Some environments or systems are simple enough that every piece can be specified and reproduced on the computer, together with all the relationships among pieces. Once the system becomes the least bit complex, it becomes increasingly difficult to specify all its parts, to represent those parts in a program, and to reproduce the tangle of relationships among the parts. Representing those relationships becomes particularly difficult if they change in complicated, perhaps unpredictable ways. Simulations in the social sciences are especially difficult to produce because of the complexity of social systems. Special criteria need to be applied to simulations, then, in order to assess their match with reality and, thus, their effectiveness for instruction.

Faced with the challenge of reducing complexity into a computerized facsimile, simulation designers use simplified models of systems or environments that deviate from reality in certain respects. It is important for simulation software packages to describe the model on which the simulation is based. We need to know what assumptions about the system or environment form the basis for the model. Of course, we want to see what assumptions have been excluded as well.

Among the assumptions to be examined is how the parts of the model relate to each other. Given a change in one part, do the other parts change in a manner that matches reality? For example, consider a simulation of an international confrontation centered on Berlin. Given a range of possible U.S. responses to a Soviet threat on Berlin, are the consequences of these responses credible? We would question the accuracy of the model if, for example, the Soviets back down at the slightest expression of U.S. opposition.

While it is unrealistic to expect that simulation designers will include all possible parts of an environment in their model, the assumptions of the designers determine which parts of the environment are most important to include in the model. Evaluating simulations requires you to judge whether the designers really have included the key factors, and have not omitted important ones. In a simulation that reproduces the motion of an object along an inclined plane, we would want to be sure that the effect of friction is included in the model. Otherwise, the simulated environment is an incomplete representation of reality (assuming that the intended reality is earth-bound).

Beyond the assumptions about the simulated environment, teachers evaluating simulations should assess the nature and quality of learner intervention allowed by the software. Not only should the learner be able to become directly involved in the environment or system, but that intervention should occur at credible points in the simulation. The kinds of decisions students make in the simulation should model the decisions made by real people in the actual environment or system. The decision alternatives should be believable and consistent with key assumptions about the workings of the system or process simulated. The consequences of student decisions must also be credible, again based on the model's assumptions. Finally, a good simulation allows the teacher (and perhaps the student) to alter some of the simulation's assumptions and to examine the results of those changes.

Tips for Evaluation, Documentation, and Preview of Software

Understanding what makes software good is only one half of the challenge of evaluation. The other half is applying those criteria in some systematic way and communicating your judgments to your colleagues.

Helpful Steps in Evaluating Software

SPECIFY YOUR EXPECTATIONS IN ADVANCE   As you sit down at a computer to evaluate software, one can assume you are doing so for one of two reasons: you have requested this piece of software, in the hope that it will be appropriate for your students, or this is one of several programs you have been asked to evaluate for other teachers. Whichever of these pertains determines your initial approach to the issue of *objectives*. If the former is the case, your first step in the evaluation process is to identify the objectives you wish this software to help accomplish. (We assume you have decided at this point that these objectives cannot be met by existing materials, print-based or otherwise.) Consider whether your objectives are realistic, given the amount of computer time your students are likely to have. What will be your expectations and requirements as you approach this software? Be explicit. You might even write them down. Doing so will avoid the temptation to mold your objectives to the software, rather than the other way around.

The prespecification of objectives is more difficult, of course, if you find yourself previewing software for someone else, perhaps someone in a subject area that is unfamiliar to you (more likely at the secondary school level). Teachers who assume the role of in-house computer expert are often put in this position. If this becomes *your* role, you have several alternatives. Check to see if a colleague in that subject area would like to collaborate with you in evaluating the software. If not, solicit from that teacher and from others what objectives they'd like to see addressed in software. Course outlines generally would be helpful in establishing expectations. And do this *before* the software is viewed and evaluated.

READ ALL ACCOMPANYING DOCUMENTATION FIRST   Documentation includes manuals, teacher's guides, and student workbooks or activity sheets. Reading this material *first* has several benefits. First, the print material often states explicitly what the objectives of the program are. If they do not, you should expect either to see objectives stated in the software or to assign the program low marks for making you guess. This is one point at which you should compare your own objectives with those stated (or inferred) in the documentation. In the case of simulations, this initial reading should provide you with an overview of the model used by the developer(s). At the very least, you should be able to infer some of the model's structure and assumptions at this point. Second, you can begin to gauge the classroom-friendliness of the software, based on the quantity and quality of suggestions for preparing the students for the program, for running the software in a variety of classroom settings, and for postcomputer activities or readings. Third, the documentation can suggest to you how much time you and your students will need to learn how to use the program effectively. Complex directions making frequent reference to "what is on the screen" may mean more preparation and training for everyone. This is not necessarily bad, since greater complexity may translate into greater flexibility of use and a bigger instructional payoff. You need to know, however, how much time it will cost to gain the promised benefits.

Of course, not all educational software is accompanied by manuals or other supplemental material. Some products claim that all you need to know about the program and its operation appears on the disk or cassette. And yet since considerable information is needed by teachers and students to use programs effectively, one should approach such a claim with healthy skepticism. In many cases, what the producers have provided on the disk is wholly inadequate. In the absence of even this amount of accompanying information, the usefulness of the software to the teacher and students is severely diminished. Indeed, teachers may have to spend as much time reconstructing the missing information or creating the necessary supplements as they would have to spend on preparing non-computer-based instructional materials.

THE FIRST RUN-THROUGH   After you've made your way through the material that accompanies the software, assuming any is provided, the next step is to run through the program once. Play it straight, making a sincere effort to follow the instructions provided. If students need to take notes or complete tables, you might try it yourself or at least make an estimate of how long that writing would take.

At the completion of this first run, you should have accomplished four things. Any monumental errors will have been readily apparent; for example, the program crashes (such as "BREAK IN 405," which forces the program to end abruptly) or hangs (no cursor appears on the screen and no user actions can move the program forward). There is no guarantee that you'll find these problems on the first run, since a single run will not have accessed all the parts of a complicated piece of software. This is especially true for simulations and other programs with significant amounts of branching. Beyond gross errors, you will also have some feel for how long it takes to work through the software, adding time if you think your students will need it. The time factor is also dependent on the clarity and overall effectiveness of the instructions both on the screen and in the documentation. This first run is an excellent time to judge the quality of instructions. Third, you should now have some impressions about the credibility of the program and its relevance to your needs. This is the second place for you to check for a match between your expectations and objectives with those of the software. Finally, you can begin to assess the extent to which the objectives stated in the documentation (or on the disk itself) are actually addressed *and* accomplished by the program. This is also a good time to jot down your reactions and impressions thus far, based on the general and specific criteria outlined earlier.

THE SECOND RUN-THROUGH   A single stroll through a program is insufficient to evaluate a piece of software adequately. Evaluating software is a bit like buying a new car. You thought you saw all the flaws the first time you opened the hood, kicked the tires, and took it for a spin around town. It is amazing, though, how many minor (and sometimes major) annoyances crop up after driving it for a few weeks. Lemons take time to ripen. This is true with software as well, so take it for at least one more "spin" before making final judgments about its quality.

The purposes of this second run-through are threefold. First, you want to reconfirm the impressions you formed during the first run. Is the program really as good or as bad as you thought at first? Does the program really fit your objectives, or will its use require major or undesirable alterations in your curriculum? Second, you want to put the program through its paces and see how well it handles unexpected user actions. Third, you want to view branches of the program you did not see during the first run. Indeed, the more complex the software, the more times you should run it in order to view a good representation of the branches.

In this second run, assume the perspective of an absolute novice. At every opportunity, try to make mistakes. Observe how the program handles the following input errors: (1) alphanumeric instead of numeric values, (2) CTRL-C or RESET, (3) out-of-range input, and (4) nonsense input. A good program should trap input errors like these. It should let the user know that an input error has been made and provide a reminder about the type or range of input being requested. Certainly, a program shouldn't crash or hang because of a user error, and entering and leaving a program should be accomplished by responding to program options, not because of a slip of the finger. If it can happen to you, it will surely happen to your students.

When you are satisfied that you have challenged the software sufficiently and have seen all or at least a significant portion of the software under review, you'll want to put your judgments down on paper (or maybe on disk) for the benefit of others.

Writing Up Your Comments

One way of communicating your evaluation of software to others, or keeping a record of your judgments for future reference, is to complete a checklist form that rates each criterion along a continuum from poor to excellent or from disagree to agree, depending on the questions. There are numerous such checklists available commercially, or you may decide to design your own. In any case, a checklist alone does not provide adequate information. Aside from a checklist rating, you need to ask what teachers need to know about a piece of software.

Certainly, your colleagues will want to know the objectives of the program. You may have to examine the software closely before you can determine what those objectives are, but they are at least inferred. Something more than a title is due as well. Describe the type and content of the program or package in a few sentences, perhaps identifying what subjects or classes might find the software relevant. In this regard, specify as well the target audience for the program. For what grade level is it appropriate? Can it be used for remediation at the upper grade limit or for gifted younger students? Is it intended for a very specific or narrow audience (such as those with special learning needs or physical handicaps)? What prerequisite knowledge must students have in order to use this software effectively?

Teachers also need to have some feel for a program's actual classroom use. How long will it take? Is it useful only in a one student–one computer setting? Can it be used in whole group instruction or something in between? Does it keep track of student performance, that is, does it have a management component? Most importantly, has it been used successfully in real classrooms with real student? Sometimes software producers provide information about field testing, indicating that the programs have been used by students. If possible, get confirmation of what was done. If you or one of your colleagues uses the program in a class, feedback about how well or poorly it worked is very useful and should be incorporated into any written evaluation comments. Also, if you have seen a review of the program in a computing magazine or educational journal, provide the citation so others can read another evaluator's assessment.

Finally, if the fruits of your evaluative labors will be disseminated beyond your school building, or perhaps your school district, you might add information on how to acquire the program and what equipment is required for its use.

The more software you see and the more formal evaluations you perform, the easier it will be to separate the good from the bad in instructional software. Armed with all this information, you and others can make wise decisions about software that deserves a place in your classroom.

Acquiring Software for Evaluation

The purpose of evaluating software is to avoid buying and using inappropriate or inferior computer-based materials. The assumption, of course, is that you haven't already had to purchase the program you are just now about to evaluate. Until relatively recently, educators had no choice but to buy software sight unseen. The root of this situation lies in the software development industry.

When microcomputers first entered the schools, most available software was produced either by small "mom and pop" companies working out of the family basement or garage, or by more sophisticated computer software firms just entering the school market. Neither understood much about education, teaching, or schools and saw no reason to adopt what has been common within the textbook industry for years—free preview of materials prior to sale or on-approval sales. In the latter case, the school purchases the materials, but may return them for a full refund within some specified time period (usually 30 days).

Indeed, there was (and continues to be) a real disincentive to allowing preview of software; that is, software is easily copied. While copy-protection techniques have improved, so have lock-picking techniques. A school or individual could simply copy the preview disk, return it without paying a dime, and still enjoy full use of the program. It is no wonder that software developers refused to provide more than a description to potential buyers. But since textbooks companies have entered the educational software market, the 30-day approval standard has become much more widespread. Where exceptions to this exist, many companies will at least sell demonstration disks for a nominal fee, though the on-approval system is preferable from an evaluative perspective.

Teachers and schools can take positive action to increase the opportunities for on-approval purchases and even outright previewing of software, but one negative action must stop—software piracy. When you copy commercial software, you violate copyright laws and open yourself to prosecution. You send a message to producers that allowing previewing and approval sales are not worth the cost of stolen software. Moreover, no company is going to increase its investment to produce higher-quality software if it cannot recoup those development costs through sales revenues. Perhaps most importantly, you transmit a message to your students that the use of computers need not conform to ethical or legal standards.

Producers will continue to allow prepurchase evaluation if software acquired on approval is returned promptly, within the 30-day limit. Under some circumstances, companies will even send preview software without requiring a purchase order. Some organizations have been successful at persuading companies to furnish products for software preview sessions at professional meetings or staff development workshops. They have promised in writing (1) to refrain from copying the software, (2) to refrain from generating a copy of the program code or performing screen dumps (transferring individual screens to hard copy), (3) to maintain sufficient control over its use to prevent others from copying the software, and (4) to return the software in original condition within 14 days of the session. As an extra incentive, you might offer to have workshop participants fill out comment cards for each piece of software they preview and forward them to the companies when you return the programs.

If you are starting from scratch with computers, a brief letter to software distributors (see Appendix D) will yield one or more copies of their latest catalogues. Once they arrive, you can survey the available software and begin to identify potentially useful programs. Whether your next step is to purchase on approval or to request preview copies, be sure to describe the equipment your school owns or will have access to during the previewing stage. Include computer brand and size of memory (in K), together with type of input medium and available peripherals. You can save some time and confusion if you request only that software that can run on the available equipment. Once the software arrives, you're in business and ready to apply your evaluation skills.

Evaluation of Teacher Utility Software

Up to this point, we have been discussing the evaluation of courseware—software intended primarily for use by students in support of instructional content in the school curriculum. There is another type of software, however, that plays an important role in the organization and delivery of instruction. *Teacher utility software* helps the teacher maintain records of student performance, organize resources, produce instructional print material, and develop computer-based lessons. Each of these categories of teacher utilities will be described in this section, and criteria for their evaluation will be suggested.

Gradebook Programs

GRADEBOOKS DESCRIBED   There is considerable variation in the kinds of gradebook programs currently available for microcomputers, but all share the professed purpose of replacing the teacher's traditional paper-and-pencil gradebook. The teacher enters the roster of students for each class and thereafter enters grades on whatever assignments, projects, quizzes, and tests have been required during the term.

The real advantage of computerized gradebooks appears at the end of a grading period, when the computer automatically calculates the summative grade of each student, saving the teacher considerable time. Current levels of student performance can also be calculated and obtained at any time during a term. With the ability of most gradebooks to provide a hard copy of its contents, these programs can reduce some of the paperwork usually associated with grading. Moreover, depending on the gradebook's sophistication, the teacher can generate a greater amount of information on student performance in a relatively short time. This can help the teacher to keep track of student progress and to transmit information on that progress regularly to parents.

EVALUATING GRADEBOOKS   Given the variety of gradebooks available and the even greater variety of grading policies and preference among teachers and schools, these utilities require evaluation just as much as the other programs we have discussed. In fact, perhaps the first criterion to apply is the extent to which the particular gradebook matches your or your school's grading policies or preferences. For example, some teachers prefer to use letter grades in assessing student work. How much work will be involved in converting letter grades into a form acceptable to the particular gradebook program? If numerical equivalents for letter grades are built into the software, do these values match your own system of equivalence? Can grades be weighted to reflect the variation of importance of assignments, quizzes, or tests? How complicated is the weighting system, and does it match the way you weight grades? Finally, how can more subjective evaluation of student performance be integrated into this electronic gradebook? If you find yourself overhauling your current grading system unnecessarily to fit the software, you'd probably be better off looking for another gradebook program or keeping your book and pen.

Another consideration in evaluating a gradebook program is whether its reporting capabilities match your needs and those of your school. Ideally, a gradebook should generate an end-of-term report than can be submitted directly to the school office without having to transfer it again by hand to some other form. You need to collaborate with the administrators in your school (and they with district administrators) to find the most acceptable reporting format that is compatible with available software. If agreement is not possible, then you should seek out the gradebook program that will require the least amount of extra work to transfer to the approved report form.

Size and flexibility are also important qualities to assess. With respect to size, can the program store and process all of the grades you will give for each of your students across all your classes? This might mean 50 grades for each of 150 students, or more. If there is not enough room on the gradebook disk to store this much, can you use separate data disks? If so, you've solved the storage part (it would be almost essential to have two disk drives in this case), but if the program cannot process this much data, it's time to look for another program. In the case of flexibility, you are looking for a gradebook that can arrange and display students in a variety ways (alphabetically, rank order, placing new students at the end of the roster), can account for late or excused assignments, and can accept changes in grade values and weighting with a minimum of effort. A gradebook that is compatible with other software, such as attendance programs and CMI software, would be a real plus.

You cannot take for granted that a gradebook program calculates grades accurately, especially where incompletes, grade changes, class averages, and standard deviations are included functions. You would be well advised to enter a sample roster and double check the calculations to ensure the accuracy of the program. Using the computer to generate more information more quickly is futile if the information is incorrect.

Teachers are always concerned, and rightly so, about the security of gradebooks, whether the paper-and-pencil version or electronic. It is important, then, to examine the security features that have been designed into the software. Two levels of security are typical in software. The first limits access to any of the programs just after the disk is booted. The user must enter a secret password in order to continue in the program. The teacher needs to be sure that unauthorized persons do not learn the password. A good security system allows the user to change the password periodically. The second level of security rests in standard copy protection techniques that prevent users from obtaining program listings. A bright student who can access the program code can circumvent the security measures. Ultimately, though, if someone is determined enough, almost any software security system can be broken, so teachers' need to observe commonsense measures to prevent their gradebooks from falling into the wrong hands.

Gradebooks have the potential of saving teachers both time and effort. If the gradebook program you are evaluating seems to do neither, look elsewhere.

Materials Generation

Computer programs are available that can help the teacher create print material for classroom use. The software can be placed in two general categories: general purpose programs and single-purpose programs. The former is represented in the range of word processing software. The latter includes test generators, puzzle makers, and similar programs.

WORD PROCESSORS   A word processor is a type of software that turns your computer into a sort of electronic typewriter. Instead of typing words on a paper, though, your words are stored in the computer's memory, displayed on the monitor, saved (if you wish) on a disk, and eventually printed out on paper.

There are several advantages to using a word processor. First, editing is extremely easy and fast. In an instant, spelling can be changed, words can be deleted, sentences can be added, paragraphs can be moved, and dates can be changed. The program makes all the other changes that are needed when you edit, keeping in mind the line length, margins, and page lengths you have selected. Second, because the editing is so easy, you can compose and edit at the keyboard—no worrying about having to retype an entire document when changes are made. Once you store the edited version of a handout or worksheet, just attach your computer to the printer and generate an updated copy at 80 to 120 (characters per second), a typical range for dot-matrix printers.

For the teacher, all the handouts, worksheets, assignments, quizzes, and tests you use in the course of a year can be stored on disk. One disk can store sixty or more double-spaced pages of text. The next time you need a particular document, you recognize that some changes are needed—perhaps the information is outdated or you've learned that some part didn't work very well last time. No need to start from scratch; just load the old worksheet, make your changes, and print it out. The paper used in most printers found in schools can be replaced with ditto masters, so with lightening speed you have a ditto ready to run off, and you can save the revised document on disk until you need it again.

Students enjoy many of the same advantages as teachers when they use a word processor for their own writing. The ease of editing encourages students to overcome their reluctance to view their work as simply a first draft. Students whose poor handwriting was a personal obstacle to writing can take pride in the polished appearance of the work they produce on a word processor. Reluctant writers can become enthusiastic writers; enthusiastic writers may become prolific writers. Both come to recognize that good writing is the result of both initial creation and ongoing improvement.

Evaluating word processors could itself take an entire chapter, given the dozens of individual features available in various programs. For purposes of this section, we will limit the discussion to some general criteria you can use in evaluating word processors for support of materials generation for the classroom.

A general rule of thumb is to look for the simplest and least expensive program that has the functions you are actually going to use, allowing some leeway for future, unanticipated word processing needs. Expensive programs allow you to produce footnotes and to generate all sorts of character enhancements (boldface, underlining, subscripts, superscripts, italics, and the like). If you are teaching math or science at the secondary level, you are likely to need subscripts (for chemical formulas) and superscripts (for exponents). If you teach English composition and require your students to learn footnoting, superscripts, and a fairly sophisticated footnoting routine then these are necessary elements in a word processor. If you rarely produce documents that require these and other "bells and whistles," why pay for them? Moreover, the more sophisticated word processors take a good deal of time to learn and master. This point is particularly important as you consider an appropriate word processor for your students to learn and use. So, take a look at the kinds of print materials that you and your students create now and see what features are really needed.

A second rule of thumb is to seek a word processor whose screen display is a close facsimile of what you'll see on the printed page. It is simply easier to use a program that does not force you to do a lot of visualizing as you try to edit and format a document the way you want. For student use, you certainly do not want more time spent visualizing the appearance of the end product than in considering the quality of its substance. Thus, finding a program that displays at least sixty-four columns (or even better, eighty columns) and upper/lower case on the screen will end up being easier to use. Some computers need to be modified to allow eighty columns, requiring the purchase of a special circuit board inserted inside the computer. Some word processors get around this added expense by producing a sixty-four to eighty column display within their own software. Also, newer computers have upper/lower case capability built in, but older models require a modification to produce lower case. Again, some word processors produce lower case artifically by means of the software.

This brings us to a third rule of thumb: be sure the word processor you like matches your equipment. This includes not only the computer brand, but the computer's ability to produce sufficiently wide screen display and to display upper-and lower-case characters. This also includes the kind of printer you have. Word processing software needs to be "configured" for particular printers and their features, so be sure yours is on the list of compatible printers.

Finally, keep your eye out for articles in computer and consumer magazines that compare word processors and their features. Since new programs and improved versions of old ones appear on the market regularly, review articles also appear often. And ask friends and colleagues: they are equally rich sources of information.

SINGLE-PURPOSE MATERIALS GENERATORS   One of the great advantages of word processors is their flexibility in generating documents. This flexibility is gained, however, by requiring the user to learn the dozens of commands that give the word processor its power. While editing time is accelerated, the time required to design special forms is still considerable. For example, word processors do not save much time when your document is a crossword puzzle. Where time is at a premium and ease of first use is important, single-purpose programs may be more desirable, though sacrificing some flexibility.

Among these utility programs are those that produce wordfinds, crossword puzzles, banners, and posters. For wordfinds and puzzles, you may be instructed to enter the words you wish to use, followed by clues or hints. The computer does the work of placing the words in a maze of letters or in a crossword matrix. For these materials, as well as for banners and posters, the program takes care of the design and formatting of hard copy, a distinct advantage over the word processor.

Another class of material-generating software—the test generators—helps the teacher in evaluating student performance. Some are sold with a large pool of prepackaged questions, and most allow teachers to write their own questions. Most are very simple to use, requiring only that the teacher enter the question, followed by the acceptable answers. That collection of questions is given a test title, and students can take the test either at a computer or by completing a printed copy, if the latter feature is available in the test generator program. A major advantage of test generators is that a large pool of questions can be maintained, edited, and administered very efficiently. The potential exists for more frequent evaluation of student performance and thus more knowledge of student needs. Since only objective-type tests are produced by test generators, the teacher cannot rely solely on this kind of software for evaluating student work; therein lies an important limitation of this class of teacher utility.

The fundamental standard to use in evaluating a single-purpose materials generator is whether its final product conforms to your needs. Therefore, the first step in the evaluation process is to specify the kinds of materials you use or would like to use. For example, do you design crossword puzzles as part of instruction, or *would* you use crosswords if they could be easily produced? If so, what vocabulary would be present? Can the crossword puzzle program you are evaluating support that vocabulary? Specifically, does this program accept a large enough base of words, words of sufficient length, clues of sufficient complexity?

You should apply this standard to test generators as well. Given the nature of these programs, you must ask yourself whether you use, or wish to use, objective tests as one measure of student performance. Do you write such tests with an eye to explicit instructional objectives (or would you like to do this)? If so, does the test generator you are evaluating allow you to key questions to instructional objectives? Do you like to use a variety of question formats for objective tests, such as multiple choice, fill-ins, matching, and short answer? If so, are varying formats available in this test generator or are you locked into a single format? Will the program allow more than one correct answer for each question? Is there sufficient storage capacity on the disk for all the students to whom you would administer the test or tests? And don't forget to check how the security of information on the disk is handled by the program, if at all. If you will not have access to multiple computers, will the program generate hard copies of the test? Can it produce different forms of the same test (useful when administering tests to students who were absent on the day the test was given)?

As with other teacher utility software, you should expect the programs to be relatively easy to use, both with respect to entering information and editing it at a later date. The time and energy required to use materials generators must be weighed against the benefits you believe their use will bring. If the benefits lose, wait until another program comes along.

Resource Management

RESOURCE-MANAGEMENT PROGRAMS DESCRIBED   Good teachers are, by nature, savers. Articles, posters, photographs, lesson outlines from years past and hundreds of other odds and ends are squirreled away with the idea that next week, or next year, they will come in handy for making an instructional point with students. Of course, a resource is only useful if it can be found and put to use by the teacher, or by the student. Amazingly, a good many teachers can put their hands on any one particular item at a moment's notice; yet, as time passes, the management of these resources can become a big job. The computer with the right kind of software might be an answer to these teachers' needs.

While the word processor can be used to help manage resources, there is a category of software specifically designed for this task. These are called *data-base management (DBM)* programs. The data base is the collection of resources you need to keep track of. The program manages that data base by allowing you to call up information about those resources quickly. Conversely, a DBM program allows you to store information about resources in an orderly fashion and in a way that allows for rapid recall of that resource. Programs range in flexibility and complexity from simple filing and inventory programs to full-blown data-base management systems. Let's examine an example of how a typical DBM program might work for the you.

One of your students expressed an interest in learning more about the nuclear energy industry. You know you have some resources that would be helpful, but you haven't used them in some time. You take your DBM program and your own data disk to the computer and type in "NUCLEAR ENERGY," which happens to be a keyword you used to label this group of resources when you set up your data base. In a flash, a list of items appears on the screen, all relating to the student's interest. For each item, you have recorded a brief description and have indicated where you stored it—the kind of information you might write on index cards. Fortunately, the computer does the work of flipping through the "cards." The next time you see your student, you'll be able to provide the resources needed to pursue that interest.

EVALUATING RESOURCE-MANAGEMENT PROGRAMS   Inventory or DBM programs are not for everyone. The purpose of this class of software is to maintain control over what has become an unmanageable amount of resources. If your own resources are still at your fingertips, and few items get lost and thus underused, there seems little reason to invest the time in learning to use a resource-management package. On the other hand, if you've accumulated a sizable amount of material, or if you are in charge of a resource collection (such as a library or media center), this sort of tool may be the answer to a growing headache. The ultimate goal is to maximize the usefulness of resources while minimizing the time required to access them.

As with word processors, choose the simplest program that still satisfies your needs. Those needs include the amount of information to be stored, the compatibility with existing hardware, the required detail of reports (communicating information on the desired subset of resources), and the complexity of keyword structure, where applicable. The latter two features require some explanation.

If you are in charge of a school's or department's resources, you may be required to produce reports that describe some of those resources, perhaps in response to someone's inquiry. The most sophisticated programs give you maximum flexibility in designing your own report forms, determining the most useful way to display the requested information. Simpler programs provide only crude output, requiring additional work to put the information into the needed form. If you use the program just for yourself, though, you may not need more than "just the facts." If flexibility of report format is not important to you, the simpler program would be easier to learn and to use.

The sophistication of keyword structure is partly determined by the amount and range of resources you must manage. In the example of nuclear energy, only one keyword was needed to access the relevant information. That teacher probably does not need to specify subcategories of nuclear energy materials. But what if you were asked for a list of teaching materials for grades seven to twelve in the area of nuclear energy? This request assumes that you are managing a resource base that is rather extensive; that is, it assumes that you also have nuclear energy resources that are *not* teaching materials and are *not* for grades seven to twelve. In this case, at least three keywords are needed ("nuclear energy," "grades 7–12," and "teaching materials"), and all must be present for a particular resource to appear on the list. This second example requires a more sophisticated program, while the first can be accomplished by simpler filing software. Even more sophisticated software allows you to specify relationships among keywords; like a library's card catalog, it may suggest that you "see also" items under different keywords.

Resource management software varies in its flexibility and power. The bottom line in choosing the right program for you is this: determine how much flexibility and power you need, add a bit more of each to allow for later unanticipated needs, and use the program that does no more than the sum of these needs. It makes little sense to buy the "cutting-edge" software if it is too complex for most people to use effectively.

Authoring Tools

Teachers sometimes decide that they would like to try their hand at creating some of their own computer-based lessons. Perhaps the impetus for doing so will arise from the absense of software in a particular topic area or from impatience with the poor quality of available software. Of this group of teachers, a number will invest their energies in learning to program in BASIC or Pascal or some other standard computer language. Most cannot afford such a time commitment but would still like to create some of their own CAI. For them, the answer may well be an authoring tool.

AUTHORING SYSTEM VERSUS AUTHORING LANGUAGE While we introduced the concept of authoring languages in Chapter 4, it is important to note that these are only half of what may be referred to generally as authoring tools. The other half consists of authoring systems. *Authoring systems* are little more than lesson frameworks on which teachers can hang the information to be presented, the questions to be asked, and the feedback to be supplied. For example, some such systems simply ask you to type in a question, then prompt you to provide the answer you will accept as correct. The framework provided by authoring systems is relatively inflexible and relies on the fact that many simple CAI lessons share the same basic format. The final product is a simple tutorial program, with drill practice features tied in. *Authoring languages* are more sophisticated tools, allowing the teacher to design the lesson framework as well as the content of the framework. In a sense, authoring languages share many characteristics of general computer languages but are designed for a special purpose. Authoring languages differ from languages like BASIC or Pascal in that they are designed for a level of communication that is more understandable to the user; that is, as BASIC is more understandable to the user than is machine language, an authoring language is more understandable to the user than is BASIC.

Authoring systems are easier to use than authoring languages. This ease of use, though, is gained at the expense of flexibility. Each new lesson produced by an authoring system tends to look the same as the last lesson produce. Authoring languages help you avoid this rut, but flexibility comes at the expense of easy use. Ease of use is a relative term, of course, and it is significant to note that an authoring language is considerably easier to learn than a general purpose computer language.

EVALUATING AUTHORING TOOLS   The primary question to ask when evaluating authoring tools relates to the quality of the final product: does the CAI lesson you develop with the tool compare favorably to commercially developed CAI lessons when you apply the evaluation criteria we have described earlier in this chapter? Let's face it: producing a CAI lesson, either by writing a BASIC program or by using an authoring tool, is not the same as *designing* a lesson. There is little to be gained if an authoring tool simply allows you to produce poorly designed lessons more quickly. At least two conditions must be met before quality lessons can be designed and produced by teachers using authoring tools: (1) teachers must possess a clear understanding of fundamental CAI lesson design standards and procedures, and (2) the authoring tool must have sufficient flexibility to support high-quality courseware design features that are assessed by most evaluation instruments. Since the first of these conditions lies outside the scope and purposes of this book, we will examine only the second condition.

A quick look at software evaluation criteria will provide ideas for evaluating authoring tools. For example, sound and graphics cannot be used appropriately if neither feature is available in a particular authoring tool. Your homemade CAI lesson cannot be very interactive if branching capability is absent from that tool. The ability to branch in a lesson is indicative of a tool's overall flexibility. Another sign of flexibility is the extent to which multiple correct answers are accepted. Some tools contain sentence parsers that read sections of student input, allowing answers to be accepted even if (among other things) the student has misspelled a word. Yet another sign of flexibility is the amount of detail that you can provide in feedback. Quality feedback instructs the user as well as judging his or her answers; it is shaped to fit the peculiar characteristics of incorrect responses. Can the authoring tool you are evaluating produce this kind of variable feedback?

A good authoring tool can record student performance (that is, it has a management system) and produce useful reports of that performance. You'll want to be sure that the program will support the number of students you have. Some tools allow teachers to assign specific levels of lesson difficulty to particular students. Others can record how long students take to answer questions or can allow teachers to determine how much time students can spend on particular questions. This timing feature can be helpful as a guide to both needed remediation and future revisions of the CAI lesson.

As always, you must check to see what equipment is required to use all the desired features of a given authoring tool and whether the tool can support all the peripherals you would like to use (like videotape or videodisc). Cost is also an important consideration, since the most elaborate authoring languages currently produced for the schools can cost between $100 and $300. (The most sophisticated authoring systems can cost thousands of dollars.)

Summary

The quality of software and its accompanying materials has been the focus of Chapter 7. As such, it brings closure to the discussion of contemporary uses of computers for instruction begun in Chapter 5 at a general level, and continued in Chapter 6 at a greater level of detail. We have presented a number of key concepts to help guide the evaluation process generally, followed by more specific criteria one may apply to both instructional computing packages and teacher utility programs.

In our final chapter, we switch scenes from the present to the future, and speculate about what education in the Information Age might become as educators apply computer-based technology to the teaching process.

Reference

MicroSIFT. *Evaluator's Guide for Microcomputer-Based Instructional Packages.* Eugene, OR: International Council for Computers in Education, 1983.

CHAPTER 8

Teaching in the Information Age

Introduction

Everyone is aware of the recent changes in all aspects of life as a consequence of the invention of computers. And without thinking too much about it, we all expect computers to be even more pervasive in the future. What is not quite so clear is the nature of the changes that teachers can look forward to in the future and how electronic machinery may influence them and their profession. Obviously, no one can predict with any certainty the future course of events in any occupation or profession. And yet those people who are about to enter the teaching profession are more likely to be prepared for whatever may happen if they have considered what the future could bring than those who have not.

For some educators, computing is seen as one more fad that will eventually run its course, and as such it should not be taken too seriously. After all, the last half century has given us Progressive Education, New Mathematics, teaching machines, and television; and yet a glance into a large proportion of the nation's classrooms gives no indication that concepts and devices from these sources have made much of an impact. Perhaps educational computing will go the same way and be remembered later as a bubble of excitement that burst onto the educational scene in the 1980s and 1990s and vanished just as quickly.

Another point of view is that while computing is certainly entering the schools, our educational system is traditionally slow to adopt permanent changes, so that teachers might well conclude that they should resist being swayed by the current flurry of excited activity in computing. Only when computers seem likely to contribute substantially to education will these people feel the necessity for becoming deeply involved. By no means

An increasingly familiar sight: the computer as a homework tool. *(Courtesy of Apple Computer, Inc.)*

least, for numbers of young people who are about to enter the teaching profession, as well as those who have been in the profession for some years, any kind of involvement with machinery—and particularly machinery based on mathematics and logic—is a threat to be avoided at all costs. What has been called computer-phobia (or techno-phobia) seems likely to continue inhibiting teacher involvement, because numbers of people are drawn into the profession in some measure for the very reason that in most areas it does not involve technical machinery.

Although many teachers may believe that the future of education is likely to be continuation of past practices, other educators are predicting fundamental changes in the way we educate children and young people, with electronic technology playing a significant part in bringing these changes about. This technology is compared in power with the invention of printing itself and involves transformations in the way the world conducts business and engages in the production of goods and services. Recent national studies, such as *A Nation at Risk* (National Commission on Excellence in Education, 1983) show that the educational leadership is well aware of changing needs, much as educators in the 19th century recognized universal literacy as a primary need if the nation was to prosper in the industrial world of the day. There is realization that a postindustrial economy is now emerging that requires an educational system to prepare children and youth for the Information Age, where physical skills will be subordinated to levels of brain power beyond anything we have yet experienced.

If these predictions come anywhere close to the truth, new entrants to the profession can expect substantially different career experiences from past generations of teachers. Instead of educating a physically skillful, minimally literate, comparatively passive work force to execute routine tasks, educators are predicting that the population will need to be prepared to handle ambiguous situations and to have developed the ability to participate with others in decision making much more than at present. Authority in a mass industrial society is vested in distant figures. What is now being predicted is the emergence of an environment where much responsibility will be shared—where authority will change from "They" to "We." One writer, Bentley Glass (1970), has gone so far as to declare that "the educated person of yesterday is the maladjusted, culturally illiterate misfit of tomorrow" (p. 52). If Glass is correct, then many teachers at work today who entered the profession 20 or 30 years ago may now be in great need of reeducation—partly for their own benefit but primarily for the benefit of their students.

Some Assumptions About the Future of Education

Advances in technology have far-reaching effects on people's lives whether they recognize them or not. This has happened in the past when, for example, fire was first discovered. It also occurred when metals were discovered and much later when printing with movable type was invented. The more recent inventions that harnessed the energy of coal, oil, electricity, and the atom have irrevocably altered human life and the kinds of education people need. We now live in an electronic age, and education must once again adjust to changes in demand. Particularly significant for teachers is the fact that we can now gain access to vast amounts of information of all kinds and can manipulate it in ways that a generation ago would not have been possible except for a handful of people working in highly specialized and very expensive facilities. In other words, information is becoming available to an extent that surpasses anything known to humankind before. And since the possession of knowledge has always been at the core of power, the traditional power structure—not to mention the whole of society—is changing, much as it did when the mass of people first began to read for themselves.

While anticipating the future of any dimension of education is extremely risky, several trends have special interest for people concerned with educational computing. At the risk of oversimplification, we have identified three clusters of these changes and present them here for consideration, to serve as the foundation for the predictions that appear in the rest of the chapter. They consist of the growing diversification among schools, a redefinition of what are considered basic educational skills, and the need to learn how to live with intelligent machines.

Diversification of Schools

Schools, whether public or private, seem almost certain to continue as the predominant institutions for engaging in the task of educating children and youth. With the increasing assertion of state and local control in education after a generation of considerable federal influence, schools are following increasingly unique paths that reflect the values of the communities they serve. The establishment of magnet schools designed to attract students with particular aptitudes and interests is one way in which school systems have responded to the wishes of parents for an education that serves special qualities. These experiments have been joined by increases in the numbers of parochial schools as well as secular schools and academies that lie outside the public system. This siphoning of students from public schools is likely to continue as local and parental interests replace state and federal mandates. Some children will move to alternative schools because their parents are ambitious for them and may be disillusioned with the education provided by the tax-supported schools. Other parents will send their children to other schools because of values that are integrated into those curriculums that cannot be included in public schools.

In such an environment, considerable competition can be expected as schools vie with one another to attract students. Freed from the constraints of bureaucratic processes and the interests of teacher's unions, more experimentation can be expected as these schools attempt to show their superiority over their competitors. More experimental teaching methods are also likely to be supported in nonpublic schools as the search goes on for more effective means of educating. And in place of conventional staffing, more experiments are likely to be attempted, partly in a search for greater effectiveness and partly as an effort to reduce costs. This competition will not be restricted to private schools entirely, however, since embattled public schools will be compelled to join the fight for students to avoid becoming repositories for those who are less fortunate and less able.

Redefining "Basic Skills"

Throughout this book we have described how computers can contribute to the achievement of educational goals. However, it is quite apparent that computing presents information to people in many ways other than through the conventional medium of print. For the best part of a century, printed information has had to fight off the challenges of the newer media of film, radio, and television. The recent development of instant worldwide satellite video broadcasting is yet another in a stream of challenges to the centuries-old dominance of print in educated people's lives. Print continues to be the primary carrier of information in schools today, but here also its supremacy is being challenged by the richness of what computers and computer-based methods can provide.

The textbook industry is unable, through its publications, to keep pace with changing events in the world sufficiently to satisfy the needs of numbers of subjects, where social changes and scientific discoveries continually modify understanding, while the political climate changes almost daily. In contrast, school experiences often have little to offer students compared with the immediacy of daily life. On the other hand, people in business, industry, the legal and medical professions, as well as the general public, make use of varieties of information that are of value to them in the course of their daily lives. Some of it is written, but much is visual or audio. This accessibility to diverse forms of information has been vastly increased with the invention of microprocessors to the extent that schools are sure to have to reconsider their priorities in the years to come. And educators will probably have to blend the traditional goals of education with those that are emerging where print literacy is but one of several "literacies." It may eventually be just as important for students to be highly sensitized to graphic images and sounds as it has been for them to be competent with words and computations.

Living with Intelligent Machines

As we indicated in Chapter 2, our lives are being transformed by the ever-increasing presence of intelligent machines. Inasmuch as past generations demanded that children and youth be educated in the use of the dominant intellectual tools of the time, so they will demand that students learn to use the machines that are central to the unfolding age of information. The beginnings of this concern have been felt already through the introduction of computer literacy into school curriculums and with instruction in the special applications of computers to particular subject areas, some of which were described in Chapters 5 and 6. This movement can be expected to expand as education becomes increasingly linked to electronic tools and information sources. And it will have a marked impact on the form that schooling takes in the future and consequently deserves the consideration of all who plan to enter the teaching profession.

Given the prospect of changes of this kind, it seems reasonable to believe that the education of young people for the future should already be changing from what it was 50 or 100 years ago. After all, the indicators of change have been with us for some considerable time. Evidence suggests that some responses have been occurring in spite of the resistance to change found in the profession and the lack of resources to work with. But if schools in general do not respond more positively than in the past, then other groups or institutions will emerge to undertake the work. It would be a mistake to believe that education must necessarily take place in institutions of the kind we have become accustomed to during the last century and a half.

If educators take the needed initiatives, new forms of learning content can be expected to emerge in school curriculums in the foreseeable future to meet these demands. Of major importance is the need for the educational direction and performance of children and youth to be revised, much as they were when literacy became a necessity during the 19th century.

Changes in Teacher Roles

For generations, the focus of classroom attention has been on the teacher. Teachers typically position themselves in front of a class of students and face them. From this position they direct what goes on in a room, while students remain seated at desks or tables. Furthermore, at all levels of education, the school day is divided into class periods, during which students work in predetermined curricular areas. This procedure is followed in self-contained elementary classrooms under the control of a single teacher, while in secondary schools students move from one room to another, each room staffed by a specialist teacher.

Teacher as Mentor

As a consequence of computers entering the schools, the traditional place of the teacher at the front of the classroom is likely to diminish. In fact, teachers will probably spend most of their time guiding, counseling, and leading instructional teams rather than lecturing to a room full of students. More likely than not, teachers will have teaching aides to assist them as well as people with specific technical knowledge. In this way students will have much more individual help than is possible today, though computers and computer-supported equipment will provide much of the actual instruction. These teacher-guides of the future will, in fact, coordinate everything that goes on in a room. Either alone or in teams, they will need to address the task of solving the educational problems of the students in their charge, using all the electronic and human resources available, while probably reserving for themselves the more difficult tasks. The tradition of the class period is also likely to change as instruction is individualized and as students work more and more with interactive computer programs and use a wide variety of information sources. Furthermore, the concept of a class period devoted to one single subject may decline to the extent that students work on problems that bridge traditional curricular areas.

Unlike the present-day classroom, teaching staffs will be linked increasingly with outside sources. The presence of guidelines for all kinds of instruction will be available through the computer, by means of educational data bases for all subjects and correlations among them. They will also be able to assess the interest and readiness levels of individual students to assure the best likelihood of effective learning. As that day approaches, teachers will cease being the primary sources of knowledge in the classrooms and will become mentors to their students in the process of learning and applying information to solve problems.

Diversification of the Teaching Profession

With the help of well-developed computer resources, schools will have the opportunity to be freed from the present rigid structure whereby a teacher is responsible for a roomful of students. If and when this condition is eliminated, principals will be able to begin an attack on root problems in schools and assign professional staffs to diverse tasks where their help is more needed. Some teachers may, in fact, choose to move into instructional development where they would spend a substantial proportion of their time developing software that is specially suited to a particular group or modifying existing programs for local use. Such people would also update contacts with educators and educational resources elsewhere in the state or nation through network arrangements in order to bring ideas and insights to their colleagues locally to improve instruction. Some teachers might establish contacts whereby students could communicate with students at other schools through their computers. In this way, students with special interests would be able to exchange ideas with each other, while students who have reached more advanced levels in particular areas would have opportunities to interact with a broader range of students and in so doing advance their educations far beyond what can be accomplished in isolation. With such means at their disposal, students would be able to exchange interpretations in a wide range of areas from social problems to literary criticism. They would also be able to invite peer evaluations of their own creative works by transmitting examples of literature, musical composition, and examples of visual art that are not practical at the present time. The transmission of words, sounds, and images is being done increasingly in business and industry, and teachers can expect it to become an integral part of school life. But this will happen only if they recognize that potential and take action to make it available for their students.

In sum, while the focus on the classroom teacher is likely to change from what it has been, teachers will play even more vital roles in schools than they are presently able to. More and more, they will assume roles as counselors and guides to help individual students and small groups select what is more appropriate for them. They will increasingly be able to help students individually as they encounter problems. They will have the opportunity to select methods of evaluation that are most suitable for given students or class situations, and on the many occasions where subjective evaluations are called for, more of their time will be available to apply their judgmental skills. In such an environment, the classroom of today would be an anachronism: the idea of the "front" of the room would be irrelevant. Even the prospect of individual instructors being responsible for rooms full of students is likely to be replaced by teaching teams responsible for groups of students in various locations in the school—or a district—where much of the communication might often be by means of electronic bulletin boards and conferencing. Close personal communications between students and teachers are vital in all good education, and this will be even more possible because teachers will have been liberated from many time-consuming routines by the availability of instructional programs that make them more available to students in need of more intensive and more personal instruction.

If there is a drawback to the unfolding future, it is that individual teachers will no longer be able to claim sufficient knowledge in any area to be thought of as having mastery of a particular range of subjects. This may well take its toll on the self-esteem of some people, and yet the idea of anyone—even today—having mastery of any field is really such an illusion that it should not be a continuing obstacle. Furthermore, beyond a certain point, the competencies that students are expected to master are likely to be much less subject-specific than a synthesis of numbers of areas, and that is where a teacher can look for mastery.

Whatever the actual chain of events is, one thing is certain: none of the desired changes can occur without considerable investments of time and money. Obviously, the purchase of up-to-date computer hardware is one dimension of this investment, although the overall cost of the computing power is continually declining. On the other hand, good quality educational software will always be expensive just because of the talented labor need to produce it, although wider acceptability should keep prices within reach. Most important of all, however, will be the redeployment of teachers from conventional classrooms to jobs that will better benefit the educational mission of the school and district. Piecemeal efforts at curricular modification are presently occurring as the literature of educational computing shows, and yet the real task has not yet begun to be addressed with any seriousness. It is a major enterprise and one that is certain to cause our present conceptions of a teacher's professional role to be modified considerably.

Changes in Methods of Teaching

The delivery of present-day school curriculums is accomplished by means of a mix of textbooks, subject-matter guides, materials developed by individual teachers, and various supplementary materials, equipment, and publications, together with a variety of practical experiences. For the most part, instruction is delivered by a teacher to a class of students in a linear manner, usually from a textbook. One part follows another in an order approved by a particular discipline. This is quite natural in view of the preeminence of books in our cultural tradition.

Teachers typically prepare for their classes by assessing the readiness of their students in relation to the subject matter prescribed for a particular grade level. Grade level expectations are usually set by the state and are then modified to suit the needs of the schools in a given district, while teachers at individual schools make further modifications to match the abilities of their classes. The focus of attention, nevertheless, remains on the group of students for which a teacher is responsible, whether in a self-contained classroom or in a subject-matter specialty.

In contrast with traditional teaching methods, computing is very recent and quite immature. Computing also requires expensive outlays of money for equipment at a time when school budgets are beset with commitments that range from costly busing arrangements to salaries of an increasing population of teachers who have reached the tops of their salary scales. The problems involved in purchasing computer hardware and software are often difficult in the face of these other demands, especially when the current quality and range of instructional software is evaluated. While the future appears encouraging, the present status of CAI software—with notable exceptions—is only a small improvement over books, dittoed handouts, and traditional teaching practices. Utility programs that enable students to engage in word processing and use electronic spreadsheets are uniquely valuable, however, and so is instruction in programming. Perhaps the most costly dimension of this transformation, and one that is only now beginning to be recognized, is the task of training (and retraining) teachers to make the best use of electronic materials, and this can be expected to be an ongoing task that will expand rather than contract with the passage of time.

Advances in Software

Most educational software programs contribute either as tools for using computers effectively—usually referred to as computer literacy—or as direct instruction in particular subject areas. Beyond the preliminary levels, programming belongs to the computer science curriculum rather than to teaching content in the conventional curriculum. In the foreseeable future, however, the random access capabilities of computers offer alternative tracks through any field of study and the opportunity to move across subject areas in ways that are impractical when learning is confined to books. In the past, opportunities for stepping across curricular boundaries and synthesizing knowledge have only been possible for a few fortunate individuals at the hands of talented teachers. However, rapidly improving software design has the potential for accomplishing this same goal and thus making available to infinite numbers of students what formerly was available to a lucky few or a privileged elite. Short of some catastrophe such a future is imminent and will lead to an altered state of learning that is different from anything we now know. The full realization of this goal, however, will depend very much on the investment that the nation is prepared to put into its schools during the next quarter century.

Individuality

With computing machinery becoming increasingly plentiful and its applications better understood, hardware and software will become an integral part of the entire school curriculum. Thus, school curriculums can expect to be transformed as a consequence of the use of computers and what they can do that cannot otherwise be done in the traditional classroom. Perhaps the most important change will be the opportunity for students to work individually at their own speeds on topics that appeal to them. This is a startling contrast to being restricted to the limitations of a class group working at a single task within a given period of time. Such a change will require much broader statements of what is to be learned than is expected at present, with preparations for much of the instructional and evaluational needs developed in advance or linked to published software. Teachers will be able to sponsor individuality among their students in ways that formerly have been acknowledged in textbooks but could not be addressed with any seriousness because of large enrollments.

Software packages are already available for school-level microcomputers that enable students and teachers to store and manipulate files of information for social studies and science. And while most of these machines have limited memories, the general organization of these programs is much the same as that found in the large information sources. Moreover, all such programs are rapidly becoming easier or "friendlier" to use.

Pleasure in Learning

In this unfolding social environment, teachers need to develop new skills and new attitudes. For example, they need to sensitize themselves to the benefits to be derived from the disposition to learn playfully in a wide range of fields of learning and not just in a prescribed few. This is not a new idea, but the profession can be expected to change dramatically as this idea takes on ever-increasing significance in classroom practice. One critic of the present educational system, Ivan Illich (1970), believes that only with what he calls "tools of conviviality" will students be encouraged in the naturalness of learning in contrast to the historic myth that education must necessarily be punishing or boring. And yet for such a change to occur, teachers will not only have to learn new skills, but they will also need to think differently about themselves, their tasks, and the children they teach.

Curricular Changes and the Electronic Classroom

During the Middle Ages, the only way to learn multiplication was to go to a university. In contrast, children in the fourth grade today may learn Boolean algebra without being pressured. Traditionally, however, schools have focused their efforts on preparing students for problem situations that require specific solutions. For example, children still spend much of their school time learning the rules of grammar and computation. In the minds of educators such as Alfred Bork (1984), so lengthy a period of "getting ready" to solve verbal and numerical problems is no longer acceptable.

Expansion of Subject Areas

The basic verbal and mathematical skills that have been the mainstay of school curriculums can be expected to continue in importance during the changing times that lie ahead. They are as essential to effective living in an electronic world as they ever were during the industrial period. But in themselves, they are insufficient to meet present educational needs, and with the increasing availability of computers, performance levels in these areas can be expected to increase, while the range of content to be learned is also likely to expand. The hand-held calculator has already demonstrated the impact of the microprocessor. It has changed the way mathematics is taught and has banished the slide rule forever, just as the automobile put buggy-whip companies out of business. And as a consequence of the recent growth of computing in school, learning the typewriter keyboard is no longer confined to high school students aspiring to be office workers but is found in elementary and middle schools as instruction in computer literacy continues. Word processing is just beginning to alter teachers' expectations in written composition. And spelling instruction will be increasingly under fire now that software programs are available to monitor student writing as it is being prepared.

It is fair to say that at the present time, the academic knowledge base of the school curriculum provides a stable foundation for the needs of a time when people were educated to fit into an industrial society that was far less flexible and dynamic than the one in which we are living. Future careers will require constant learning and relearning, regardless of a person's occupation. This has already begun in numbers of high technology industries including the military, and their investment in education is substantial and growing rapidly. One can begin to glimpse the beginnings of the same phenomenon in schools, where we find increasing numbers of mathematics teachers who, through retraining and experience, have transformed themselves into computer science teachers. In contrast, failure to be open to such transformations may have serious negative consequences. The lack of preparation for continual learning has already taken a toll among redundant workers from old-line heavy industries in recent years, creating a pool of men and women who have difficulty finding employment following the loss of their jobs.

Until recently the development of general learning skills was vital primarily for people in the professions and management. And yet the growth of continuous re-education in business and industry points to what lies ahead for the schools. If this need is to be met, then the complexion of the school curriculum will be required to change. Students will need to be helped to develop those skills required for constant adjustment to change, one consequence of which is that they will find themselves in more face-to-face situations involving risks to their self-esteem.

New Basics

From these concerns arises a need for rethinking the meaning of "basic skills," which could challenge the foundations of education. Programming computers is considered by such educators as Seymour Papert (1980) as an extension of intelligence, and it is this general quality that is truly "basic" for education in the future. An involvement with computers is thus seen as engaging in a new sphere of thinking, where information is manipulated to solve problems, often in individual ways.

Oral and memory skills that have been losing ground for several generations may also have an opportunity to break the grip of the print tradition based on books that has dominated school curriculums. The voice synthesizer, for example, may well encourage the rebirth of these skills. And educators such as Arthur Combs (1981) have gone so far as to suggest that while everyone will need to read, not everyone may need to write. Thus student aptitudes in such diverse areas as seeing, speaking, and listening may acquire new places in education rather than being subordinated as they are in present-day school curriculums.

Robert Molek (1984) declares the computer to be a unique machine that allows young people to chart a course between the verbal and non-verbal worlds. At the moment, he writes that only a small proportion of the populations are able to communicate and think with visual images, although strong evidence exists to support the value of such learning. Visual learning enables people to complement their verbal and computational needs with visual images that may be organized into categories or compared with each other and perhaps be modified or reorganized to communicate with others or to solve particular problems.

Thinking with visual images calls for active participation, since graphics is a natural quality in computing and is being used increasingly by business and industry. The future expansion and manipulation of visual images seems to be one that all teachers should be seriously considering as they plan for the future, though this can only succeed if students are more in control of their own learning than is traditionally the case.

Cultivating Diverse Abilities

Were an emphasis to be embraced that focused on learning new kinds of material or learning familiar information more efficiently, many students who today enjoy success in school would probably find themselves in competition with others possessing different but complementary aptitudes. And if, as Harold Shane (Shane and Tabler, 1981) proposes, "real world experiences" come to be emphasized more than they have in traditional schooling, then it is quite likely that still other students will rise to prominence who in the present school climate are not recognized. The world outside school is a dynamic environment that calls on diverse talents to solve a variety of problems, and yet rigid boundaries have isolated the subjects in the curriculum from that world as well as from each other. These subject-matter separations may not crumble, but they can be expected to bow to the needs of a broader conception of general education as electronic means for data storage, retrieval, and interaction advance during the next few decades.

Finally, educators are expressing doubt about the idea that all children need to share a common body of content in school. They are realizing that as educational needs become more personal and individual as a consequence of improved accessibility to information, a univerally shared base may no longer be essential or even desirable. They believe that an education offers a world of choices for students, which could well eliminate the boredom that presently estranges many bright adolescents and postadolescents trapped in classroom "convoys" moving at a speed approaching that of the slowest. Computerized instruction offers the means to help many of these students at their own speeds, while future advances are certain to open the way to even better methods. And yet, what is true for the two extremes of students in heterogeneous classrooms is also true for all students. All students possess qualities that are as diverse as those found across the range of the academic continuum, but these qualities are less often noticed by teachers who are preoccupied with more obvious classroom problems.

While individualization deserves consideration, any excess would threaten such fundamental educational goals as social cohesion and cultural unity. Were such an excess of individualism to occur, public reactions could then be expected that would lead to a more suitable balance. Given the present circumstances, however, the schools would have to change very considerably before such a condition would begin to exist.

Expansion of Expectations

One conclusion reached by Anne Peistrup (1984) as a consequence of her software development is that children can learn far more than they are normally credited with, including handling quite complex logic problems. She believes that learning need not be tied to traditional levels of expectation. For example, she describes seven-year-olds who are doing "college-level" work. In her opinion schools are not aware that children can do far more than has ever been asked of them, and that these latent abilities can be tapped by computerized instruction. As a consequence, she and others like her see the computer serving to broaden the range of intellectual performance vastly by raising the lower levels of learning while expanding it at the upper levels.

The heart of this issue of new skills lies in the increasing availability of information and the need to be able to use it. In such professions as medicine, law, and engineering, electronic machinery has been essential in order for practitioners to remain in business. Students and teachers alike also need to learn how to gain rapid, easy access to useful information. One alternative to disregarding this, as Alan Hald (1981) has said, is that we may "become overwhelmed to the point of inaction" by the sheer quantity of available information.

Students will also need to consider what it means to be human in a world populated with intelligent machines. They will have to learn to use machines for instruction. They will have to learn that education is a continuing process throughout life. Such issues have had little or no place in traditional school curriculums.

The impact on students would be considerable were some or all of these reforms to occur. And yet individual students are more likely than not to pass through an educational system without really realizing what changes, if any, are taking place around them because each person only travels the route through school once. Teachers, on the other hand, encounter new students every year. And they often remain in the profession for as long as 40 years. The challenge to teachers, therefore, is potentially much more exciting as well as more threatening. In addition, self-renewal becomes progressively more difficult with age unless individuals have been exercising their learning skills. Not least, the teaching profession is becoming a less reliable occupation: tenure no longer holds out a lifetime of security as it once did, and there is a strong likelihood that this protection will diminish even more in the future. Perhaps teachers themselves need to recognize their own career needs as much as people in other occupations.

Classrooms of the Future

Although a century ago school desks were commonly bolted permanently to the floors and today they are movable, in many instances that may be just about the only significant difference. In effect, the fundamental organization of school classrooms has not changed for over a century.

Remodeling of Facilities

With the arrival of computing in schools, every facet of school life will need to be reconsidered. Existing classroom space is likely to continue in use well into the foreseeable future just because school buildings already exist, and no major surge in the birthrate is anticipated that would stimulate more building. However, our present schools will need to be remodeled to accommodate the changes in curriculum and methods of instruction that result from the use of electronic instructional equipment. The focus of classrooms in the future will almost certainly be on electronic work stations, with each student having immediate access to a terminal. And yet desks and tables are likely to remain in use, because pencil-and-paper activities will continue to be useful for planning strategies and synthesizing ideas.

Although to all outward appearances, school buildings will probably remain more or less as they are, internal remodeling needs can be expected. Among the more obvious ones will be controls over temperature, lighting, and dust. Wherever computing equipment is used, temperature controls must exist; otherwise information may be lost from memory. Any extreme of heat or cold can become a problem, so air conditioning will take on a new importance in schools. Air conditioning might even contribute to a lengthening of the school year to make fuller use of facilities that traditionally remain unused during the summertime.

Researchers studying people who work at computers in business and industry have learned that poor lighting leads to fatigue and inefficiency, and consequently factory and office lighting is now being more carefully planned to avoid problems. Dust and static electricity are also major enemies of electronic machinery, and while such a thing as a dust-free environment is not imaginable in any school when children are present, carpeting and dust covers can be used to minimize problems. Carpeting will also need to be treated to help reduce static electricity, which can cause loss of information from computer memories.

Sources of Information

School-quality microcomputers of today typically have auxiliary memory storage in the form of floppy disks, and, occasionally, tape cassettes and cartridges. The presence of hard disk storage is increasing as schools acknowledge the insatiable appetite for information and for increasingly flexible ways of manipulating it. Hard disks offer advantages to multiple floppy disk drives in that maintenance is minimized. Optical memory will also provide immediate information in areas throughout the curriculum; videodiscs will present visual information for areas where pictures are of fundamental importance. The capacity of optical storage together with future approaches to auxiliary memory (bubble memory, bio-chip memory) will continue to feed this information demand.

In addition to these changes will be an exploding demand for access to information from outside the school. Connections with large data bases in school districts, states, regions, and even the nation will require appropriate wiring to be installed. Students will be able to go directly to a primary source for information about geography assignments, or they will be able to access reports from any newspaper on a given topic. For some time to come, students can expect to go to central locations in schools, such as libraries, to make these connections, although in time access points are likely to be dispersed throughout schools.

Service Personnel

Although computing machinery has far fewer moving parts than a movie projector or a typewriter, the almost certain abundance of computing equipment in the future will increase the dependency of schools on these machines, and this will require that maintenance staffs be employed to handle the machinery of the time but also the equipment to be anticipated in the future.

It may even be that schools as we know them today may not be needed. Some have suggested that schooling may eventually be almost entirely electronic and much of it conducted at home. Wherever schools are needed in the sense we understand them today students might have a voucher system that would enable them to attend the school that serves their needs best. Were this to occur, many school buildings might be closed except for social and sports events, or converted to some other purpose. Educational experiments can be expected during the next 30 years that explore some of these possibilities, and selected private and public schools may incorporate the more successful results. From the perspective of the present, however, such revolutionary shifts seem unlikely, at least during much of the career time of the readers of this book.

In sum, while some changes in schools will be physical, most of the change will be technological and psychological. Schools will continue to house students in traditional ways, but because of advances in electronic technology, instruction and information will be accessible from such a variety of sources that considerable pressure will be brought to push the concept of schools and schooling beyond a building with walls.

Preparing for Your Own Future

The most important aspect of the future for any individual is what is likely to happen to that person. General statements about computers in present-day schools or schools of the more distant future are abstract and may not become part of the experience of any single person who reads this book. And yet with such possibilities already in mind, this chapter closes with some ideas that may prove useful to someone who looks forward to a satisfying career as a teacher in what is likely to be a period of great change in education.

As we have explained throughout this book, numbers of future teachers (and current teachers as well) are excited by the prospect of working with computers in schools. They may have been introduced to electronic machinery as a home hobby, or through computer games, or they may have been among the fortunate ones who received good instruction while at school. Among this group will be those with aptitudes for the kind of logical thinking that is specially valuable while programming and using specialized program packages. Others may have encountered computers as a result of studies in mathematics or science. In contrast, numbers of other people find computers threatening to them personally or believe that computers will remove the all-important warmth of human contact from school, especially at the elementary levels. These people are less likely to have strong backgrounds in the sciences or mathematics. They are also less likely to have had successful encounters with computers either at school or at home.

It is convenient to think of these two extreme positions, because most people fall somewhere between them. For this reason, the following set of suggestions addresses either one extreme or the other. Each reader will then be free to take whatever seems relevant. And since those who feel uncomfortable probably need more help than those who possess both knowledge and confidence, we begin with the problem of confidence first of all.

Acquiring a Level of Confidence in Computing

The first and most important goal is to become reasonably comfortable with the computer, and it does not matter much how this is achieved. For most people, the last thing that should be attempted to begin with is to learn how to program in a high-level language. It is far better to look for the solution in work where you feel very much at home and then search to see whether computers are used in any way in that preferred area. For example, numbers of software programs may be purchased that enable people to balance their checkbooks and maintain control of their personal accounting. Others enable users to file all the good food recipes they have collected and be able to find them much more quickly than by card files. Such programs also allow additional recipes to be added quickly and easily. Computer programs exist that help improve typing skills. And if you can already type, then the move to using a simple word processing program is an easy step. Furthermore, if you do not spell well or if you have a difficult time thinking of the best choice of words, then spelling and thesaurus programs would be very helpful.

Those people with musical or artistic interests will discover that programs exist that cause the computer to make musical sounds or generate pictures. Inexpensive graphics pads offer easy yet pleasing ways to become involved with the ways in which computers work while producing appealing art. A more hedonistic approach yet might be to begin using a computer program to play bridge or poker. While all these programs have much to offer, the purpose here is simply to help beginners overcome fears and at the same to develop a familiarity with computer programs. As time goes by, it will become apparent that all computer programs have numbers of qualities in common, so that each new program is more quickly understood than earlier ones.

During this process, it often helps to work with someone who is much like you. In this way a mutual support system is developed that helps weather some of the inevitable frustrations and magnify the delight of successes of working in a new and strange field. And in the event that you do not have easy access to a machine, then splitting the rental of a microcomputer is less of a burden. For much of the same reasons, it is wise at these early stages to give a wide berth to those people who like nothing more than to impress others with their knowledge of computers and continually use computer jargon.

As confidence increases, you may want to make yourself familiar with the kinds of software that have been written for the subject you expect to teach, and especially those you enjoy most. The manuals supplied with some of this software can be quite formidable, though with continued use, you will eventually reach the point where you do not need to turn to the documentation any longer. At that point you will have acquired a sense of familiarity with the programs that will enable you to enjoy a high degree of freedom when using them and with that a much more profound understanding of the potentials—and limitations—of the programs.

At some point, you will want to attempt programming using a high-level language like BASIC, Logo, or Pascal. Only from such an experience can you become fully aware of the ways in which computers work. From then on you will become a better critic of computer programs of all kinds. You will be able to recognize what a programmer did to achieve a certain goal and also be able to visualize how a particular program might have been designed and how it might be improved. Finally, after some experience with learning to program, you will recognize the potential for developing problem-solving skills inherent in the act of programming, as discussed in Chapter 6.

Advancing Your Computing Skills

People who bring to teaching a strong background in computing have a great deal to contribute to education. Perhaps the greatest threat to this being realized, however, is that such people are often recruited to jobs outside education and thus are lost to the profession. For those who have no desire to work in business and industry, numbers of opportunities are available.

An obvious one is to become an educational expert in computing. Many states now offer teaching endorsements in computing that enable a person to be recognized and be used for computer assignments in one or more schools or throughout a school district. While such work is not intended to place a teacher in competition with a professional computer scientist, preparation for such an endorsement usually requires moderate competence in one or two of the more familiar languages used in schools.

Most teachers with an expertise in computing will probably not want to be identified as specialists, though they will want to be able to make as full use as possible of the resources that computing makes available. While extensive reading in the computing literature for educators will probably help, an even better strategy is frequent visits to schools to observe what is happening firsthand. In some districts teachers with special interests in computing make a point of sharing their ideas and insights with each other. A related approach is to attend educational computing conferences; one example is the annual National Educational Computing conference (see also the educational computing associations in Appendix E). Alternatively, you can plan to attend those sections of general conferences that address computing issues. The conferences of educational specialties in such areas as mathematics, language arts, music, social studies, special education, and the sciences are also likely to have parts of their programs devoted to the use of computers and computer-based technology (see Appendix E). While at conferences, it is always interesting and often enlightening to visit the commercial exhibits, though considerable caution has to be exercised in assessing the pitches of the salespeople.

Not least, you may gain considerably from getting to know a user group of the brand of computer that you either own or use at school. While these people may include teachers, the primary interest is in making full use of the machinery, and this can be invaluable, since manufacturers do not publish all the information about what their products will do. Inquisitive members of user groups delight in uncovering this information and sharing it with anyone who is interested. The task that faces the teacher is then to assess all the various tricks and determine which ones are valid for the classroom.

Conclusion

In attempting to peer into the future of education, we hope we have presented a provocative picture of possibilities. Although the tone of that presentation seems tuned to where technology will take us, it is still our contention that the future of schools and schooling will be very much the story of where *we* choose to take *technology*. Regardless of the forces technology seems to apply on its own, reflective educators will play key roles in shaping the direction of those forces. And while it is imperative that educators pick up the challenges electronic technology places before them, being skilled, thoughtful, and committed teachers first and foremost will always be of paramount importance and value, regardless of the particular technological tools that appear on the horizon.

Nonetheless, it seems clear that the teaching profession is on the verge of major upheavals, in spite of its much longer tradition as an institution that is slow to accept change. The more seasoned teachers who are well along in their careers may believe that the forces of tradition and institutional inertia will persist and that few major changes will occur. Like-minded but younger people may align themselves with conservative forces, since such a prospect for continuity in an otherwise turbulent outside world may be the reason why some people choose to become teachers in the first place, and it is true that the history of education supports those who predict that little change will take place. Many young people about to enter teaching may find the prospect of entering a profession that at last seems about to become more dynamic will be stimulated by what they read here. Whatever position a person adopts, however, no one who is about to embark on a career in education should be unaware of the forces at work in present-day educational thinking. For these reasons, this chapter described some of the possibilities that face teachers, particularly where computers and education meet.

References

Bork, Alfred. "Computers in Education Today—and Some Possible Futures," *Phi Delta Kappan* 66 (1984), pp. 239–243.

Combs, Arthur W. "What the Future Demands of Education," *Phi Delta Kappan* 62 (1981), pp. 446–51.

Glass, Bentley. *The Timely and the Timeless.* New York: Basic Books, 1970.

Hald, Alan P. "Toward the Information-Rich Society," *The Futurist*, August 1981, pp 20–21+.

Illich, Ivan. *Deschooling Society.* New York: Harper & Row, 1970.

Luehrmann, Arthur. "A Nation at Risk: Implications for Computer Science Education," *AEDS Monitor* 22, nos. 5–6 (1983), pp. 22–26.

Molek, Robert, "Visual Technology and the Development of Active Visual Learning," *AEDS Monitor* 22, nos. 11–12 (1984), pp. 8–12.

National Commission on Excellence in Education. *A Nation at Risk.* Washington, D.C.: U.S. Department of Education, April 1983.

Papert, Seymour. *Mindstorms.* New York: Basic Books, 1980.

Peistrup, Anne M. "A Computer in the Nursery School." In Dale Peterson (ed.), *Intelligent Schoolhouse.* Reston, VA: Reston Publishing Company, 1984.

Shane, Harold, & Tabler, M. Bernadine. *Educating for a New Millennium.* Bloomington, IN: Phi Delta Kappa, 1981.

Bibliography and Suggested Reading

Chapter 1

BOOKS

BELL, DANIEL. *The Coming of the Post-Industrial Society.* New York: Basic Books, 1973.

BITTER, GARY. *Computers in Today's World.* New York: John Wiley & Sons, 1984.

GOLDSTINE, HERMAN H. *The Computer from Pascal to von Neumann.* Princeton, NJ: Princeton University Press, 1972.

HOPPER, GRACE MURRAY, & MANDELL, STEVEN L. *Understanding Computers.* New York: West Publishing Company, 1984.

NAISBITT, JOHN. *Megatrends.* New York: Warner Books, 1982.

POLANYI, KARL. *The Transformation.* Boston: Beacon, 1944.

TIME-LIFE (EDS.). *Understanding Computers,* Book 1, *Computer Basics.* Alexandria, VA: Time-Life Books, 1985.

ARTICLES

AUSTRIAN, GEOFFREY D., "VITA: Herman Hollerith." *Harvard Magazine,* July–August 1982, p. 41.

CLEMENT, FRANK. "Digital Made Simple," *Instructional Innovator,* March 1982, pp. 18–20.

"Computers' Next Frontiers," *U.S. News & World Report,* August 26, 1985, pp. 38–41.

FRIEDLAND, LOIS. "The Incredible Shrinking Microchip," *Sky,* April 1984, pp. 20–26.

SALSBERG, ARTHUR. "Jaded Memory," *InfoWorld,* November 12, 1984, p. 7.

Chapter 2

BOOKS

BELL, DANIEL. *The Coming of Post-Industrial Society: A Venture in Social Forecasting*. New York: Basic Books, 1973.

BITTER, GARY. *Computers in Today's World*. New York: John Wiley & Sons, 1984.

EVANS, CHRISTOPHER. *The Micro Millennium*. New York: Washington Square Press, 1979.

FEIGENBAUM, EDWARD A., & McCORDUCK, PAMELA. *The Fifth Generation*. Reading, MA: Addison-Wesley, 1983.

HOPPER, GRACE MURRAY, & MANDELL, STEVEN L. *Understanding Computers*. New York: West Publishing Company, 1984.

NAISBITT, JOHN. *Megatrends*. New York: Warner Books, 1982.

TOFFLER, ALVIN. *The Third Wave*. New York: Morrow, 1980.

WEIZENBAUM, JOSEPH. *Computer Power and Human Reason: From Judgment to Calculation*. San Francisco: W. H. Freeman, 1976.

ARTICLES

BERNSTEIN, HARRIET T. "The Information Society: Byting the Hand That Feeds You," *Phi Delta Kappan*, October 1983, pp. 108–109.

DEDE, CHRISTOPHER, BOWMAN, JIM, & KIERSTEAD, FRED. "Communications Technologies and Education: The Coming Transformation," in Howard F. Didsbury (ed.), *Communications and the Future: Prospects, Promises, and Problems*. Bethesda, MD: World Futures Society, 1982.

FRIEDLAND, LOIS. "The Incredible Shrinking Microchip," *Sky*, April 1984, pp. 20–26.

KURLAND, NORMAN D. Have Computer, Will Not Travel: Meeting Electronically," *Phi Delta Kappan*, October 1983, pp. 124–126.

SANDERS, WILLIAM H. "Going Digital," *Instructional Innovator*, March 1982, pp. 14–16.

Chapter 3

BITTER, GARY. *Computers in Today's World*. New York: John Wiley & Sons, 1984.

HAROLD, FRED. *Introduction to Computers*. New York: West Publishing Company, 1984.

HOPPER, GRACE MURRAY, & MANDELL, STEVEN L. *Understanding Computers*. New York: West Publishing Company, 1984.

TIME-LIFE (EDS.). *Understanding Computers,* Book 1, *Computer Basics*. Alexandria, VA: Time-Life Books, 1985.

Chapter 4

BITTER, GARY. *Computers in Today's World*. New York: John Wiley & Sons, 1984.

HOPPER, GRACE MURRAY, & MANDELL, STEVEN L. *Understanding Computers.* New York: West Publishing Company, 1984.
SHELLY, GARY B., & CASHMAN, THOMAS J. *Introduction to Computers and Data Processing.* Brea, CA: Anaheim Publishing Company, 1980.
TIME-LIFE (EDS.). *Understanding Computers,* Book 1, *Computer Basics.* Alexandria, VA: Time-Life Books, 1985.

Chapter 5

BOOKS

BITTER, GARY G., AND CAMUSE, RUTH A. *Using a Microcomputer in the Classroom.* Reston, VA: Reston Publishing Company, 1984.
PAPERT, SEYMOUR. *Mindstorms.* New York: Basic Books, 1980.

ARTICLES

ANDERSON, RONALD E., KLASSEN, DANIEL L., & JOHNSON, DAVID C. "In Defense of a Comprehensive View of Computer Literacy—A Reply to Luehrmann," *Mathematics Teacher* 74 (December 1981), pp. 687–690.
BORK, ALFRED. "Interactive Learning," *American Journal of Physics* 47, no. 1 (January 1979).
FORMAN, DENYSE. "Search of the Literature," *The Computing Teacher* 9, no. 5 (January 1981).
JOHNSON, DAVID C., ANDERSON, RONALD E., HANSEN, THOMAS P., & KLASSEN, DANIEL L. "Computer Literacy—What Is It?" *Mathematics Teacher* 73 (February 1980).
LUEHRMANN, ARTHUR. "Computer Literacy—What Should It Be?" *Mathematics Teacher* 74 (December 1981).

Chapter 6

READING AND LANGUAGE ARTS

GEOFFRION, LEO D., & GEOFFRION, OLGA P. *Computers and Reading Instruction.* Reading, MA: Addison-Wesley, 1984.
LOHEYDE, KATHERINE M. JONES. "Computer Use in the Teaching of Composition: Considerations for Teachers of Writing," *Computers in the Schools* (1984), pp. 81–86.
MONTGOMERY, JIM. "Cloze Procedure: A Computer Application," *The Computing Teacher,* May 1984, pp. 16–17.
RUBIN, ANDEE. "The Computer Confronts Language Arts: Cans and Shoulds for Education." In A. C. Wilkinson (ed.), *Classroom Computers and Cognitive Science.* New York: Academic Press, 1982.
SHARPLES, MIKE. "The Use of Computers to Aid the Teaching of Creative Writing," *AEDS Journal,* Winter 1983, pp. 79–91.
WRESCH, WILLIAM (ED.). *The Computer in Composition Instruction.* Urbana, IL: National Council of Teachers of English, 1984.

ZACCHEI, DAVID. "The Adventures and Exploits of the Dynamic Storymaker and Textman," *Classroom Computer News*, 2 (1986), pp. 28–30, 76, 77.

MATHEMATICS AND GEOMETRY

GRADY, M. TIM, & GAWRONSKI, JANE D. (EDS.). *Computers in Curriculum and Instruction*. Arlington, VA: Association for Supervision and Curriculum Development, 1983.
MAIER, GENE. "We Have a Choice," *Mathematics Teacher* 76, no. 6 (September 1983), pp. 386–387.
PIELE, DONALD, "Computer-Assisted Mathematics." In M. Tim Grady & Jane D. Gawronski (eds.), *Computers in Curriculum and Instruction*. Arlington, VA: Association for Supervision and Curriculum Development, 1983.
SCALZITTI, JOYCE. "Added Dimension to Literacy," *Arithmetic Teacher* 32, no. 1 (September 1984), pp. 14–15.
STEELE, KATHLEEN J., BATTISTA, MICHAEL J., & KROCKER, GERALD H. "Using Micro-Assisted Mathematics Instruction to Develop Computer Literacy," *School Science and Mathematics* 84, no. 2 (February 1984), pp. 119–124.
SUYDAM, MARILYN N. "What Research Says: Microcomputers and Mathematics Education," *School Science and Mathematics* 84, no. 4 (April 1984), pp. 337–343.
USISKIN, ZALMAN. "The Arithmetic Curriculum is Obsolete," *Arithmetic Teacher* 30, no. 9 (May 1983), p. 2.

SOCIAL STUDIES

BRAUN, JOSEPH A., JR. *Microcomputers and the Social Studies*. New York: Garland Publishing, 1986.
BUDIN, HOWARD, KENDALL, DIANE S., & LENGEL, JAMES. *Using Computers in the Social Studies*. New York: Teachers College Press, 1986.
DIEM, RICHARD A. (ED.). "Technology and the Social Studies" (special section), *Social Education* 47 (1983), pp. 308–343.
GLENN, ALLEN & RAWITSCH, DON. *Computing in the Social Studies Classroom*. Eugene, OR: International Council for Computers in Education, 1984.
MARTORELLA, PETER. "Software: Side by Side (Six Election Simulations)," *Electronic Learning*, September 1984, pp. 63–64.
ROOZE, GENE E., & NORTHRUP, TERRY. *Using Computers to Teach Social Studies*. Littleton, CO: Libraries Unlimited, 1986.
ROSE, STEPHEN A., BRANDHORST, ALLAN R., GLENN, ALLEN D., HODGES, JAMES O., & WHITE, CHARLES S. "Social Studies Microcomputer Courseware Evaluation Guidelines," *Social Education* 48 (1984), pp. 573–576.
WHITE, CHARLES S. "PFS:File Review," *Social Education* 49 (1985), pp. 228, 230–231.
WHITE, CHARLES S. "Software: Side by Side (Six Economics Simulations)." *Electronic Learning*, September 1984, pp. 60–61.
WHITE, CHARLES S., & GLENN, ALLEN D. "Computers in the Curriculum: Social Studies," *Electronic Learning*, September 1984, pp. 54–55.

SCIENCE EDUCATION

BORK, ALFRED. "Computer-Based Instruction in Physics." In Dale Peterson (ed.), *The Intelligent Schoolhouse*. Reston, VA: Reston Publishing Company, 1985, pp. 117–130.

FAZIO, ROSARIO P., & BEVENTY, FRANCIS J. "Everyone Wins in Group Programming," *The Science Teacher* 50, no. 7 (September 1983), pp. 56–58.

GRAEF, JEAN L. "The Computer Connection: Four Approaches to Microcomputer Laboratory Interfacing," *The Science Teacher* 50, no. 4 (April 1983), pp. 42–47.

MACE, SCOTT. "Science for the Home," *InfoWorld*, July 23, 1984, pp. 34–35.

THE VISUAL ARTS

CLEMENTS, ROBERT D. "Adolescents' Computer Art," *Art Education* 38, no. 2 (March 1985), pp. 6–9.

ETTINGER, LINDA. "Talk about Teaching Computer Art Graphics," *The Computing Teacher*, October 1983, pp. 16–18.

HUBBARD, GUY. "Computer Literacy and the Art Program," *Art Education* 38, no. 2 (March 1985), pp. 15–18.

HUBBARD, GUY, & BOLING, ELIZABETH. "Computer Graphics and Art Education," *School Arts* 83, no. 3 (November 1983), pp. 18–21.

HUBBARD, GUY, & LINEHAM, THOMAS E. "Arcade Games, Mindstorms, and Art Education, *Art Education* 36, no. 3 (May 1983), pp. 18–20.

LINEHAM, THOMAS E. "Computer Graphics: Opportunity for Artistic Vision," *Art Education* 36, no. 3 (May 1983), pp. 11–14.

WHITE, DENNIS W. "Creative Microcomputer Graphics with the Koala Pad," *Art Education* 38, no. 2 (March 1985), pp. 10–13.

FOREIGN LANGUAGES

HOPE, GEOFFREY R., TAYLOR, HEIMY F., & PUSACK, JAMES P. "Using Computers in Foreign Language Teaching." Unpublished manuscript, February 1984. (Contact James P. Pusack, Department of German, Schaeffer Hall 102, The University of Iowa, Iowa City, Iowa 52242.)

PUSACK, JAMES P., & OTTO, SUE E. K. "Blueprint for a Comprehensive Foreign Language CAI Curriculum," *Computers and the Humanities* 18 (1984), pp. 195–204.

WYATT, DAVID H. "Computer-Assisted Language Instruction: Present State and Future Prospects," *System* 11, no. 1 (1983), pp. 3–11.

MUSIC

JONES, DOROTHY STEWART. "Now Is the Hour," *The School Musician* 54, no. 3 (November 1982), pp. 8–9.

SLIND, L. H. "A New Look at Elementary Music Education," *Canadian Music Educator* (1971), pp. 3–6.

UPITIS, RENA. "The Synthesizer: A Bridge from Reality to Ideals in Music Education," *The Computing Teacher*, August 1983, pp. 54–57.

WHITTLICH, GARY. "Computers and Music: Evaluating Microcomputers for the Delivery of Music Instruction," *The School Musician* 55, no. 5 (January 1984), pp. 38–39.

WHITTLICH, GARY. "Computers and Music: Evaluating Microcomputers for the Delivery of Music Instruction, Part II," *The School Musician* 55, no. 7 (March 1984), pp. 18–19.

WHITTLICH, GARY. "Computers and Music: Music Rudiments Programs," *The School Musician* 55, no. 9 (May 1984), pp. 14–15.

BUSINESS EDUCATION

EGATZ, LAURA B. "How Does Telecommunications Fit into the Curriculum?" *Business Education Forum* 38, no. 7 (March 1984), pp. 25–29.

GRADY, M. TIM, & GAWRONSKI, JANE D. (EDS.). *Computers in Curriculum and Instruction.* Arlington, VA: Association for Supervision and Curriculum Development, 1983.

KORNBLUHN, MARVIN. "The Electronic Office: How It Will Change the Way You Work," *The Futurist,* June 1982, pp. 37–42.

McMULLEN, LINDA. "Is Shorthand Dead, Terminally Ill, or Just Ailing?" *Business Education Forum* 38, no. 8 (April 1984), pp. 3–7.

NIGRO, JOHN S. "Prepare for Microcomputers with or without Hardware," *Business Education Forum* 38, no. 9 (May 1984), pp. 20–22.

STAGG, BEVERLY. "The Automated Office: What Will You Do with It?" *Business Education Forum* 38, no. 9 (May 1984), pp. 13–15.

TITEN, HAROLD. "Computer Instruction in Marketing and Distributive Education," *Business Education Forum* 38, no. 1 (October 1983), pp. 28–29.

HOME ECONOMICS

BURKHART, AUDREY C., MULLER, ELAINE, & O'NEIL, BARBARA. "Computers in the Home Economics Classroom," *Journal of Home Economics* 77, no. 3 (1983), pp. 24–31.

FEINBERG, RICHARD, & WALTON, KATHY. *Home Economics Research Journal* 11, no. 4 (1983), pp. 319–326.

ILLINOIS STATE BOARD OF EDUCATION, "Microcomputer Applications in Vocational Education: Home Economics." Springfield, IL: Author, n.d. (Available from Curriculum Publications Clearinghouse, Western Illinois University, Horrabin Hall 46, Macomb, IL 61455).

SPECIAL EDUCATION

BEHRMANN, MICHAEL M. *Handbook of Microcomputers in Special Education.* San Diego, CA: College Hill Press,1984.

BEHRMANN, MICHAEL M., & LAHM, L. (EDS.). *Proceedings of the National Conference on the Use of Microcomputers in Special Education.* Reston, VA: Council for Exceptional Children, 1984.

BUDOFF, M. *Microcomputers in Special Education.* Cambridge, MA: Brookline Books, 1984.

HAGEN, D. *Microcomputer Resource Book for Special Education.* Reston, VA: Reston Publishing Company, 1984.

HOFMEISTER, A. M., & THORKILDSEN, R. J. "Videodisc Technology and the Preparation of Special Education Teachers," *Teacher Education and Special Education* 4, no. 3 (Summer 1981), pp. 34–39.

JONES, WAYNE A., & CARMEN, JEFFREY. "Computer Services for the Training and Education of Handicapped Children," *AEDS Monitor,* May/June 1984, pp. 27–28.

MARTIN, C. DIANNE, & HELLER, RACHELLE S. *Capitol-izing on Computers in Education.* Proceedings of the 1984 Association for Educational Data Systems Annual Convention. Rockville, MD: Computer Science Press, 1984.

METZGER, M., OUELLETTE, D., & THORMAN, J. *Learning Disabled Students and*

Computers: A Teacher's Guide Book. Eugene, OR: International Council for Computers in Education, 1983.

RAGAN, ANDREW L. "The Miracle Worker: How Computers Help Handicapped Students," *Electronic Learning* 1, no. 3 (January–February 1983), pp. 57–58, 83.

Specialware Directory, LINC, 3857 N. High Street, Columbus, OH 43214.

PROGRAMMING

DIJKSTRA, EDSGER. "GOTO Statement Considered Harmful," *Communications of the Association for Computing Machinery* 11, no. 3 (March 1968), pp. 147–148.

PAPERT, SEYMOUR. *Mindstorms: Computers, Children, and Powerful Ideas.* New York: Basic Books, 1980.

POLYA, G. *How to Solve It,* 2d ed. New York: Doubleday, 1957.

COMPUTER SCIENCE EDUCATION

APPLE PUGET SOUND PROGRAM LIBRARY EXCHANGE. *Call-A.P.P.L.E. in Depth— All about Pascal.* Renton, WA: A.P.P.L.E., 1982. (304 Main Avenue South, Suite 300, Renton, WA 98055.)

COLLEGE ENTRANCE EXAMINATION BOARD. *Advanced Placement Course Description: Computer Science.* Princeton, NJ: CEEB, 1984.

COLLEGE ENTRANCE EXAMINATION BOARD'S ADVANCED PLACEMENT COMPUTER SCIENCE DEVELOPMENT COMMITTEE. *Teacher's Guide to Advanced Placement Courses in Computer Science.* Princeton, NJ: CEEB, 1983.

TAYLOR, HARRIET G., & POIROT, JAMES L. "The Certification of High School Computer Science Teachers." In *Capitol-izing on Computers in Education.* Proceedings of the 1984 Association of Educational Data Systems Annual Convention. Rockville, MD: Computer Science Press, 1984.

Chapter 7

"The Computer as Super-typewriter," *Consumer Reports* 48 (1983), pp. 540–551.

FISHER, GLENN. "Where to Find Good Reviews of Educational Software," *Electronic Learning* 3, no. 2, (1983), pp. 86–87.

JAY, TIMOTHY B. "The Cognitive Approach to Computer Courseware Design and Evaluation," *Educational Technology* 32, no. 1 (1983), pp. 22–26.

KLEIMAN, GLENN, & HUMPHREY, MARY. "Writing Your Own Software: Authoring Tools Make It Easy," *Electronic Learning,* 1, no. 5 (1982), pp. 37–41.

MICROSIFT. *Evaluator's Guide for Microcomputer-Based Instructional Packages.* Eugene, OR: International Council for Computers in Education, 1983.

ROBLYER, M. D. "Courseware Criteria from an Instructional Design Perspective," *AEDS Monitor* 21, nos. 1–2 (1982), pp. 42–45.

Chapter 8

BORK, ALFRED. "Computers in Education Today—and Some Possible Future," *Phi Delta Kappan* 66 (1984), pp. 239–243.

COMBS, ARTHUR W. "What the Future Demands of Education," *Phi Delta Kappan* 62 (1981), pp. 446–51.

EVANS, CHRISTOPHER. *The Micro Millennium.* New York: Washington Square Press, 1979.

HALD, ALAN P. "Toward the Information-Rich Society," *The Futurist,* August 1981, pp. 20–21+.

KURLAND, NORMAN D. "Have Computer, Will Not Travel; Meeting Electronically," *Phi Delta Kappan* 64 (1983), pp. 124–126.

LUEHRMANN, ARTHUR. "A Nation at Risk: Implications for Computer Science Education," *AEDS Monitor* 22, nos. 5–6 (1983), pp. 22–26.

MOLEK, ROBERT. "Visual Technology and the Development of Active Visual Learning," *AEDS Monitor* 23, nos. 11–12 (1984), pp. 8–12.

NAISBITT, JOHN. *Megatrends.* New York: Warner Books, 1982.

PETERSON, DALE (ED.). *Intelligent Schoolhouse: Readings on Computers and Learning.* Reston, VA: Reston Publishing Company, 1984.

SHANE, HAROLD, & TABLER, M. BERNADINE. *Educating for a New Millennium.* Bloomington, IN: Phi Delta Kappa, 1981.

STURDIVANT, PATRICIA. "Courseware for Schools: Present Problems and Future Needs," *AEDS Monitor* 22, no. 7–8 (1984), pp. 25–27.

TURKLE, SHERRY. *The Second Self: Computers and the Human Spirit.* New York: Simon & Schuster, 1984.

WILLIS, JERRY. "Educational Computing: Current Status and Future Directions," *Computers in the Schools* 1, no. 1 (1984), pp. 3–12.

YOUNG, JON I. "Videodisc Simulation: Tomorrow's Technology Today," *Computers in the Schools* 1, no. 2 (1984) pp. 49–57.

Programming Languages

BASIC:
: Beginner's All-purpose Symbolic Instruction code. Designed in 1963 by John Kemeny and Thomas Kurtz at Dartmouth College to teach students programming. It is widely available for microcomputers and lauded for its ease of use. A more sophisticated version that requires greater program structure, TrueBASIC, was developed by BASIC's originators in 1984.

FORTRAN:
: FORmula TRANslator, or FORTRAN, was developed for scientific and engineering applications in the 1950s. It resembles BASIC in many respects and is widely used in large computer systems.

COBOL:
: Designed in the late 1950s to satisfy the computing needs of business and government. Rear Admiral Grace Hopper played a major role in the development of COmmon Business Oriented Language.

Pascal:
: Named for Blaise Pascal (see Chapter 1), Pascal entered the scene in the early 1970s and is becoming more common in the nation's high schools, due in large part to its selection by the Educational Testing Service as part of its Advanced Placement Computer Science test. Pascal is a highly structured program that demands considerable discipline on the part of the programmer.

Prolog:
: A language gaining in popularity within the field of artificial intelligence. Prolog has been selected as the programming language base for Japan's ambitious fifth-generation projects.

LISP: LISP, or LISt Processing, is a language of artificial intelligence research.

Logo: Drawn from his work in artificial intelligence at M.I.T., Seymour Papert developed Logo, a language derived from LISP and designed particularly for educational uses. With its highly motivating graphics and Turtle, Logo is designed to allow children to discover powerful ideas and ways of thinking, according to Papert. Logo is becoming widely used in elementary school computing programs. For more information about Logo's philosophy and development, see Papert's book *Mindstorms* (New York: Basic Books, 1980).

C: This compiled language is associated most closely with a particular operating system called UNIX. It is a highly structured language resembling Pascal.

APL: Developed in the early 1960s by Kenneth Iverson at IBM, APL (A Programming Language) is used extensively for science applications. Many businesses have also found APL useful.

PL/1: Also developed in the 1960s, PL/1 (Programming Language 1) was intended as a universal programming language, combining features of both FORTRAN and COBOL. Also demanding structured program design, PL/1 is used for scientific and business applications. Because of its considerable memory requirements, PL/1 is currently a language for large computer systems.

Forth: Another language with an IBM connection, Forth is particularly well suited to engineering and graphics uses.

Smalltalk: A newcomer to the family of programming languages, Smalltalk was developed at the Xerox Research Center at Palo Alto, California. It shares many of the user advantages of Logo.

Ada: Named for Charles Babbage's gifted supporter and collaborator, Lady Ada Lovelace, Ada has become the programming language of choice within the U.S. Defense establishment.

RPG: Requiring little involvement in specifying the logic involved, RPG (Report Program Generator) allows the data-processing user to generate business reports. After providing the necessary specifications, little actual programming knowledge is required to obtain the desired result.

Selected Programming Texts

Each of the languages described is supported by textbooks available for the kindergarten to twelfth grade teacher and student audience. Below is a partial list of those texts.

BASIC

CARLSON, EDWARD H. (1983). *Kids and the TRS80*. Reston, VA: Reston Publishing Company. (Also available for the Atari, Apple, Pet, Commodore 64, and IBM microcomputers.)

CRITCHFIELD, MARGOT, & DWYER, THOMAS A. *A Bit of Applesoft BASIC*. Reading, MA: Addison-Wesley, 1985.

LUEHRMANN, ARTHUR, & PECKHAM, HERBERT. *Computer Literacy: A Hands-On Approach*. New York: McGraw-Hill, 1983.

SHANE, JUNE GRANT. *Programming for Microcomputers: Apple II BASIC*. Boston: Houghton Mifflin Company, 1983.

Logo

BILLSTEIN, RICK, LIBESKIND, SHLOMO, & LOTT, JOHNNY W. *Apple Logo: Programming and Problem Solving*. Reading, MA: The Benjamin Cummings Publishing Company, 1986.

BILLSTEIN, RICK, LIBESKIND, SHLOMO, & LOTT, JOHNNY W. *MIT Logo for the Apple*. Reading, MA: The Benjamin-Cummings Publishing Company, 1985.

CONLAN, JIM, & INMAN, DON. *Spirits, a Turtle, and TI Logo*. Reston, VA: Reston Publishing Company, 1983.

SHARP, PAMELA. *TURTLESTEPS: An Introduction to IBM Logo and Dr. Logo*. Bowie, MD: Brady Communications Company, 1984.

THORNBURG, DAVID. *Beyond Turtle Graphics: Further Explorations of Logo.* Reading, MA: Addison-Wesley Publishing Company, 1986.

WATT, DANIEL. *Learning with Atari Logo.* New York: McGraw-Hill, 1983. (Also available for the Apple and Commodore microcomputers.)

WATT, MOLLY, & WATT, DANIEL. *Teaching with Logo: Building Blocks for Learning.* Reading, MA: Addison-Wesley Publishing Company, 1986.

Pascal

COOPER, DOUG, & CLANCEY, MICHAEL. *Oh! Pascal!* New York: W. W. Norton & Company, 1983.

DALE, NELL, & ORSHALICK, DAVID. *Introduction to Pascal and Structured Design.* Lexington, MA: D. C. Heath and Company, 1983.

LUEHRMANN, ARTHUR, & PECKHAM, HERBERT. *Apple Pascal: A Hands-On Approach.* New York: McGraw-Hill, 1981.

PATTIS, RICHARD. *Karel the Robot.* New York: John Wiley & Sons, 1981.

WALKER, H. M. *Introduction to Computing and Computer Science with Pascal.* Boston: Little, Brown, 1986.

Computer Science Curriculum

A. Programming methodology
   1. Specification
      a. Problem definition and requirements
      b. Functional specifications for programs
   2. Design
      a. Modularization
      b. Top-down vs. bottom-up methodologies
      c. Stepwise refinement of modules and data structures
   3. Coding
      a. Structure
      b. Style, clarity of expression
   4. Program correctness
      a. Testing
         (i) Relation to design and coding
         (ii) Generation of test data
         (iii) Top-down vs. bottom-up testing of modules
      b. Verification
         (i) Assertions and invariants
         (ii) Reasoning about programs
      c. Debugging
   5. Documentation
B. Features of programming languages
   1. Types and declarations
      a. Block structure
      b. Scope of identifiers
         (i) Local identifiers
         (ii) Global identifiers

2. Data
   a. Constants
   b. Variables
3. Expressions and assignments
   a. Operations and operator precedence
   b. Standard functions
   c. Assignment statements
4. Control structures
   a. Sequential execution
   b. Conditional execution
   c. Iteration (loops or repetitive execution)
5. Input and output
   a. Terminal input and output
   b. File input and output
6. Procedures
   a. Subroutines and functions
   b. Parameters
      (i) Actual and formal parameters
      (ii) Value and reference parameters
   c. Recursive procedures
7. Program annotation
   a. Comments
   b. Indentation and formatting
C. Data types and structures
   1. Primitive data types
      a. Numeric data
         (i) Floating-point real numbers
         (ii) Integers
      b. Character (symbolic) data
      c. Logical (Boolean) data
   2. Linear data structures
      a. Arrays
      b. Strings
      c. Linked lists
      d. Stacks
      e. Queues
   3. Tree structures
      a. Terminology
         (i) Nodes: root, leaf, parent, child, sibling
         (ii) Branches and subtrees
         (iii) Ordered and unordered trees
      b. Binary trees
      c. General tree structures (optional)
   4. Representation of data structures

      a. Sequential representation of linear structures

      b. Pointers and linked data structures

D. Algorithms

  1. Classes of algorithms

      a. Sequential algorithms

      b. Iterative or enumerative algorithms

      c. Recursive algorithms

  2. Searching

      a. Sequential (linear) search

      b. Binary search

      c. Hash-coded search

      d. Searching an ordered binary tree

      e. Linear vs. logarithmic searching times

  3. Sorting

      a. Selection sort

      b. Insertion sort

      c. Exchange or bubble sort

      d. Merge sort

      e. Sorting using an ordered binary tree

      f. Quicksort (optional)

      g. Radix sort (optional)

      h. Quadratic vs. $n*\log(n)$ sorting times

  4. Numerical algorithms

      a. Approximations

         (i) Zeroes of functions by bisection

         (ii) Monte Carlo techniques

         (iii) Area under a curve (optional)

      b. Statistical algorithms

         (i) Measures of central tendency

         (ii) Measures of dispersion

      c. Numerical accuracy

         (i) Round-off effects

         (ii) Precision of approximations

  5. Manipulation of data structures

      a. String processing

         (i) Concatenation

         (ii) Substring extraction

         (iii) Matching

      b. Insertion and deletion in linear structures, trees,

      c. Tree traversals

E. Applications of computing

  1. Text processing

      a. Editors

      b. Text formatters

   2. Simulation and model
      a. Continuous simulation of physical processes
      b. Discrete simulation of probabilistic events
   3. Data analysis
      a. Statistical packages
      b. Graphical display of data
   4. Data management
      a. Information storage and retrieval
      b. Typical business systems
   5. System software
      a. File management routines (e.g., mail systems)
      b. Graphical software
      c. Syntax analysis routines
         (i) Command scanners
         (ii) Evaluation of arithmetic expressions
   6. Games
      a. Simple puzzles (e.g., Tower of Hanoi)
      b. Simple games (e.g. tic-tac-toe)
      c. Searching game trees (optional)
F. Computer systems
   1. Major hardware components
      a. Primary and secondary memory
      b. Processors
      c. Peripherals
   2. System software
      a. Language processors
      b. Operating systems
      c. Graphical output facilities
   3. System configuration
      a. Microprocessor systems
      b. Time-sharing and batch processing systems
      c. Networks
G. Social implications
   a. Responsible use of computer systems
   2. Social ramifications of computer applications
      a. Privacy
      b. Values implicit in the construction of systems
      c. Reliability of systems

SOURCE: Reprinted with permission from *Teacher's Guide to Advanced Placement Courses in Computer Science*, pp. 118–121, copyright © 1983 by College Entrance Examination Board, New York.

Software Sources

Software Directories

Addison-Wesley Book of Apple Computer Software, The Book Company, 16720 Hawthorne Blvd., Lawndale, CA 90260

The Apple Software Directory, Vol. 3—Education, WIDL Video, 5245 West Diversey, Chicago, IL 60639

Atari Program Exchange, Atari, Inc., P.O. Box 427, Sunnyvale, CA 94086

Commodore Software Encyclopedia, Commodore Business Machines, Software Group, 681 Moore Road, 300 Valley Forge Square, King of Prussia, PA 19406

Educational Software Directory, Sterling Swift Publishing Company, P.O. Box 188, Manchaca, TX 78652

Educator's Handbook and Software Directory, Vital Information, Inc., 350 Union Station, Kansas City, MO 64108

The Educational Software Selector (TESS), EPIE Institute, P.O. Box 620, Stony Brook, NY 11790

Educational Software Sourcebrook, Catalog No. 26-2756, Radio Shack, Education Division, 400 Atrium, One Tandy Center, Fort Worth, TX 76102

School Microware, Dresden Associates, P.O. Box 246, Dresden, ME 04342

Texas Instruments Program Directory, Texas Instruments, P.O. Box 53, Lubbock, TX 79408

Software Producers/Distributors

Apple Computer, 20525 Mariani Avenue, Cupertino, CA 95014

Appleware, Inc., 6400 Hayes Street, Hollywood, FL 33024

Atari, Inc., P.O. Box 427, Sunnyvale, CA 94086

Bertamax, Inc., 958 Church Street, Baldwin, NY 11510

Borg-Warner Educational Systems, 600 West University Drive, Arlington Heights, IL 60004

Borland International, 4585 Scotts Valley Drive, Scotts Valley, CA 95065

Brain Bank Software, 220 Fifth Avenue, New York, NY 10001
Broderbund Software, 17 Paul Drive, San Rafael, CA 94903
Charles Clark Company, 168 Express Drive South, Brentwood, NY 11717
CONDUIT, University of Iowa, Box 388, Iowa City, IA 52242
Control Data Corporation, 8100 34th Avenue South, P.O. Box 0, Minneapolis,
    MN 55440
Developmental Learning Materials, One DLM Park, P.O. Box 4000, Allen, TX
    75002
Educational Activities, Inc., P.O. Box 392, Freeport, NY 11520
Encyclopedia Britannica Educational Corporation, 425 North Michigan Ave-
    nue, Chicago, IL 60611
Focus Media, 839 Stewart Avenue, Box 865, Garden City, NY 11530
Follet Library Book Company, 4506 Northwest Highway, Crystal Lake, IL
    60014
J. L. Hammett Company, Box 545, Braintree, MA 02184
Hartley Courseware, Inc., Box 431, Dimondale, MI 48821
Holt, Rinehart & Winston School Department, 383 Madison Avenue, New
    York, NY 10017
Houghton Mifflin, 777 California Avenue, Palo Alto, CA 94304
Intellectual Software, 798 North Avenue, Bridgeport, CT 06606
IBM, P.O. Box 1328, Boca Raton, FL 33432
K-12 MicroMedia, P.O. Box 17, Valley Cottage, NY 10989
Krell Software Corporation, 1320 Stony Brook Road, Stony Brook, NY 11790
The Learning Company, 4370 Alpine Drive, Portola Valley, CA 94025
Lightning Software, P.O. Box 11725, Palo Alto, CA 94306
Macmillan Publishing Company, 866 Third Avenue, New York, NY 10022
Marck, 280 Linden Avenue, Bradford, CT 06405
McGraw-Hill Company, School Division, 1221 Avenue of the Americas, New
    York, NY 10020
Merlan Scientific, 247 Armstrong Avenue, Unit 6, Georgetown, Ontario, Can-
    ada L7G 4X6
The Micro Center, P.O. Box 6, Pleasantville, NY 10570
MICRO-Ed, Inc., P.O. Box 24156, Minneapolis, MN 55424
MicroLab, 2699 Skokie Valley Road, Highland Park, IL 60035
Micro Learningware, Box 2134, North Mankato, MN 56001
MicroMedia, 172 Broadway, Woodcliff Lakes, NJ 07675
Milliken Publishing Company, 1100 Research Boulevard, St. Louis, MO 63132
Milton Bradley Software, 443 Shaker Road, East Longmeadow, MA 01028
Minnesota Educational Computing Consortium (MECC), 2520 Broadway Drive,
    St. Paul, MN 55113
Muse Software, 330 North Charles Street, Baltimore, MD 21201
Opportunities for Learning, Dept. L-4, 8950 Lurline Avenue, Chatsworth, CA
    91311.
Oronoque Computer Concepts, Inc., Williamstown, VT 05679
Prentice-Hall, Inc., Computer Programs, Englewood Cliffs, NJ 07632
Rand McNally, P.O. Box 7600, Chicago, IL 60680
Random House, School Division, Department 985, Suite 201, 2970 Brandywine
    Road, Atlanta, GA 30341
Scholastic Software, Scholastic, Inc., 730 Broadway, New York, NY 10003

Science Research Associates (SRA), 155 North Wacker Drive, Chicago, IL 60606

Scott, Foresman & Company, 1900 East Lake Avenue, Glenview, IL 60024

Tom Snyder Productions, Inc., 123 Mt. Auburn Street, Cambridge, MA 02138

Spinnaker, 215 First Street, Cambridge, MA 02142

Strategic Simulations, Inc., 465 Fairchild Drive, Suite 108, Mountain View, CA 94043

Sunburst, Room Y B, 39 Washington Avenue, Pleasantville, NY 10570

Associations

General Computing Associations

Associations for Computing Machinery, Inc.
1133 Avenue of the Americas
New York, NY 10036

Association for the Development of Computer-Based Instructional Systems (ADCIS)
ADCIS Headquarters
Computer Center
Western Washington University
Bellingham, WA 98225

Association for Educational Communications and Technology (AECT)
1126 Sixteenth Street, N.W.
Washington, DC 20036

International Association for Computing in Education (IACE)
1230 Seventeenth Street, N.W.
Washington, DC 20036

International Council for Computers in Education
Department of Computer and Information Science
University of Oregon
Eugene, OR 97403

Young People's Logo Associations (YPLA)
P.O. Box 855067
Richardson, TX 75085

Reading and Language Arts Associations and Contacts

Computers, Reading and Language Arts (CRLA)
P.O. Box 13039
Oakland, CA 94661

Computer Technology and Reading Committee
International Reading Association
800 Barksdale Road, P.O. Box 8139
Newark, DE 19714

Andee Rubin
Bolt, Beranek and Newman, Inc.
50 Moulton Street
Cambridge, MA 02238

Dr. Harold Nugent
229 Main Street
Keene State College
University of New Hampshire
Keene, New Hampshire 03431

Committee on Technology and Reading
                and
ERIC Clearinghouse on Reading and Communication Skills
National Council of Teachers of English
1111 Kenyon Road
Urbana, IL 61801

Mathematics Associations

National Council of Teachers of Mathematics (NCTM)
1906 Association Drive
Reston, VA 22091

Association for Computers in Mathematics and Science Teaching
P.O. Box 4
Austin, TX 78765

Social Studies Associations

SIG-CASE
(Special Interest Group–Computers And Social Education)
National Council for the Social Studies
3501 Newark Street, N.W.
Washington, DC 20016

National Council for the Social Studies (NCSS)
Instructional Media and Technology Advisory Committee
3501 Newark Street, N.W.
Washington, DC 20016

Science Associations

Association for Computers in Mathematics and Science Teaching
P.O. Box 4
Austin, TX 78765

National Science Teachers Association (NSTA)
1742 Connecticut Avenue, N.W.
Washington, DC 20009

Foreign Language Education Associations and Contacts

American Council on the Teaching of Foreign Languages
579 Broadway
Hastings-on-Hudson, NY 10706

CALICO
Computer Assisted Language Learning and Instruction Consortium
233 SFLC
Brigham Young University
Provo, UT 84602

Home Economics Associations

Computer Software Committee
American Home Economics Association
2010 Massachusetts Avenue, N.W.
Washington, DC 20036

Computer-Based Home Economics SIG
Association for the Development of Computer-Based Instructional
    Systems (ADCIS)
Miller Hall 409
Western Washington University
Bellingham, WA 98225

Vocational Education Associations and Contacts

American Vocational Association
2020 North Fourteenth Street
Arlington, VA 22201

Special Education Associations and Contacts

The Council for Exceptional Children
1920 Association Drive
Reston, VA 22091

Technology in Special Education Program
c/o Prof. Michael Behrmann
Department of Curriculum and Instruction
George Mason University
4400 University Drive
Fairfax, VA 22030

Alan M. Hofmeister
Professor of Special Education
Exceptional Children Center
Utah State University
Logan, UT 84322

Visual Arts Association
National Art Education Association (NAEA)
1916 Association Drive
Reston, VA 22091

Journals, Magazines, and Other Resources

Classroom Computer Learning, 19 David Drive, Belmont, CA 94002

Closing the Gap [focuses on special needs], P.O. Box 68, Henderson, MN 56044

Computers in the Schools, The Haworth Press, Inc., 28 East 22nd Street, New York, NY 10010

Computer-Using Educators Newsletter, Computer-Using Educators, Independence High School, 1776 Education Park Drive, San Jose, CA 95133

DBKids, c/o Beverly Hunter (DBKids coordinator), Targeted Learning Corporation, Route 1, Box 190, Amissville, VA 22002

Digit Magazine [for children], P.O. Box 29996, San Francisco, CA 94129

Educational Computer, P.O. Box 535, Cupertino, CA 95015

Educational Technology, 140 Sylvan Avenue, Englewood Cliffs, NJ 07632

Electronic Education, Electronic Communications, Inc., Suite 220, 1311 Executive Center Drive, Tallahassee, FL 32301

Electronic Learning, 902 Sylvan Avenue, Englewood, NJ 07632

Enter [for children], Children's Television Workshop, 1 Lincoln Plaza, New York, NY 10023.

Journal of Computer-Based Instruction [ADCIS], Computer Center, Western Washington University, Bellingham, WA 98225

Journal of Computers in Mathematics and Science Teaching [ACMST], P.O. Box 4455, Austin, TX 78765

Journal of Computers, Reading and Language Arts [CRLA], NAVA, 3150 Spring Street, Fairfax, VA 22031

Journal of Educational Computing Research, Baywood Publishing Company, Inc., 120 Marine Street, Box D, Farmingdale, NY 11735

Journal of Educational Technology Systems, Baywood Publishing Company, Inc., 120 Marine Street, Box D, Farmingdale, NY 11735

Journal of Research on Computing in Education [IACE], 1230 Seventeenth Street, N.W., Washington, DC 20036

The Logo and Educational Computing Journal, Suite 219, 1320 Stony Brook Road, Stony Brook, NY 11790

The Mathematics Teacher, NCTM Publication, 1906 Association Drive, Reston, VA 22091

Microcomputers: The Voc Ed Connection. Resource Handbook (Spring 1983). Vocational Education Services, 840 State Road 46 Bypass, Room 111. Indiana University, Bloomington, IN 47405

The Science Teacher [NSTA], 1742 Connecticut Avenue, N.W., Washington, DC 20009

Social Education [NCSS], 3501 Newark Street, N.W., Washington, DC 20016

Specialware Directory, LINC, 3857 North High Street, Columbus, OH 43214

Teaching and Computers, 902 Sylvan Avenue, Englewood, NJ 07632

The Computing Teacher [ICCE], Department of Computer and Information Science, University of Oregon, Eugene, OR 97850

T.H.E. Journal, Information Synergy, Inc., 2626 South Pullman, Santa Ana, CA 92705

Turtle News [for children]. Young People's Logo Association (YPLA), P.O. Box 855067, Richardson, TX 75085

Computer Literacy Curricula

The Bitter Curriculum

Computer Literacy Scope and Sequence
Grades K-3

Topics	Computer Awareness K	1	2	3	4	5	6	7	8	9	10	11	12	Programming K	1	2	3	4	5	6	7	8	9	10	11	12
K																										
What a Computer Is	IA	C	C	C	C	C	C	C	C	R	R	R	R													
Following Directions	IA	C	C	C																						
Vocabulary	IA	C	C	C	C	C	C	C	C	C	C	C	C													
Programming Programmable Devices														IA	C	M										
Turtle Graphics (Making Shapes)														IA	C	C										
1ST GRADE																										
What a Computer Can Do		IA	C	C	C	C	C	C	C	R	R	R	R													
Learning to Use a Computer		IA	C	C	C	C	C	C	C	C	C	C														
Using the Keyboard		IA	C	C	M																					
Turtle Graphics (Moving Shapes)															IC	C	C									
2ND GRADE																										
Computer Advantages			IA	C	C	C	C	C	C	C	C	C														
Computer Disadvantages			IA	C	C	C	C	C	C	C	C	C														
Computers in Our Lives			ID	C	C	C	C	C	C	C	C	C														
Everyday Applications			ID	C	C	C	C	C	C	C	C	C														
Future			ID	C	C	C	C	C	C	C	C	C														
Turtle Graphics (Rotations, etc.)																IA	C	C	C							
Logo (Sprites)																IA	C	C	C	C	C	C	C	C	C	C
3RD GRADE																										
History				ID	C	C	C	C	C																	
Logic				IA	C	C	C	C	C	C	C	C					IA	C	C	C	C	C	C	C	C	
How a Computer Works				IA	C	C	C	C	C	C	C	C														
Parts of a Computer				IA	C	C	C	C	C	C	C	C														
Logo Programming																	IA	C	C	C	C	C	C	C	C	
Problem Solving with Logo																	IA	C	C	C	C	C	C	C	C	

LEGEND: IA—Introduction with Activities ID—Introductory Discussion C—Expansion of Discussion from Previous Grades R—Review M—Mastery

(Continued)

227

Computer Literacy Scope and Sequence
Grades 4-6

	Topics	Computer Awareness													Programming												
		K	1	2	3	4	5	6	7	8	9	10	11	12	K	1	2	3	4	5	6	7	8	9	10	11	12
4TH GRADE	Hardware					ID	C	C	C	C	C	C	C	C													
	Software					ID	C	C	C	C	C	C	C														
	Flowcharting					IA	C	C	C	C	R	R	R	R					IA	C	C	C	C	C	C	C	C
	Storyboarding					IA	C	C	C	C	R	R	R	R					IA	C	C	C	C	C	C	C	C
	BASIC: PRINT & REM																		IA	C	C	C	C	R	R	R	R
	BASIC: LET																		IA	C	C	R	R	R	R	R	R
	BASIC: INPUT																		IA	C	R	R	R	R	R	R	R
	BASIC: GO TO																		IA	C	R	R	R	R	R	R	R
	Formulas (Variables & Constants)					IA	C	C	C	C	C	C	C	C					IA	C	C	C	C	C	M		
	String Data																		IA	C	C	C	C	C	C	R	R
	Relations					IA	C	C	C	M									IA	C	C	C	M				
	Binary Numbers					IA	C	C	C	C	C	C	C	C													
5TH GRADE	Computer Generations					ID	C	C	C																		
	Counters					IA	C	C	C	M										IA	C	C	C	C	C	C	C
	BASIC: IF-THEN																			IA	C	R	R	R	R	R	R
	BASIC: ON-GO TO																			IA	C	R	R	R	R	R	R
	BASIC: READ-DATA																			IA	C	R	R	R	R	R	R
	Word Processing						IA	C	C	C										IA	C	C	C	C	C	C	C
6TH GRADE	Computer Types							ID	C	C	R	R	R	R													
	Data Handling							IA	C	C	C	C	C	C													
	Computer Languages							IA	C	C	C	C	C	C													
	Looping							IA	C	C	C	M									IA	C	C	C	C	C	C
	BASIC: FOR-NEXT																				IA	C	C	C	C	C	C
	BASIC: Random Number																				IA	C	C	C	C	C	C
	Problem Solving with BASIC																				IA	C	C	C	C	C	C
	Graphics																				IA	C	C	C	C	C	C

LEGEND: IA—Introduction with Activities   ID—Introductory Discussion   C—Expansion of Discussion from Previous Grades   R—Review   M—Mastery

228

Computer Literacy Scope and Sequence
Grades 7-12

Grade	Topics	Computer Awareness														Programming												
		K	1	2	3	4	5	6	7	8	9	10	11	12	K	1	2	3	4	5	6	7	8	9	10	11	12
7TH GRADE	Modeling								IA	C	C	C	C	C													
	Robotics								ID	C	C	C	C	C													
	Social Issues								ID	C	C	C	C	C													
	Data Bases								IA	C	C	C	C	C													
	BASIC: Arrays (One-Dimensional)																					IA	C	C	C	C	C
	BASIC: Functions																					IA	C	C	C	C	C
8TH GRADE	Computer Crime									ID	C	C	C	C													
	Algorithms									IA	C	C	C	C									IA	C	C	C	C
	BASIC: Arrays (Two-Dimensional)																						IA	C	C	C	C
	Graphics (Sound and Color)																						IA	C	C	C	C
9TH GRADE	Computer Capabilities										ID	C	C	C													
	Computer-Related Fields										ID	C	C	C													
	BASIC: Simulation Programming																							IA	C	C	C
	BASIC: Matrices																							IA	C	C	C
	BASIC: Files																							IA	C	C	C
	Pilot: Introductory Language Commands																							IA	C	C	C
10TH GRADE	Prediction, Interpretation, Generalization of Data											IA	C	C													
	Artificial Intelligence											IA	C	C													
	Pascal: Introduction																								IA	C	C
11TH GRADE	Computer Systems												ID	C													
	Sampling Techniques												IA	C												IA	C
	Statistical Application												IA	C												IA	C
	Pilot: Programming																									IA	C
12TH GRADE	Computer Survival													ID													
	Invasion of Privacy													ID													
	Pascal: Advanced																										IA
	Data Bases: Advanced																										IA

LEGEND: IA—Introduction with Activities   ID—Introductory Discussion   C—Expansion of Discussion from Previous Grades   R—Review   M—Mastery

SOURCE: Gary G. Bitter, and Ruth A. Camuse, *Using a Microcomputer in the Classroom,* © 1984, pp. 214–215, 226–227, 240–241, 252. Reprinted by permission of Prentice-Hall, Inc., Englewood Cliffs, New Jersey.

The Hunter Curriculum

Strands	Grades K – 2	Grades 3 – 4	Grades 5 – 6	Grades 7 – 8
	TEACH STUDENTS TO:			
Procedures	• Follow a procedure for a familiar task • Modify a procedure • Show different procedures can produce the same outcome • Find and correct errors in a procedure • Describe procedures used to perform a task	• Help to develop a procedure involving repetition, decision making, and variables • Find and correct errors in a procedure • Develop a procedure, demonstrate that is works • Use procedures to perform new tasks	• Apply procedures skills to new problems • Note differences between procedures for people and procedures for computers • Break problem into subproblems: plan procedures and subprocedures • Develop procedures for organizing data	• Apply procedures skills to new problems • Choose the best aid for solving a problem: calculator, computer, pencil?
Using Programs	• Use computer drills and games • Operate equipment; load and run programs • Recognize the computer needs instruction	• Read documentation that describes programs and tells how to use them • Select and operate programs without teacher's help • Select and use a program to solve a specific problem	• Use simulations as an aid in learning • Demonstrate learning from a simulation • Retrieve information from a computer data base • Apply skills in using equipment, programs and documentation	• Use word processor to improve writing • Use more complex simulations • Use new methods to retrieve information
Fundamentals	• Understand that computer instructions are contained in a program	• Understand that the computer is a general purpose machine	• Recognize tasks for which computer speed is needed • Recognize tasks requiring repetition • Recognize tasks requiring large amounts of data	• Apply knowledge of fundamentals to new situations

Strands	Grades K – 2	Grades 3 – 4	Grades 5 – 6	Grades 7 – 8
	TEACH STUDENTS TO:			
Applications	• Discover computer applications in homes and neighborhoods	• Know about computer applications in school and local government • Compare fictional and real computers	• Understand 1 or more ways - information retrieval is used in diverse fields • Understand how scientists might use computers	• Recognize uses of Word Processor • Recognize uses of computer in business and manufacturing • Recognize use of computer systems in large organizations • Recognize main components of computer systems
Impact	• Follow rules for using equipment and programs	• Follow rules for using equipment and programs	• Understand reasons to restrict access to data bases and programs • Understand advantages and disadvantages of particular uses of information retrieval	• Become aware of new social issues created by computers • Appreciate social dependence on computers • Understand effects of computer failures • Understand the kinds of computer skills needed in diverse careers • Become aware of computer professions
Writing Computer Programs	(Note: For grades K – 6, objectives and activities related to computer programming are reflected in the Procedures, Using Programs, and Fundamentals strands.)			• Modify programs • Code programs • Write documentation • Test and debug programs • Plan and develop programs

SOURCE: Beverly Hunter, *My Students Use Computers: Computer Literacy in the K–8 Curriculum,* © 1984, pp. 12–13. Reprinted by permission of Prentice-Hall, Inc., Englewood Cliffs, New Jersey.

Index

Abacus, 2, 3
ABC machine, 7
Active learning, 156
Ada, 5, 210
Adaptive devices, 141, 142. *See also* Special
    education
Address, 63, 93. *See also* Memory
Advanced placement computer science
    course outline of, 213–216
    examination, 149, 209
    goals of, 149–150
Agriculture, 31, 137, 138, 140
Aiken, Howard, 6
Algebra, 125
ALGOL, 148
Algorithms, 120, 125, 144, 145, 215
Altair, 12
ALU, 62–63
American Express, 31
Analog, 15, 17
    signal, 15, 16
Analytical Engine. *See* Babbage
Animation, 131
APL, 82, 84, 210
Applications software. *See* Software
Art education, 118. *See also* Visual arts
    association, 223
    computers in, 130–131
Artificial intelligence, 34, 48, 119, 144, 148,
    209, 210
ASCII, 61
Asimov, Isaac, 34, 50
Assistive devices, 141, 142. *See also* Special
    education
Associated Press, 31

Associations, computing, 220
Astronomy, 26, 128
Atanasoff, John Vincent, 7
Audio discs, 132. *See also* Compact discs
Authoring language. *See* Language, au-
    thoring
Authoring tools, 177–179
    authoring systems vs. authoring lan-
      guages, 177–178
    evaluation of, 178–179
Authority, 182
Automobiles, on-board navigation, 29

Babbage, Charles, 5–7, 58, 210
Back-up copy, 41
Bardeen, John, 10
BASIC, 10–11, 61, 81, 82, 83, 84, 102–103,
    119, 147–148, 209
    textbooks for, 211
Basic skills, 190
    for a democracy, 54
    industrial age, 190
    new, 191–92, 193
    redefining, 183–184
Baud rate, 75
Bell, Daniel, 45, 55
Berry, Clifford, 7
Binary
    code, 61
    number system, 7
Biochip, 47, 195
Bit, 60
Bitter, Gary, 119, 121, 227
Bitter curriculum, 119–120, 227–229
Blind, 142. *See also* Special education

BLOCKS, 82
Boole, George, 5, 62
Boolean (algebra), 5, 190, 214
Boot/bootstrap, 98, 99
Bork, Alfred, 104, 128, 152, 190, 200
Branch(ing), 107, 108, 156, 157, 166
Brattain, Walter, 10
Broadway, 26
Browsing, 19
Bubble memory. *See* Memory
Bug, 6, 7, 148, 161
Building trades, 137
Bus, 63–64, 69
  address, 98–99
  data, 98–99
  system, 64
Business
  and industry, 184, 194
  management, 135
  training and retraining in, 191
Business education, computers in, 133–135
Byte, 60

C, 82, 84, 210
CAD (computer-aided design), 27, 28, 137
CAI (computer assisted instruction), 108–
  112, 158, 177
  adjunct, 108
  effectiveness of, 112
  primary, 109
  vs. programming, 145
Calculator(s), 144, 190
  and mathematics education, 125
CAM (computer-aided manufacture), 27
Capabilities of computer medium. *See*
  Computers
Career System, 31
Cartridge, ROM, *See* ROM-pack
Cassette tape, 87
CAT scanner, 26
CB Simulator, 44. *See also* CompuServe
CD (compact discs), 24, 33
CD ROM, 25. *See also* CD
Census Bureau, U.S., 6
Child care, 135, 136
Chip(s), 13, 59, 60, 64
  production, 12–14
  8080, 12
Classroom friendly, 162, 165
Classrooms, future, 194–196
Clothing design, 135, 136
CMI (computer managed instruction), 112–
  115, 141, 142, 157
  instructional guidance, 113–114
  resource availability, 114
  tests and records, 113
COBOL, 82, 84, 209, 210
College Entrance Examination Board, 152,
  216. *See also* Advanced placement
  computer science

Compatibility, 84–85, 86
Compiler, 85
Composition, 124
CompuServe, 19, 44, 157
Computer assisted instruction. *See* CAI
Computer awareness, 117, 119. *See also*
  Computer literacy
Computer Curriculum Corporation (CCC),
  103
Computer education, teacher endorse-
  ments in, 198
Computer literacy, 39, 55, 103, 105, 115,
  117, 120, 149, 188, 190
  BASIC in, 147
  Bitter curriculum, 119–120, 227–229
  curriculum for, 119–120
  defining, 117–118
  Hunter curriculum, 120, 230–231
  purposes of general education and,
    118
  for teachers, 142
  vs. computer science, 150
Computer managed instruction. *See* CMI
Computer-phobia, 181, 197
Computer science, 143, 148
Computer science education, 149–151
  curriculum for, 118, 213–216
  general education and, 151
  teacher certification in, 150–151
  teachers of, 191
Computer scientists, 115, 198
Computers
  as instructional medium, 155
  capabilities of medium, 106–108, 155–
    158
  learning about, 115–119
  in subject areas, 123–142
CONFER, 20
Conferencing, 19, 20, 42, 44, 187
Control unit, 62–63, 66–67
Conviviality, tools of, 190
Copy protection, 168
Copyright, 37
Copyright Act of 1976, 42
Cost, computing, 14
Council for Basic Education, 53
CPR, 140
CPU (central processing unit), 58, 59–64,
  67, 68, 76, 88, 94, 98
Crash, program, 165, 166
Cray 2, 47
Crime, 34, 39
  at Brown University, 37
  and FBI, 37–38
  and 414s, The, 39
  at Los Alamos Nuclear Testing Ground,
    37, 39
  and privacy, 37, 216
  at Security Pacific Bank, 39
  software piracy, 40